A BEGINNER'S GUIDE TO

ANIMAL WOODCARVING

Learn to Sculpt Lifelike Figures from a Japanese Master

MIO HASHIMOTO

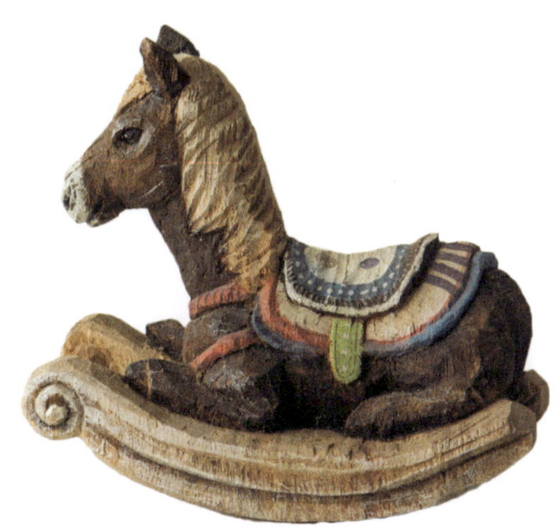

TUTTLE Publishing

Tokyo | Rutland, Vermont | Singapore

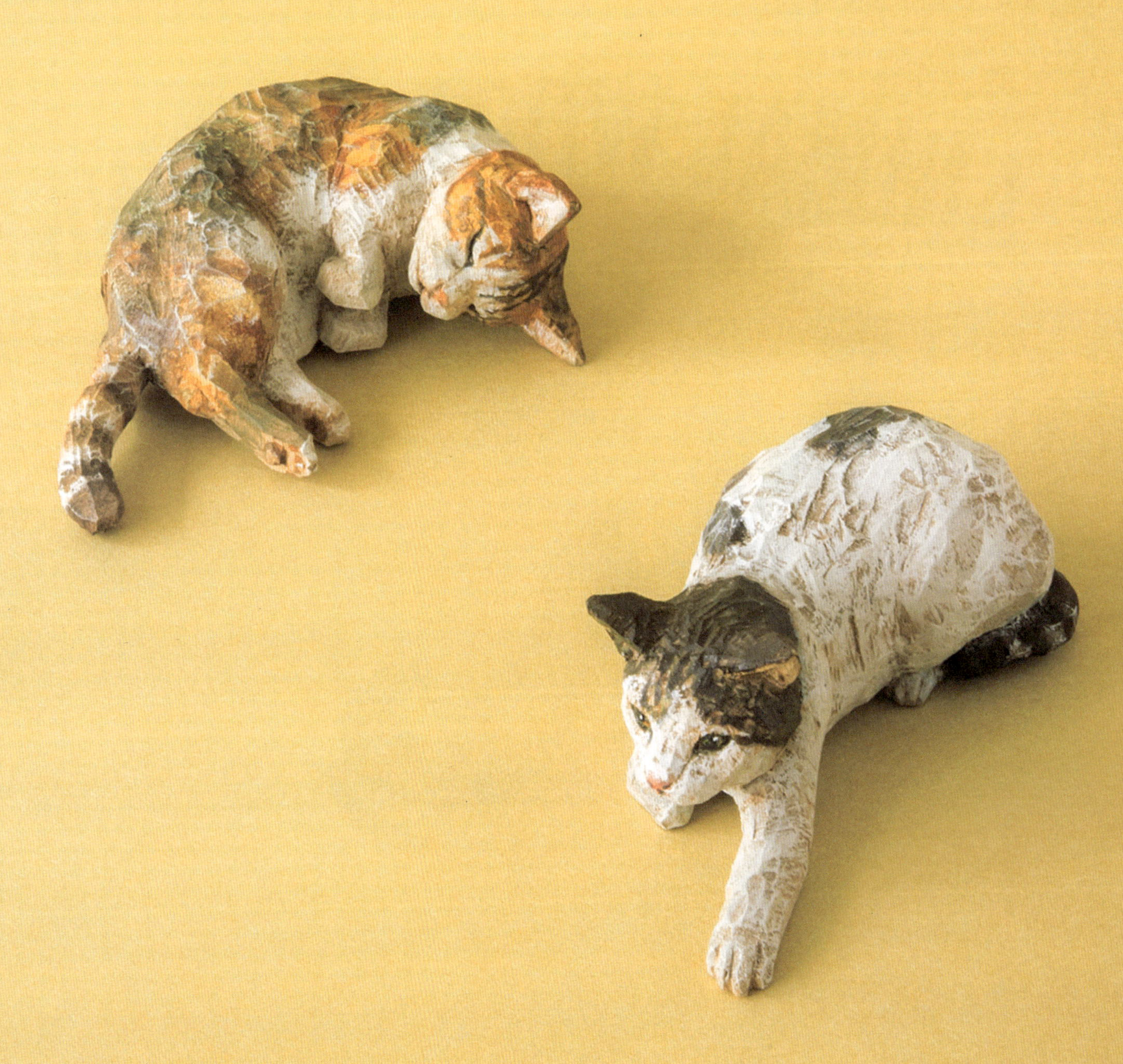

Contents

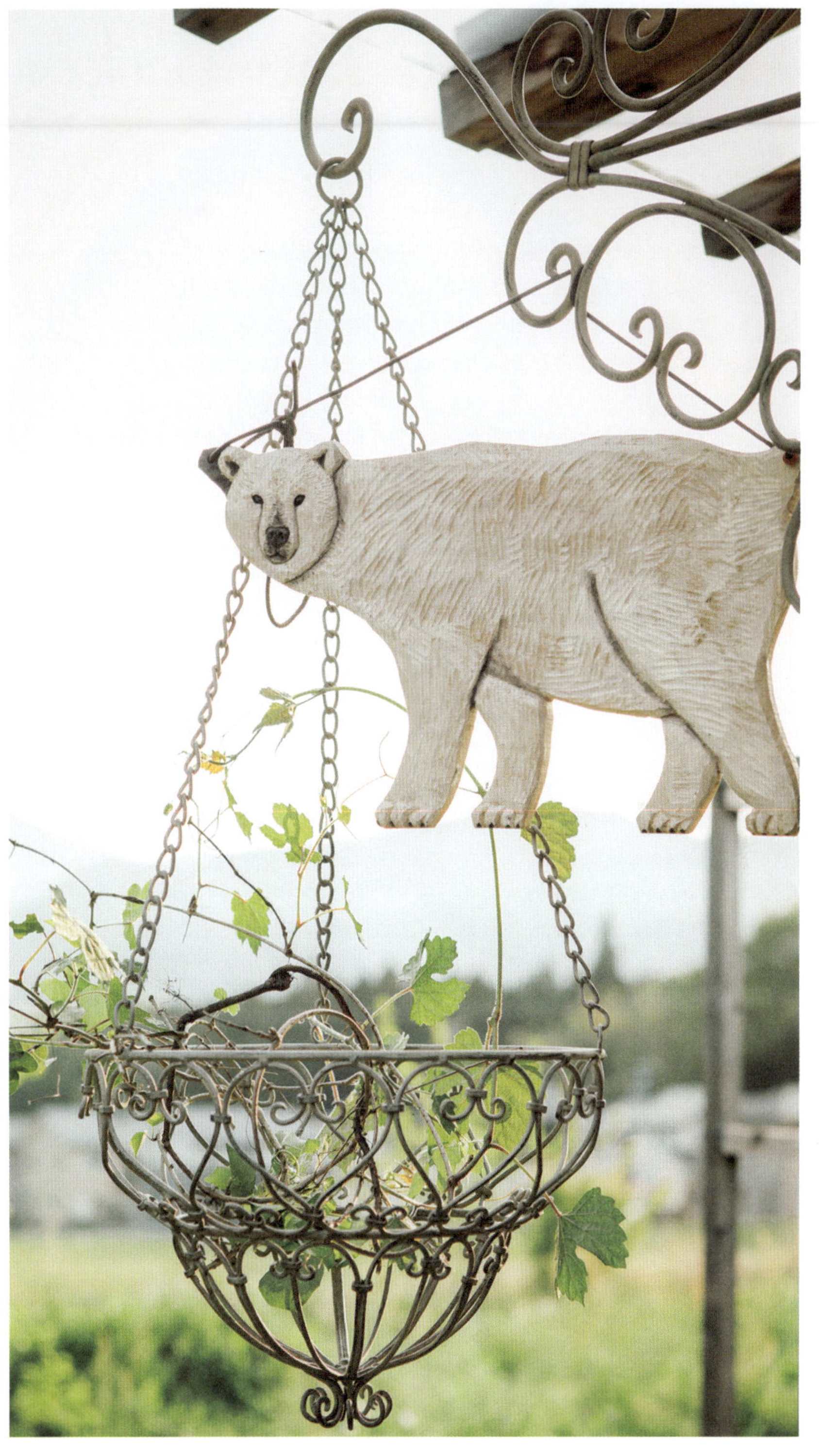

Why I Wrote This Book

Before I began my art journey, landscapes and animals were simply fascinating things that I enjoyed looking at. Before I began sculpting, trees were just part of the scenery; I thought they were pretty, but I only looked at them with passing interest. As I started to paint and carve wood, creating something meaningful based on my observations, I began to viscerally appreciate how beautiful nature is and how important each subject's characteristics are.

Fashioning objects with your hands is intrinsically bound to the process of discovering the beauty of objects. The best part of studying art is comprehending the splendor of the world around us with intention.

Whether it's an adorable cat I met on a trip, a sweet dog that's always in the neighborhood, or pets that are or were important family members, how wonderful would it be if a small wood carving could be lovingly produced to preserve these precious moments? One-of-a-kind sculptures crafted not from molds, but from one's hands and one's own mind's eye have a life all their own, even if they don't replicate the original exactly. More than making them "correctly," I believe they should be made with love and heartfelt effort.

Sculpture in the round is one of the more challenging artistic endeavors, but it's so worthwhile to create. It's okay if you don't carve well at first; keep trying again and again. When you finish, although you will feel spent, a sense of peace and achievement await, as if you've climbed a great mountain.

—Mio Hashimoto

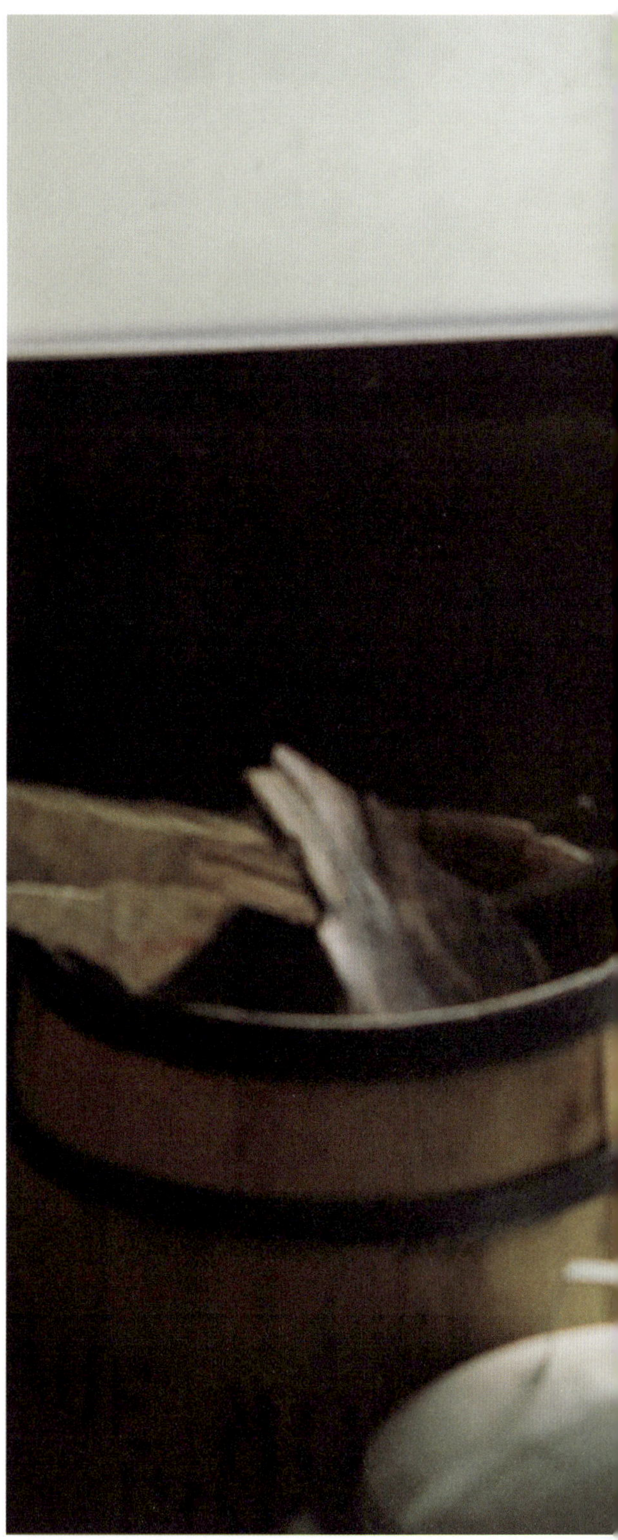

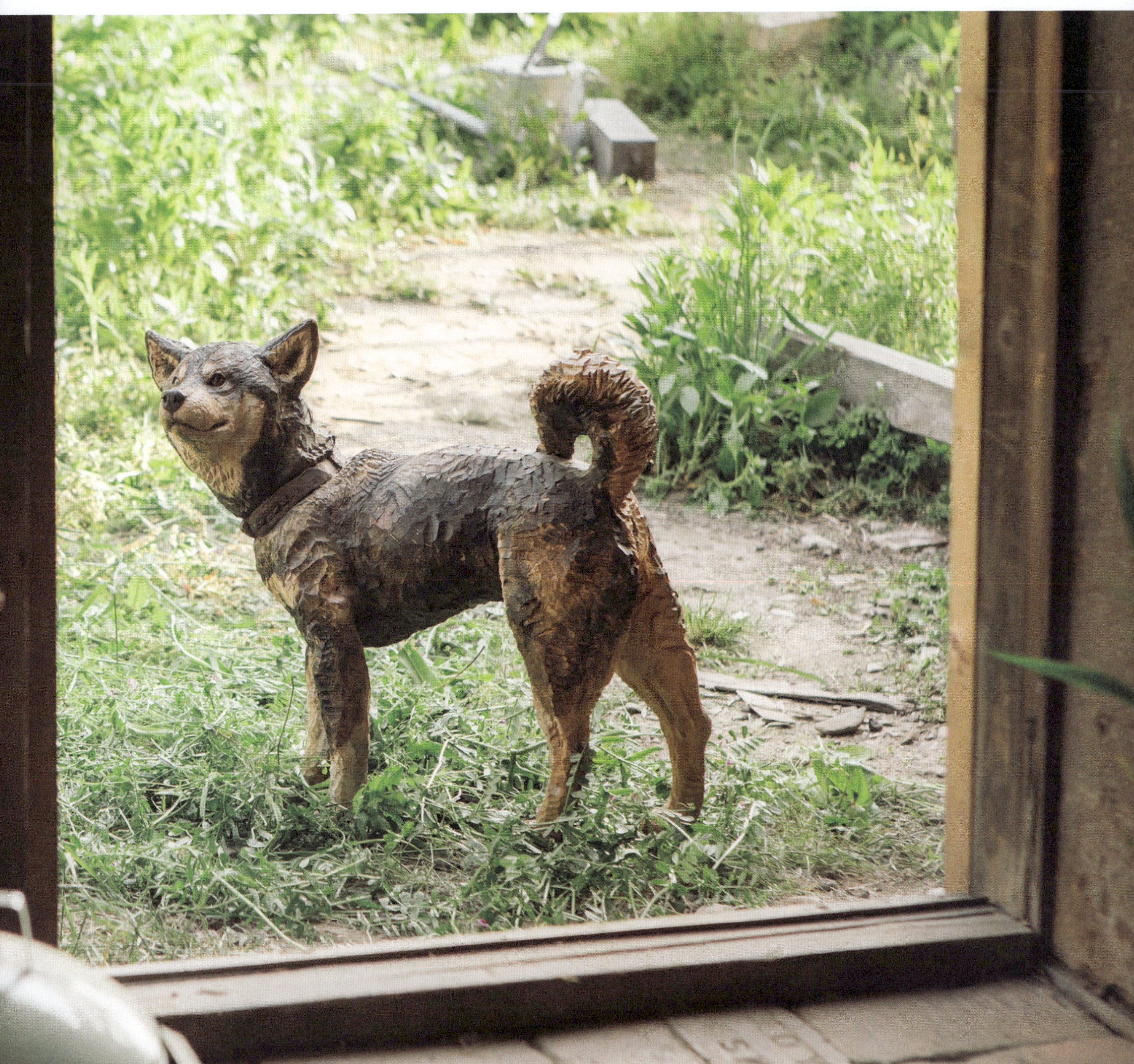

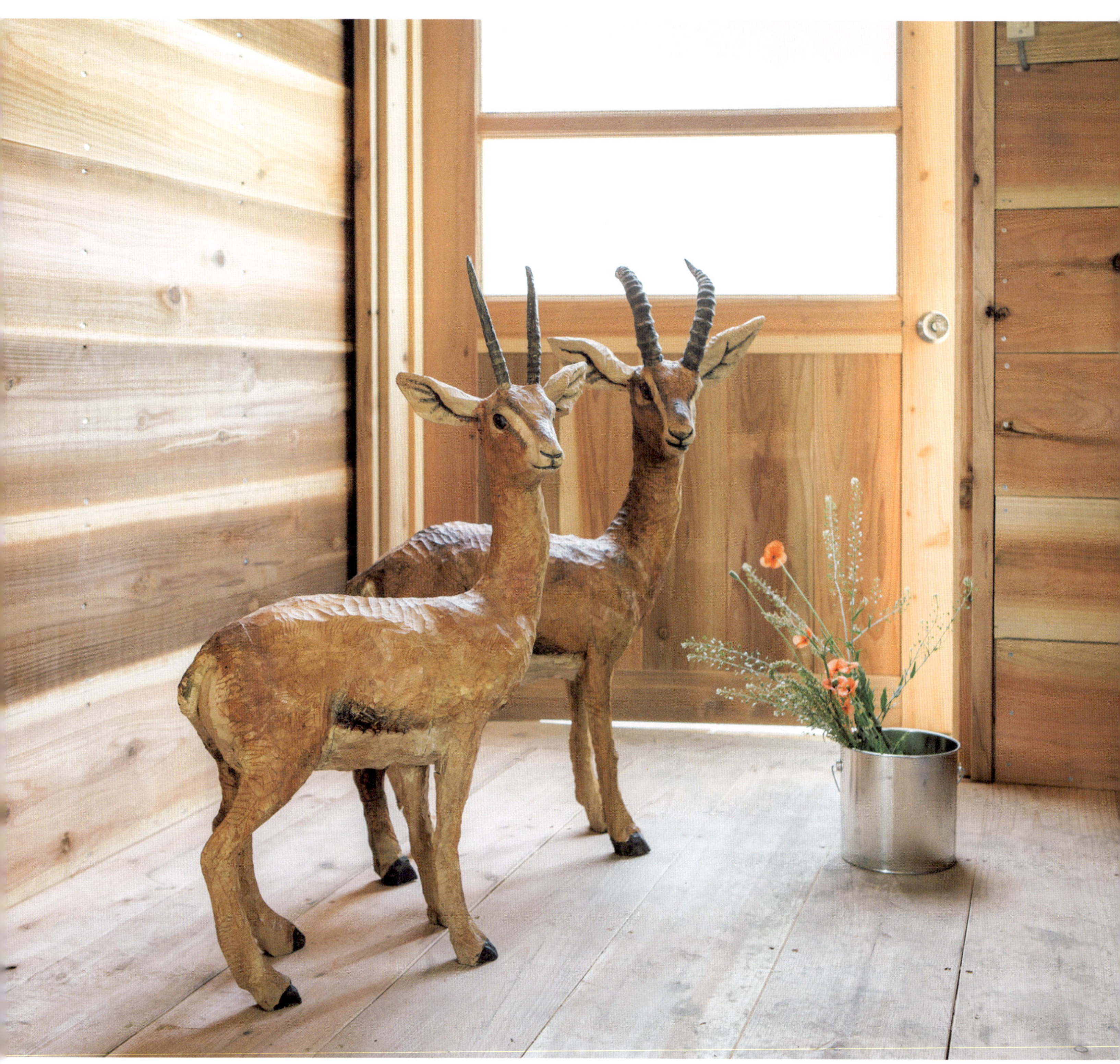

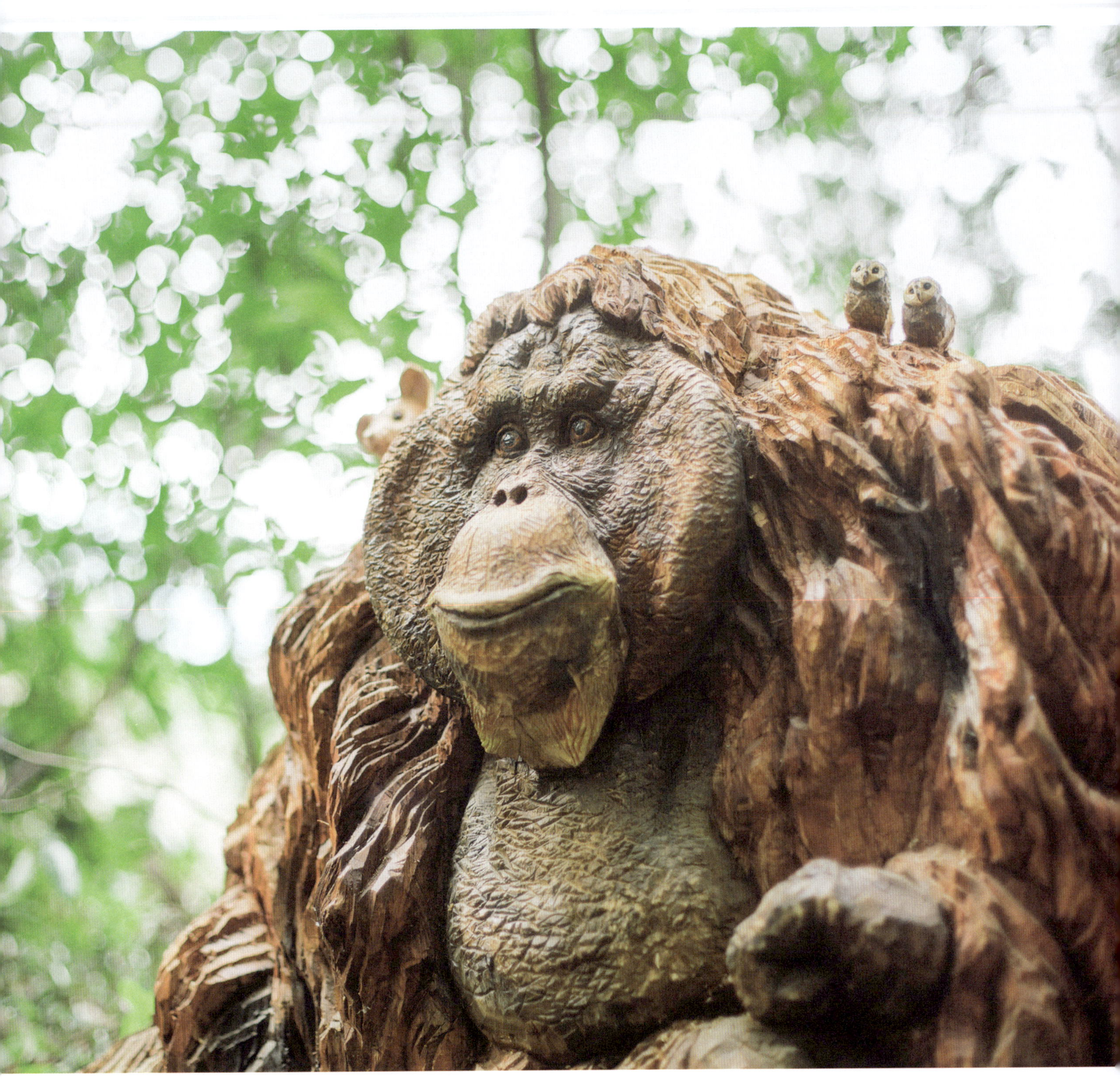

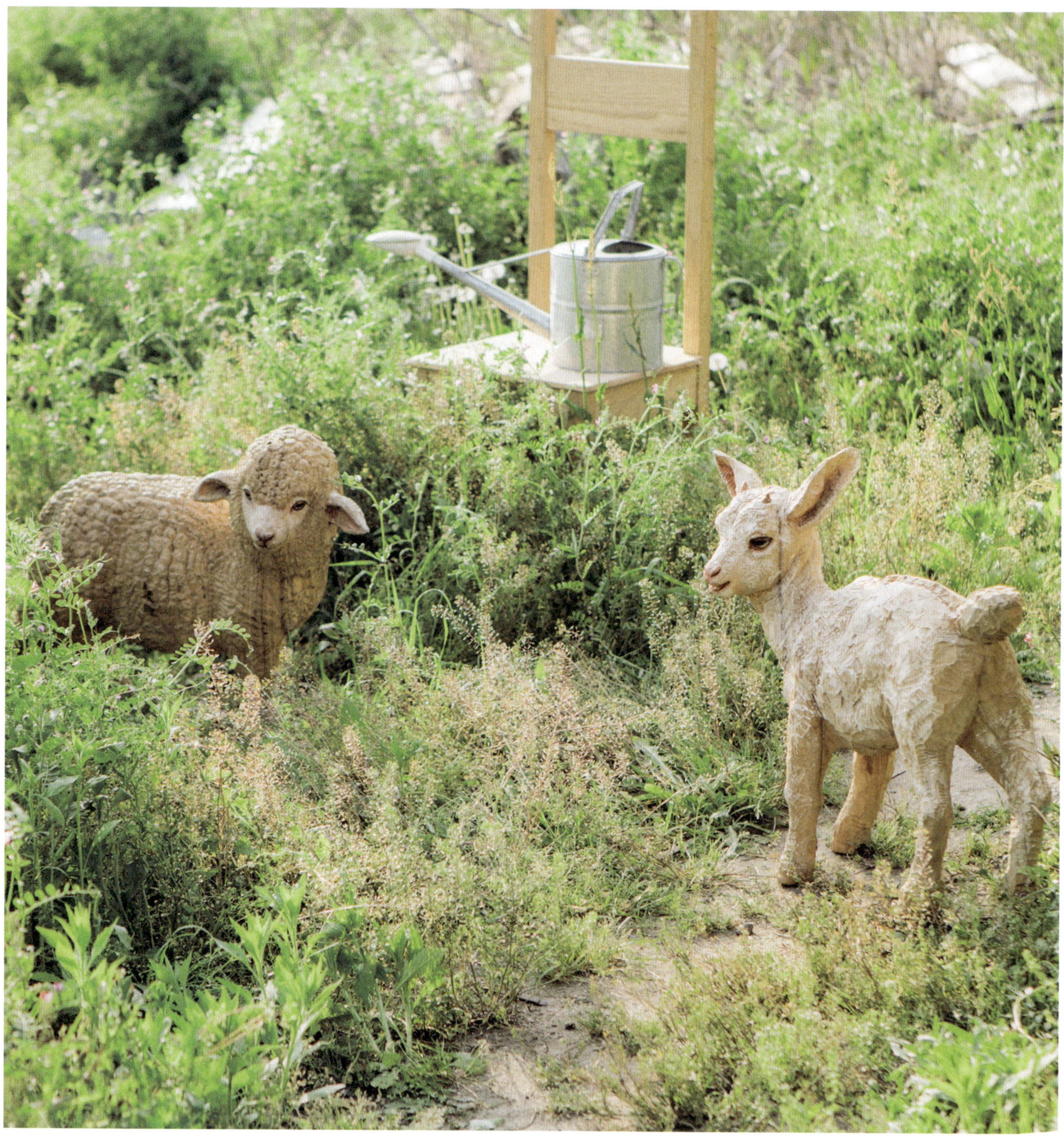

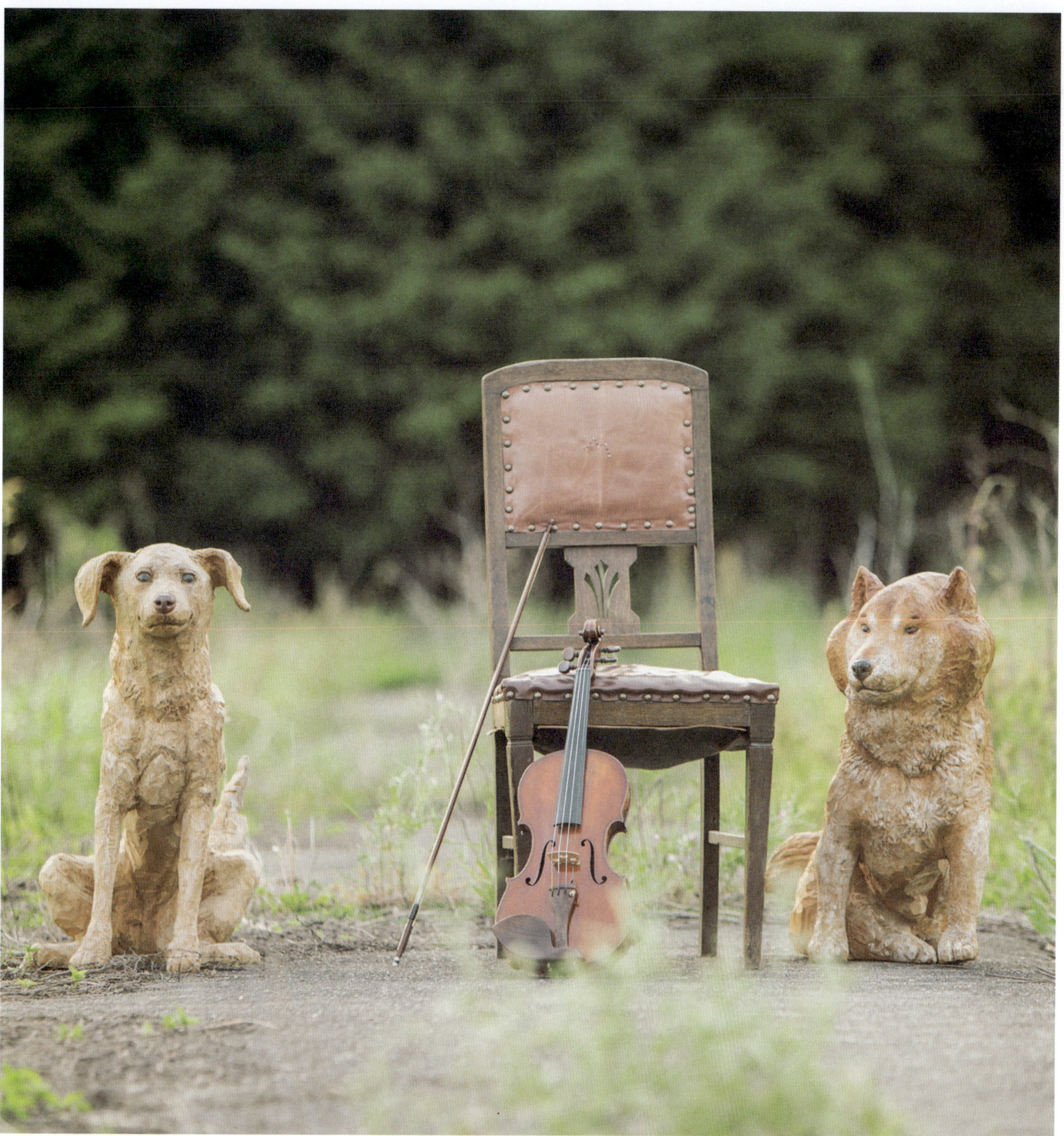

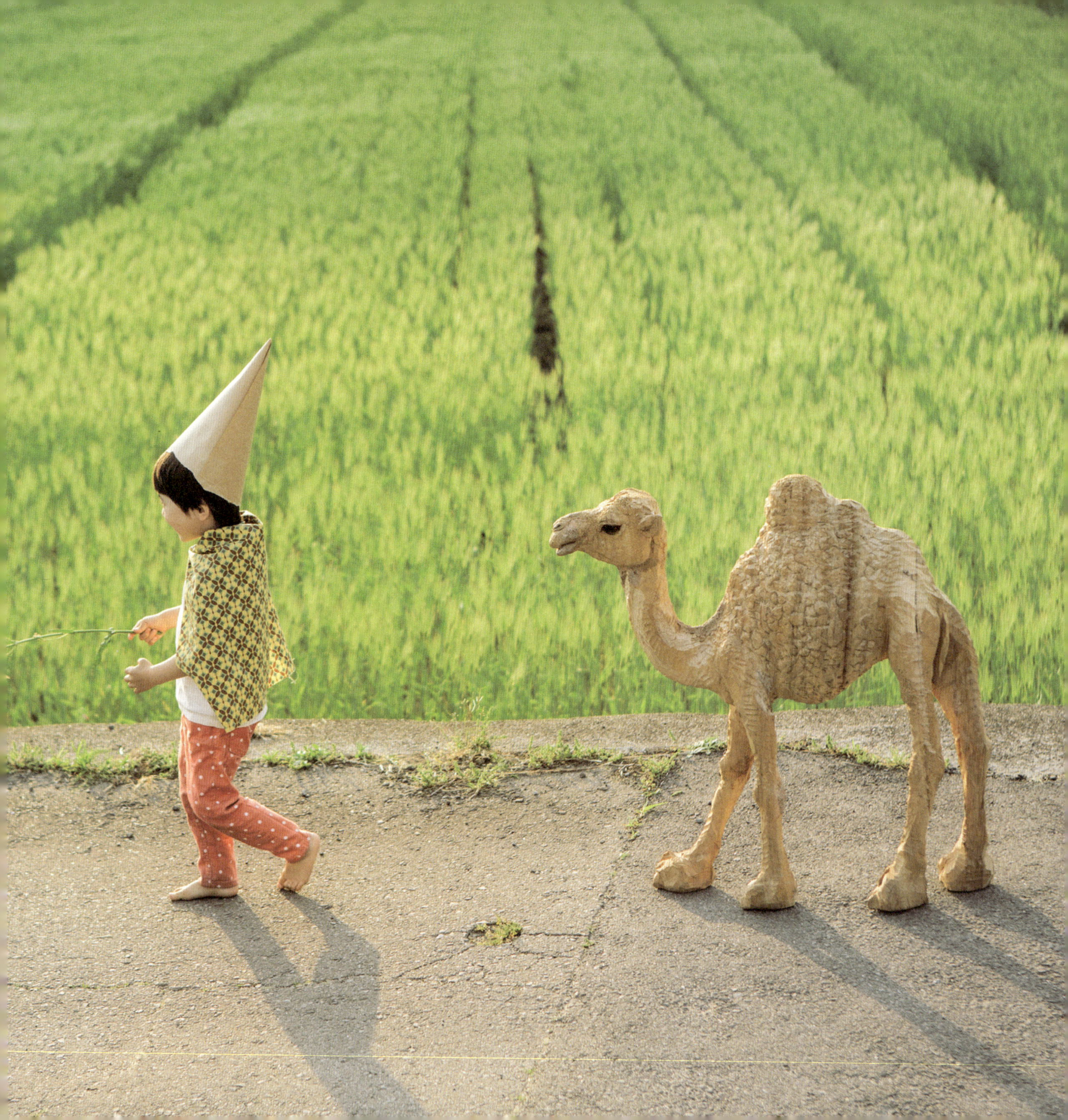

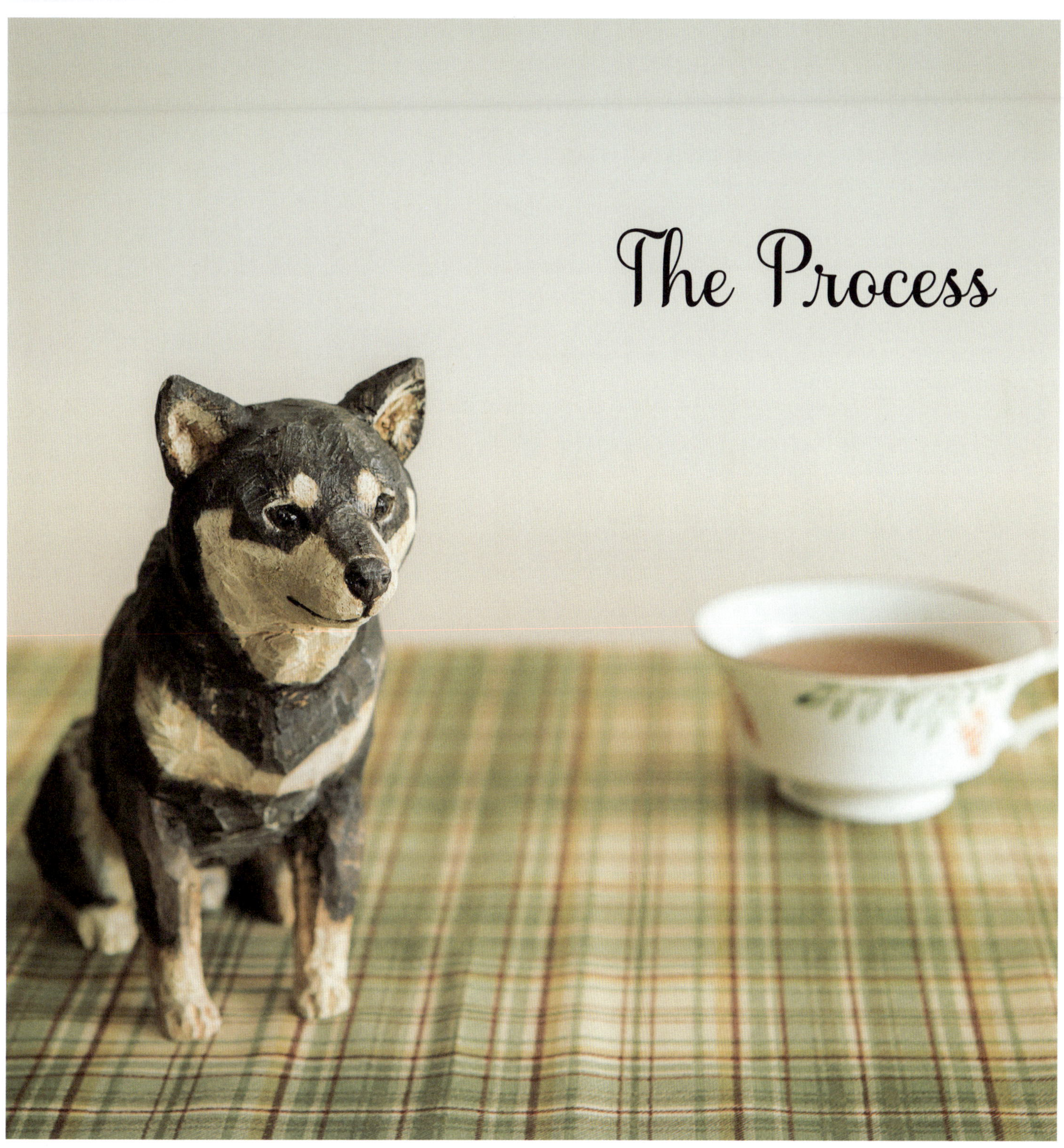
The Process

Getting Started

I want to preserve the innate charm and adorable features of the animals I encounter throughout my everyday life. At such times, carving wood and creating something with my own hands is a wonderful way to express this desire. When you encounter a fleeting moment when an animal reveals its sweet nature to you, immortalize that treasured experience with a one-of-a-kind wooden sculpture!

First, carefully observe the animal you want to use as a model. Sketch it and firmly imprint the shape in your memory based on your initial impression. Once you've found the pose you want to create, select a piece of wood that seems suitable for it, prepare the wood, and start carving the sculpture.

If possible, it's best to continue observing the model as you work on your sculpture. Discovering interesting shapes, determining areas of light and shadow within the form, and carefully observing difficult or tricky parts are essential.

Each pass of the chisel should feel like it's bringing you closer to the animal. Having an eye for realism and moving your hands with care is crucial.

While the natural color of wood is lovely, it's advisable—particularly for animal sculptures—to try your hand at adding color at least once. At the very least, I like to apply lacquer to the eyes. Witnessing the moment when the wood suddenly comes to life with shining, soulful eyes gazing back at you is truly remarkable.

The sculpture represents the beginning of a new kind of life for that creature.

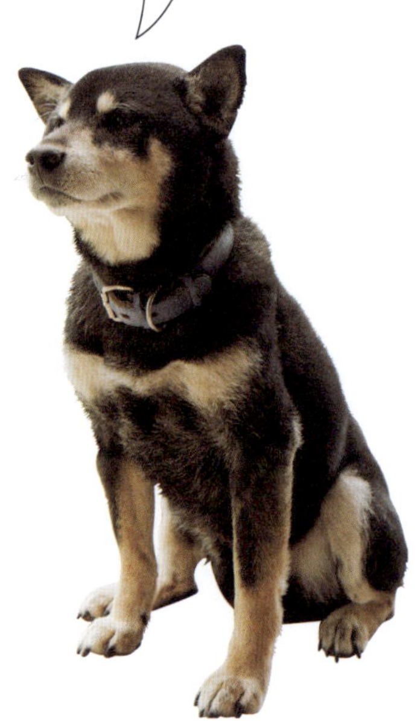

Model
Name: Tsuki (Male), 13 years old, Black Shiba Inu

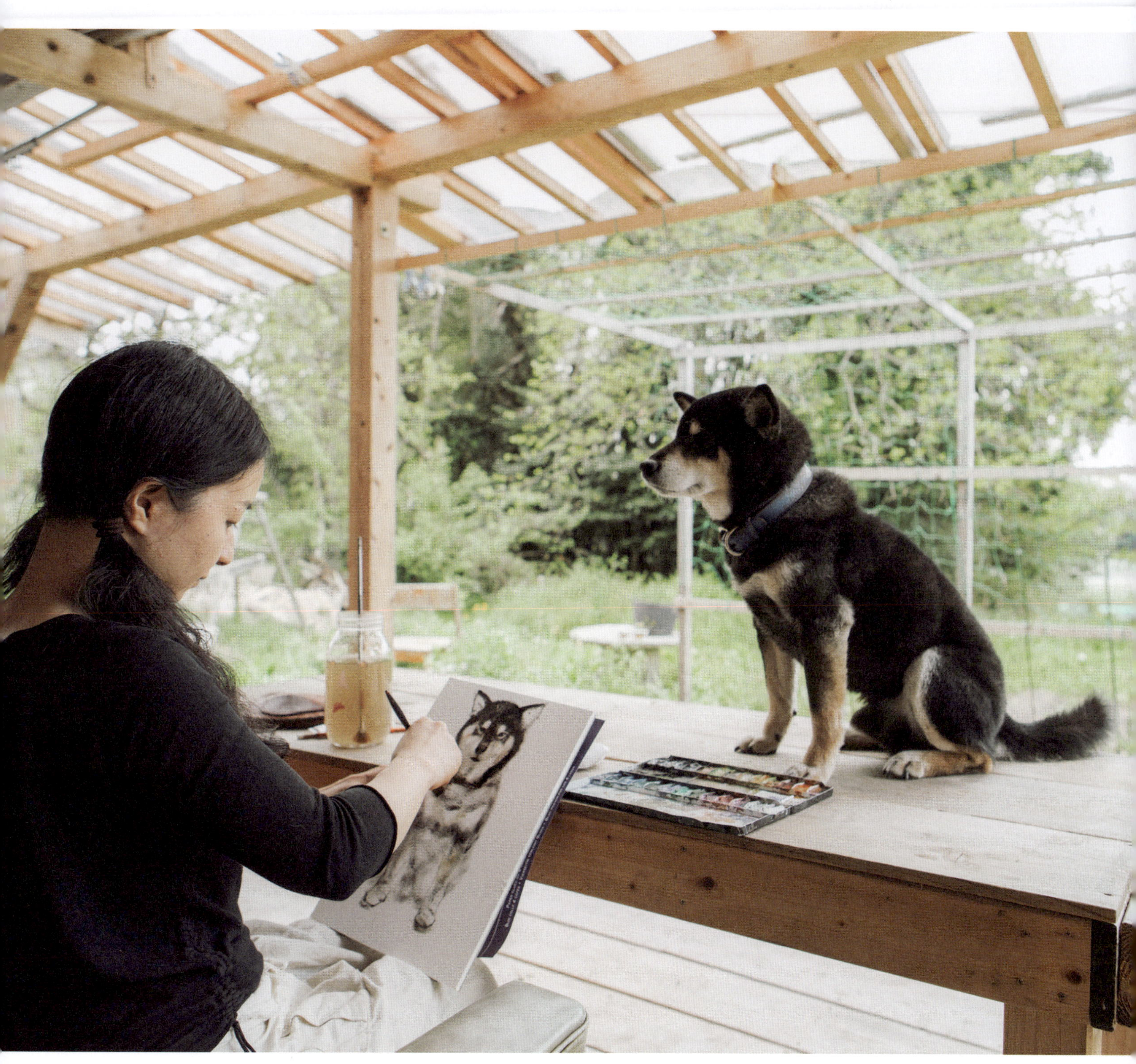

Sketching the Model

Sketching is the most crucial step in creating a sculpture. It's not about drawing well or creating a beautiful picture, but about capturing your impressions of the creature in front of you in the moment.

The purpose of sketching is to create something akin to a roadmap that helps you get to know the model well, and as you draw, you keep a three-dimensional memory of it. Each additional drawing brings you closer to the essence of the subject.

During this process of exploration, you can determine what expression the subject usually has, what makes it contented or annoyed, and decide what kind of moments you want to capture. Pursuing the answers to these questions leads to more vivid and realistic sketches.

Drawing is tied directly to observing well. Observing well leads to remembering well, and remembering well leads to creating well. Observe carefully and feel deeply as you freely sketch the forms you see with your eyes and the textures you feel with your hands.

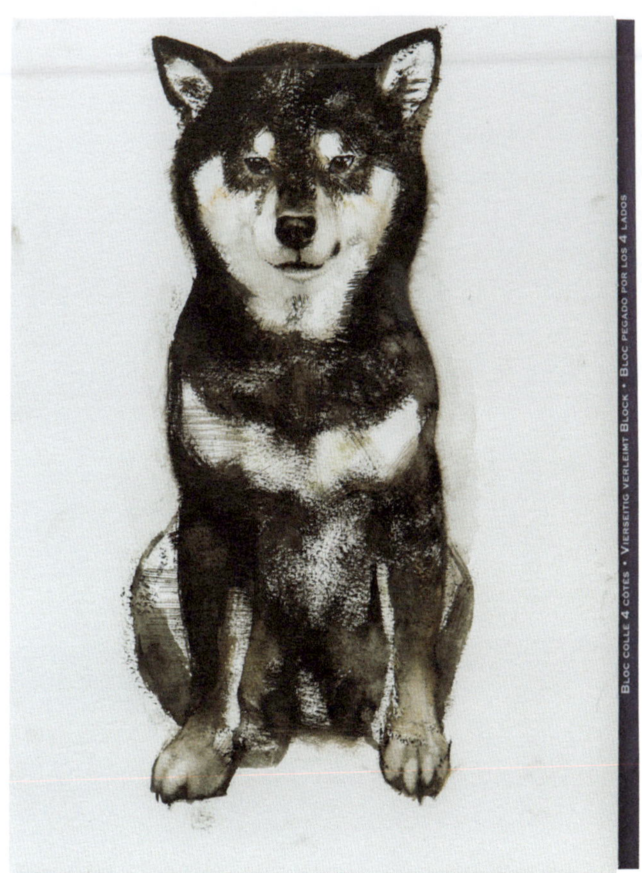

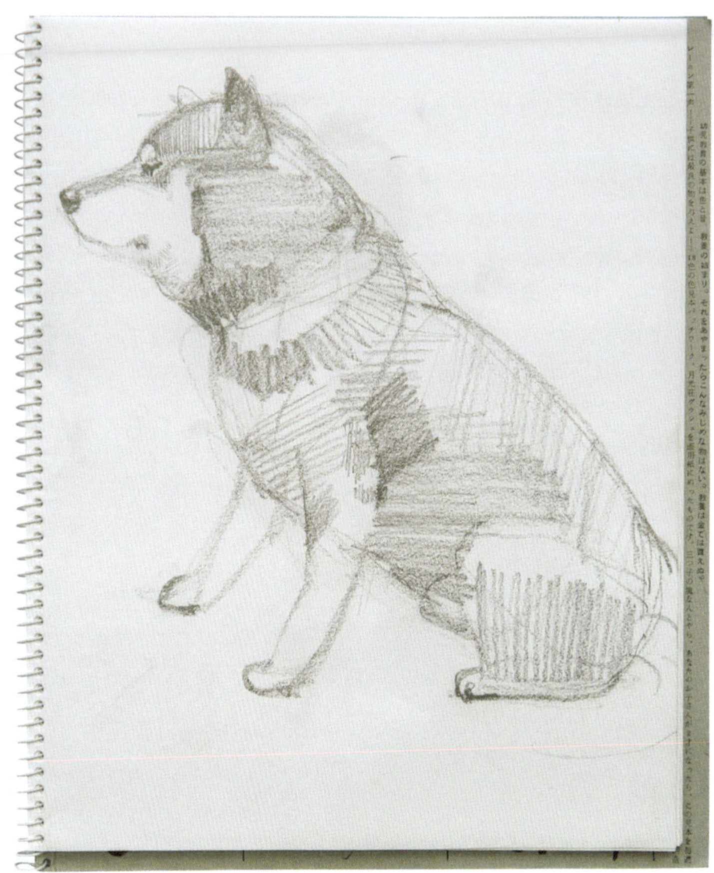

Accurately paint the features of the model as you see them. Because animals move frequently, don't worry about preliminary sketches—just start working as soon as you find a pose you want to sculpt. Watercolors, which allow for bold application and removal of color, are recommended.

Do set out to draw "well," but rather, work quickly and correct any incorrect shapes as the situation arises. Describe the forms and surfaces using the direction of the sketch lines in your own way. Conté crayons, pastels and kneaded erasers, which allow for quick corrections, are recommended.

Choosing the Wood

When selecting wood, consider the direction and character of the grain well. Select wood that exhibits a grain that runs vertically, in the direction the model stands on the ground. Choose a block that appears as if the model could be comfortably embedded within it. Because wood is a living material, rather than looking for wood that will conform to your expectations, it is better to choose wood that feels compatible with the model you want to sculpt (for a wild animal, consider using wood with gnarled grain; for a domestic animal, perhaps use consistently fine grained wood...). However, use what you like—I prefer to use camphor wood because I enjoy its scent.

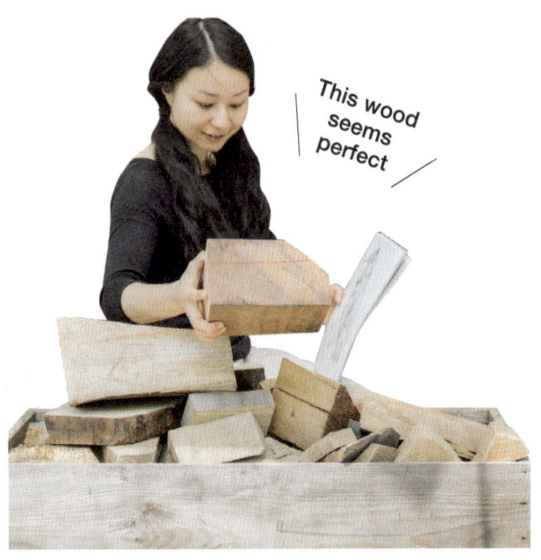

With your sketch in hand, choose a piece of wood of just the right size. If you can imagine the model within the wood, that's the one to go with.

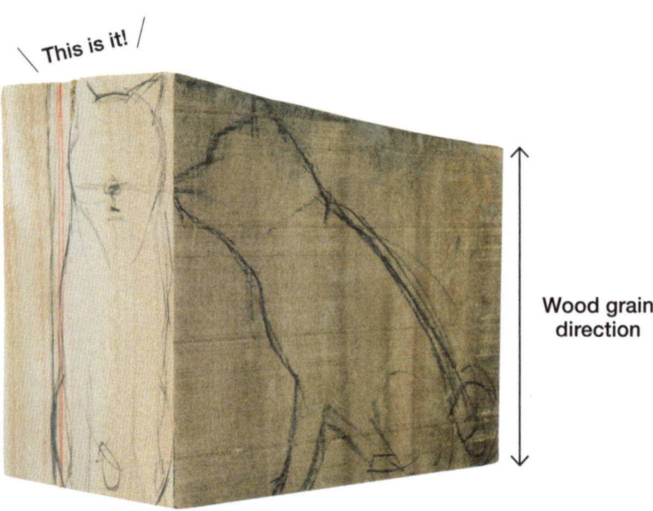

Once you've chosen the wood, draw on the shape roughly. Draw the front and side views to remind yourself of the sketched shape.

Note

Drawing

By aligning either the ground side or the front side neatly to the edge when drawing, you can avoid wasting wood, and the excess can be reused. In this case, you can see a portion of unused wood at the back that I will reserve for a future project.

Sawing the Wood to Reveal the Rough Form

Wood carving is a simple type of sculpture made with a saw and chisels, gouges and knives. For larger sculptures, sometimes chainsaws or band saws are used to speed up the process. Roughing out the shape by cutting away large portions of the wood requires boldness tempered with delicacy, focused concentration and a safety-conscious mindset.

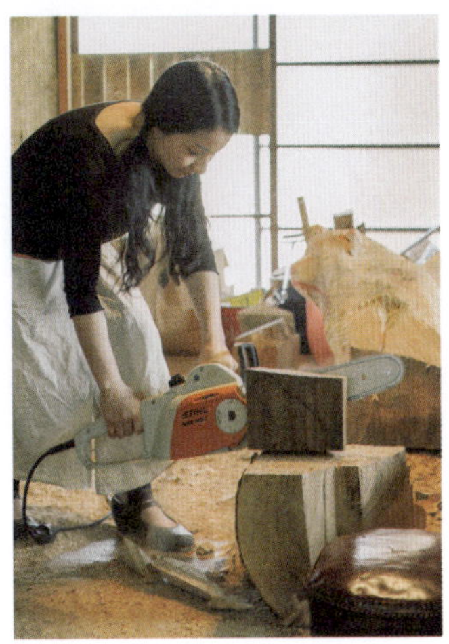

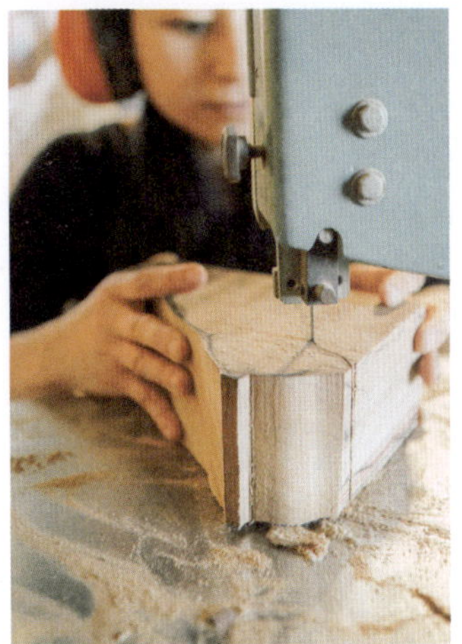

Depending on the size of your sculpture, you can quickly cut the outline with a chainsaw. In the studio, the loud sound of cutting wood echoes, and the pleasant scent of camphor wood fills the air.

Roughly cut out the shape of the model with a band saw if you have access to one. Even just cutting large, three-dimensional planes that correspond to your rough drawing can have your block of wood starting to look like the shape of a dog!

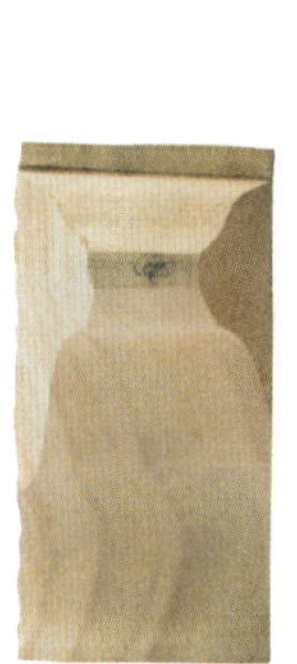

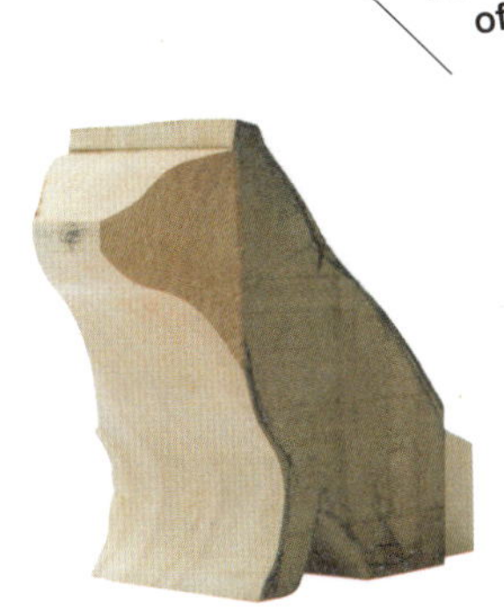

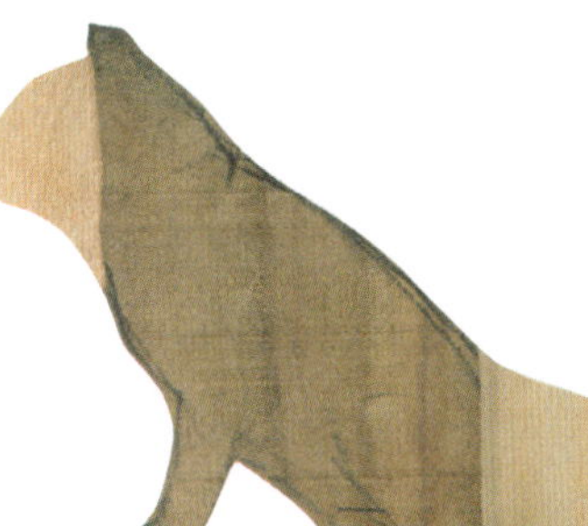

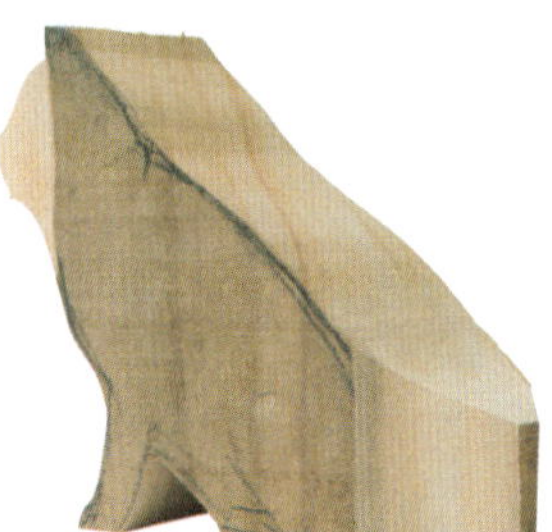

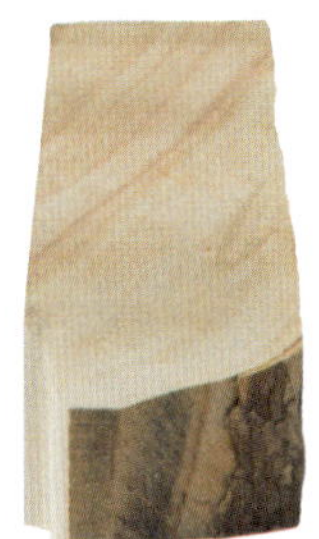

Sculpting the Animal

Wood carving is one of the oldest forms of sculpture, where a living material, wood, is carved using knives. Because knives are necessarily very sharp, they require careful concentration to be used safely.

Carving, which reveals the form "buried" within the wood block by shaping it, requires intense focus, correct judgment, courage and decisiveness. It's a very challenging endeavor, but what's important is that you swing the mallet with feeling, striving for each cut to be one that shapes the model, in the best and most perfect way possible. Thus, the shape created, no matter how humble, becomes a sculpture with the power to move those who see it. Approach the model with care, never rush, and carefully choose each cut. With courage, keep carving, pushing for more and more realism.

At a certain point, when the chisel finally reaches the edge of the model's form and it feels like it might be detrimental if you carve deeper, that's when you can swiftly carve out the rest of the figure, and suddenly, it appears before you with a "pop." Rather than breathing life into it, the life is already embedded within the wood, waiting eagerly to be revealed.

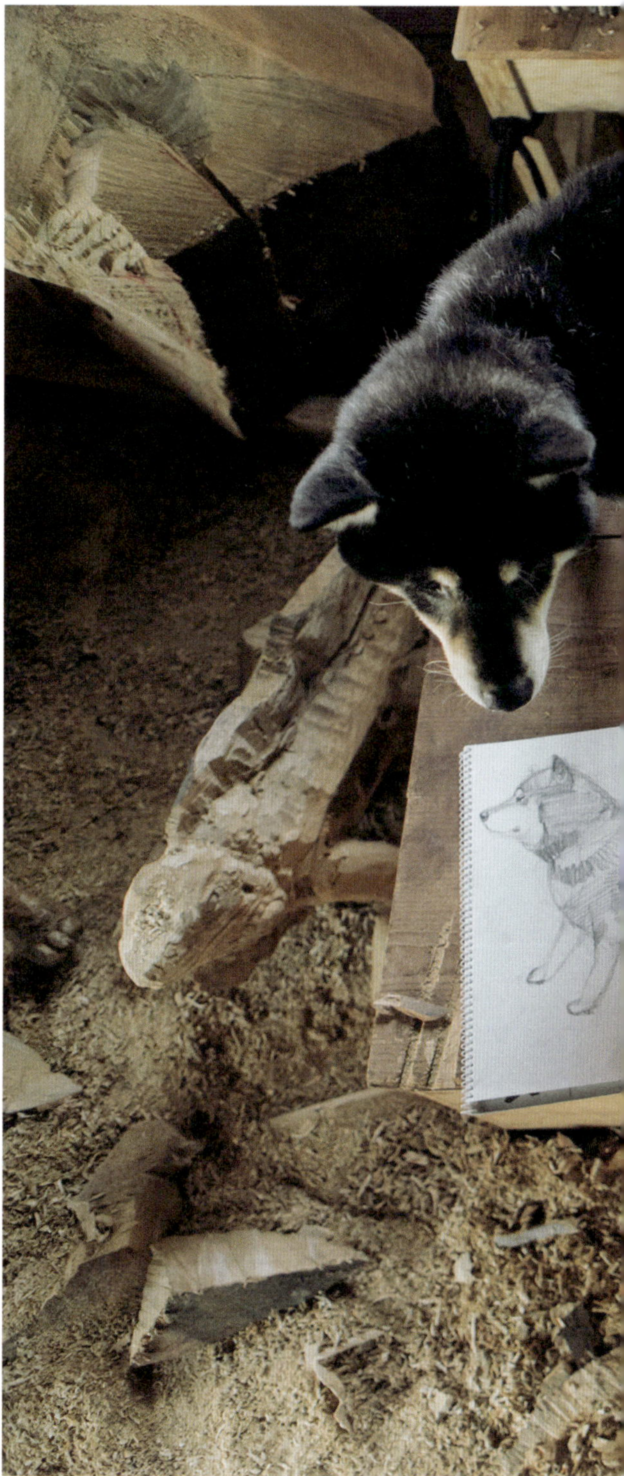

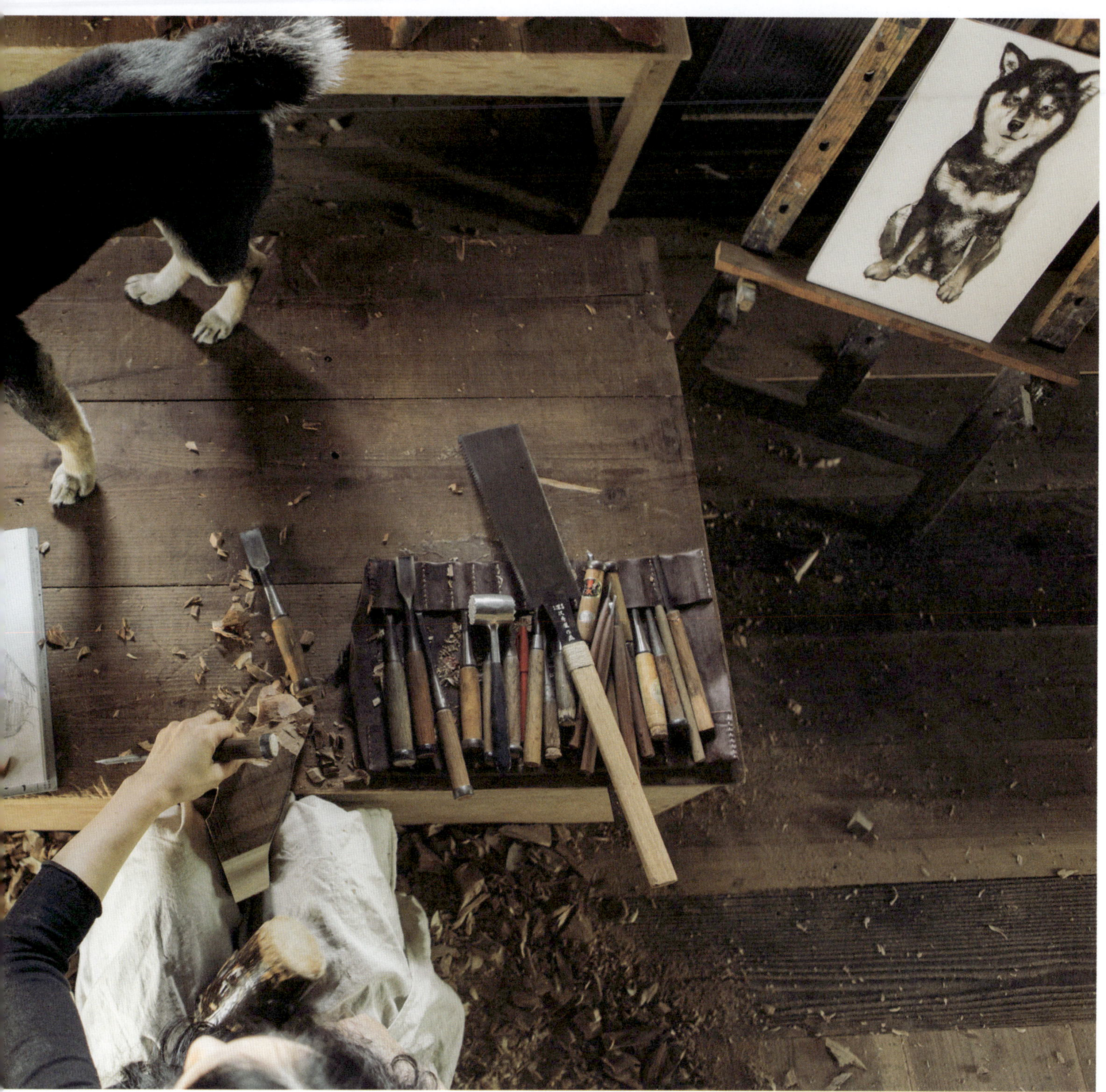

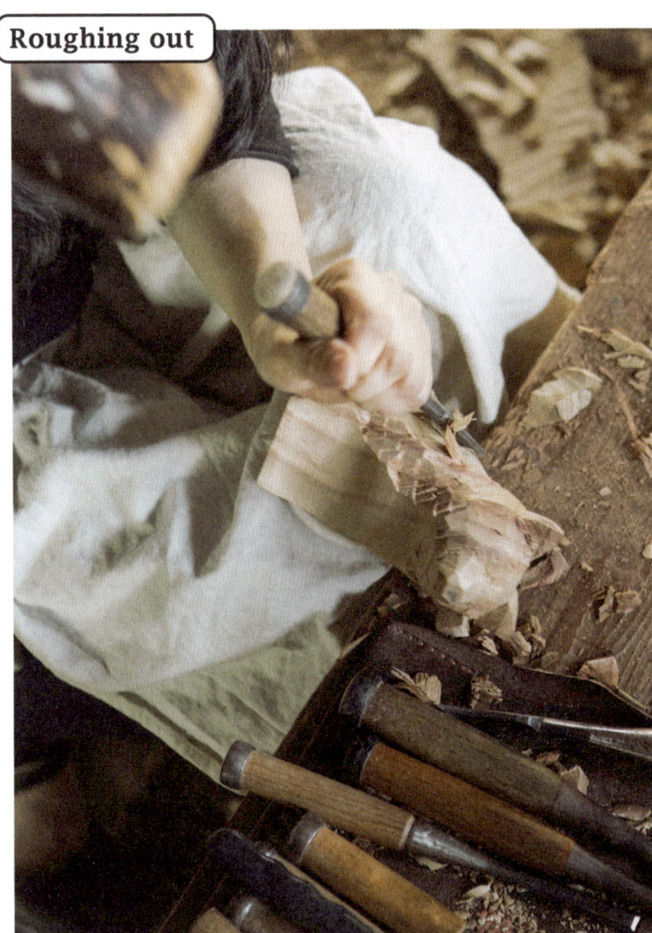

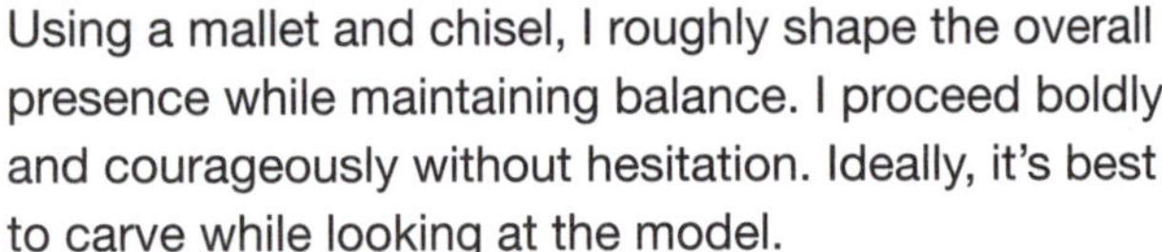

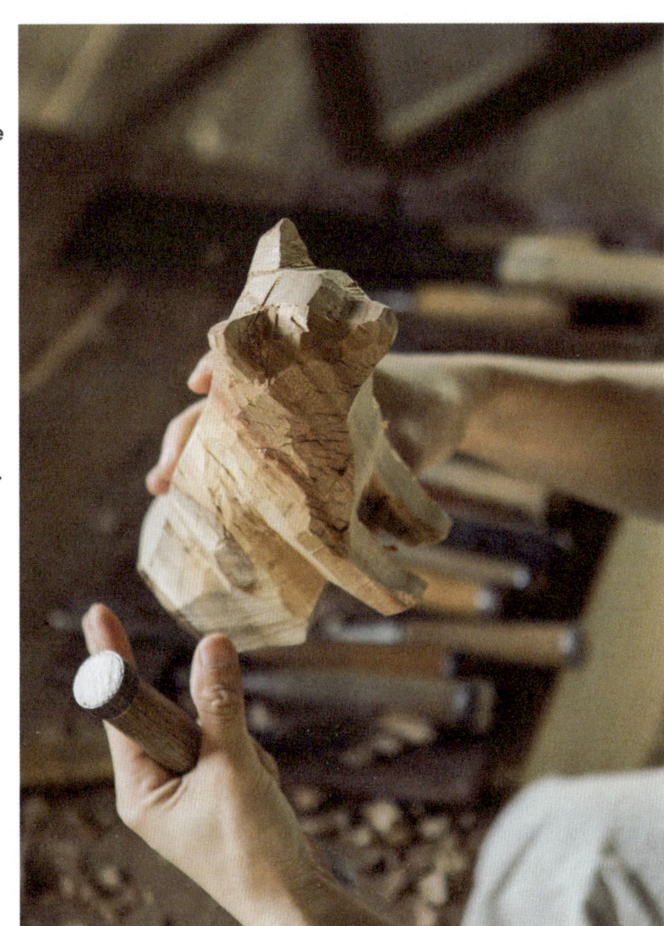

Using a mallet and chisel, I roughly shape the overall presence while maintaining balance. I proceed boldly and courageously without hesitation. Ideally, it's best to carve while looking at the model.

Instead of focusing on carving one spot at a time, I carve in the round while rotating the entire figure to achieve a cohesive look. Sometimes, I hold it up to the light to see the silhouette. It's important to produce shadows and highlights on the wooden surface that correspond to what I see when looking at the model.

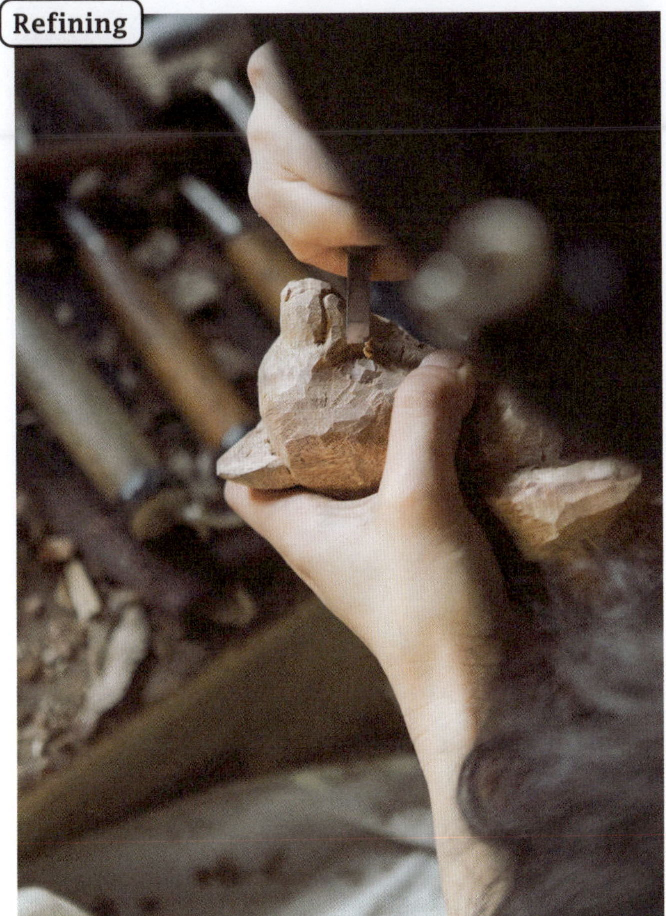

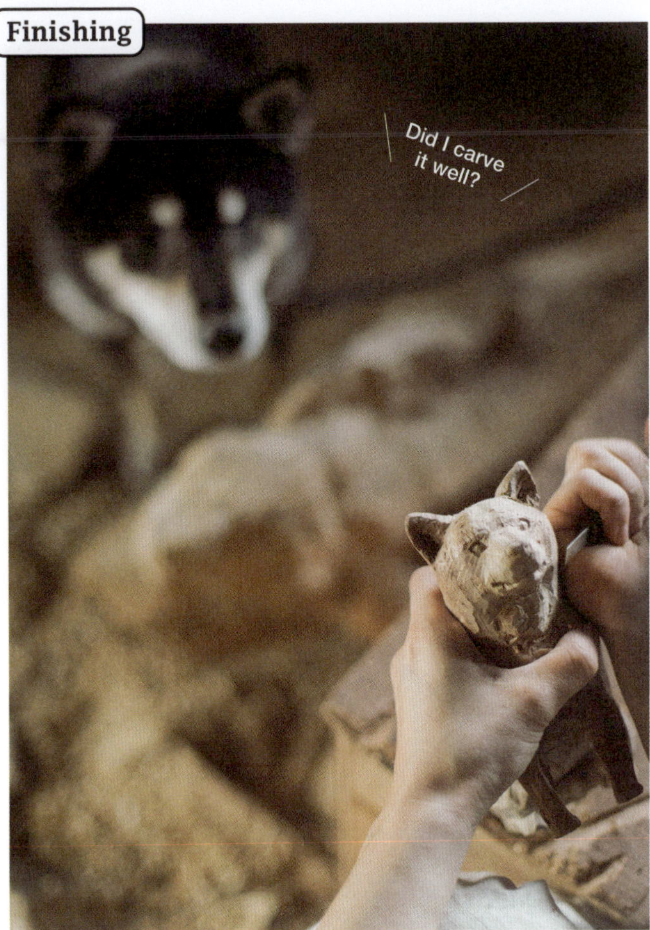

I remain engaged and aware of what I'm carving, ensuring that the model's shape and silhouette are visible from any angle. For animals that are difficult or dangerous to observe live, I refer to pictures in books or other references.

Once I complete a particular area, I consciously resist the temptation to begin honing it to a further degree. I proceed boldly yet delicately toward the finish, ensuring that I capture the animal's vitality before calling the carving "complete."

Painting the Sculpture

I consider the wood's natural color first, and then choose stains or paints that complement it for coloring. When coloring, I revisit the watercolor sketch I initially made, recalling the excitement I felt when I first saw the model. It's crucial not to paint flatly. Instead of just slapping on paint, I color with the intention of approximating the texture of the subject, treating the coloring process with thoughtfulness.

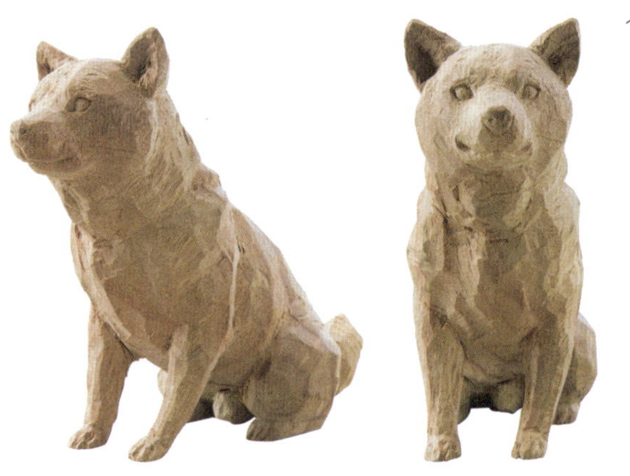

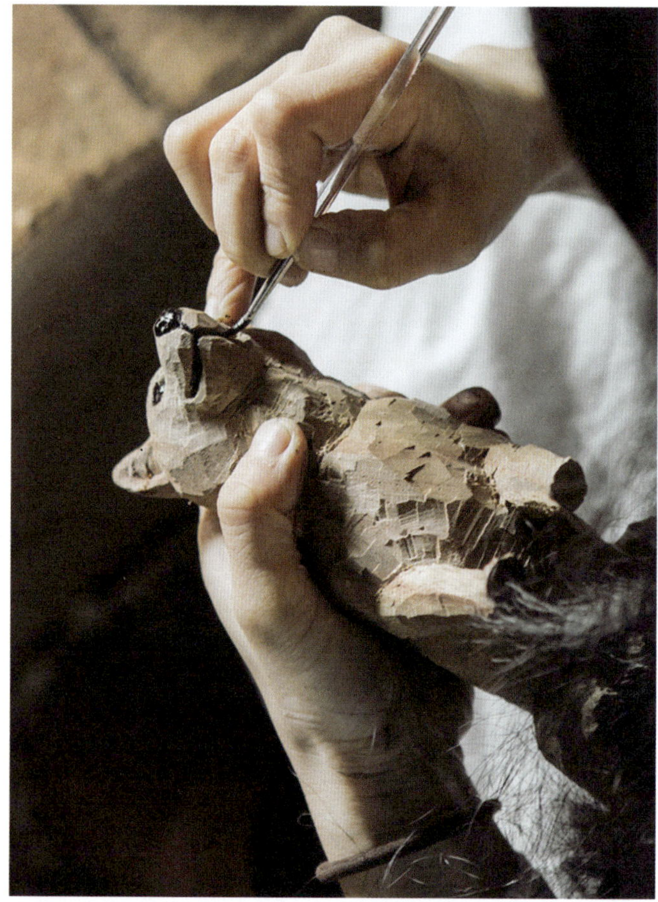

Some people are allergic to lacquer, so I recommend tracking down Cashew brand synthetic lacquer (or similar) that is less likely to cause a reaction. Paint the eyes carefully and thoroughly, and coat the body boldly with a broad brush. In this book, I call for using acrylic paints because of their ease of use, but oil-based paints are also suitable. Oil-based paints require a special thinner and require more time to dry, but they work well if you are serious about professional results.

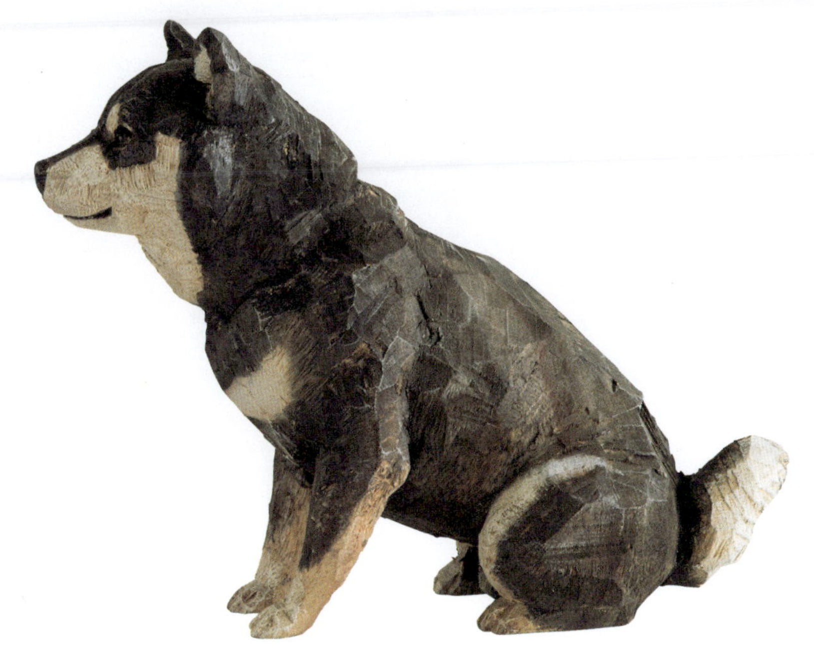

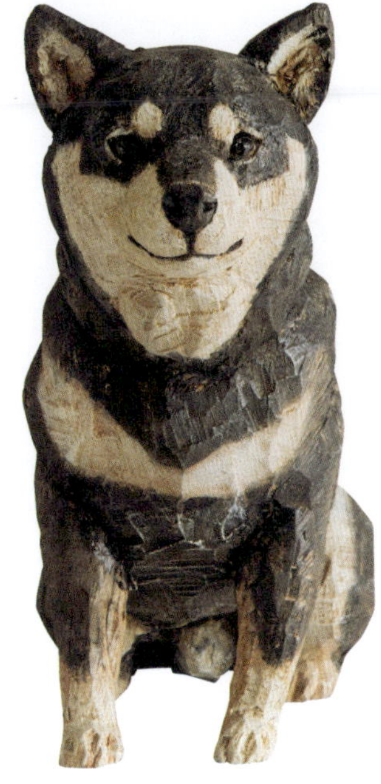

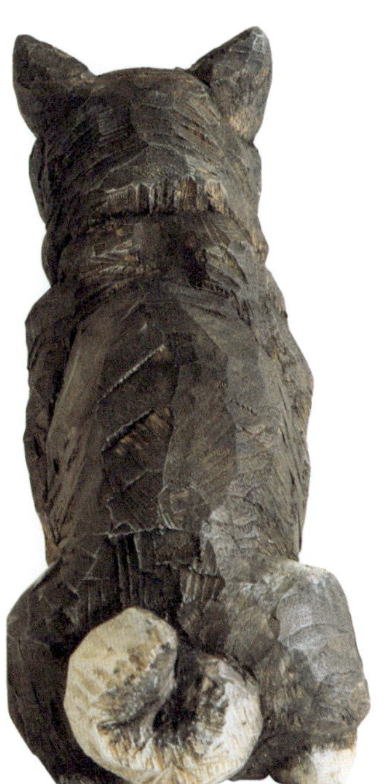

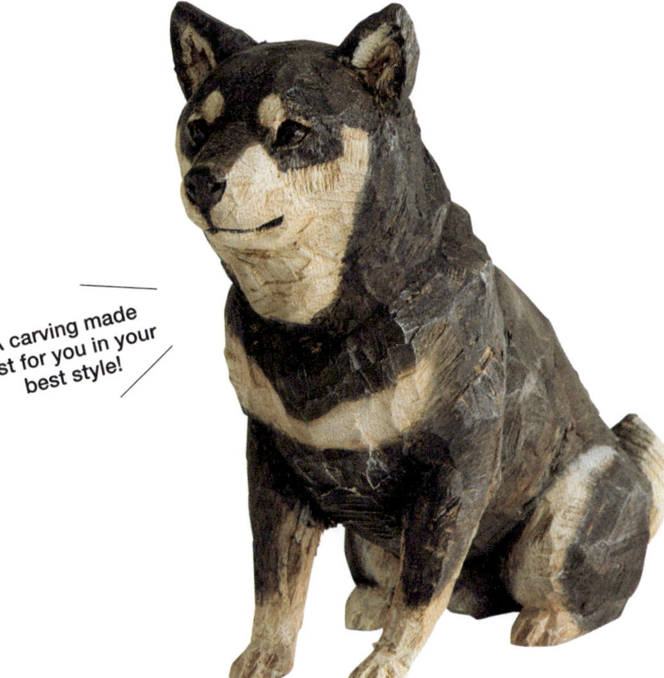

A carving made just for you in your best style!

Evaluating in Nature

Once I think it's finished, I will take a sculpture into the outdoors to evaluate whether it feels like the animal in the sculpture seems about to come to life and run off, and if it still looks realistic even under natural light. If something feels off, I repaint or recarve it as many times as necessary.

Through this process, the sculpture is refined until it looks as if it will spring to life. Hand-carved wooden animals convey a special warmth to everyone who sees and touches them. When handled, it should feel as though a miniature animal is right there in your hand—that's when you know the sculpture complete.

Remember the date it was finished as that animal's birthday. If it has no name, give it one; if it represents a pet, call it by that animal's name. If it's a small sculpture, take it with you on trips or outings and photograph it in various settings. A new "life" made of wood can go on journeys to places the real animal couldn't visit. And when you discover another animal motif you want to commemorate, buy new wood and try making it!

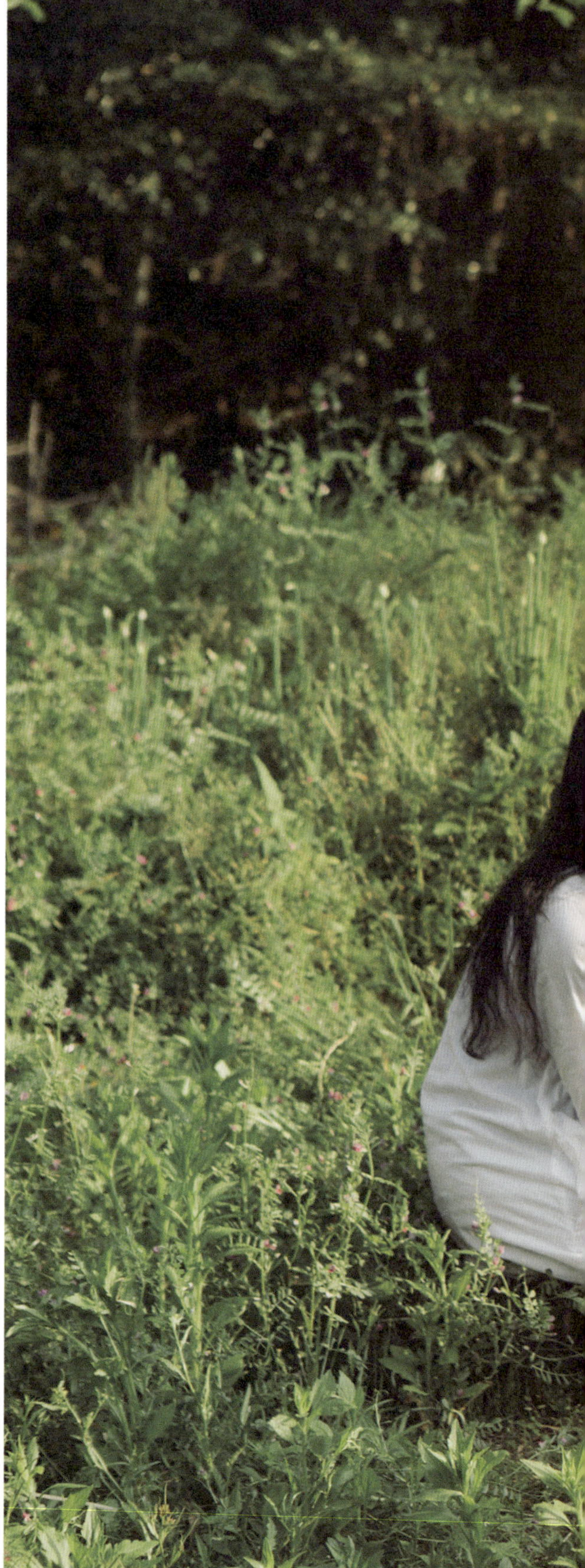

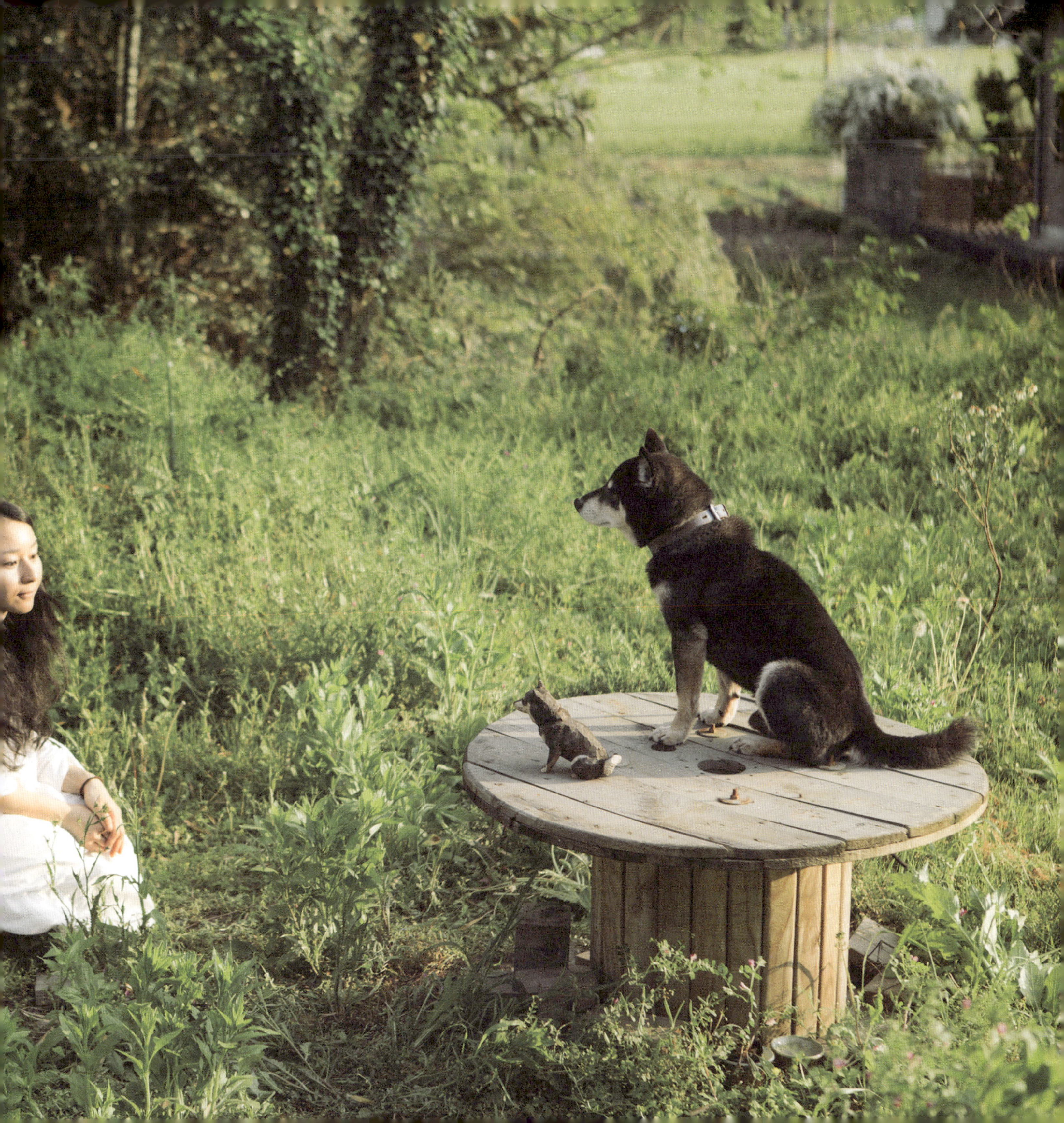

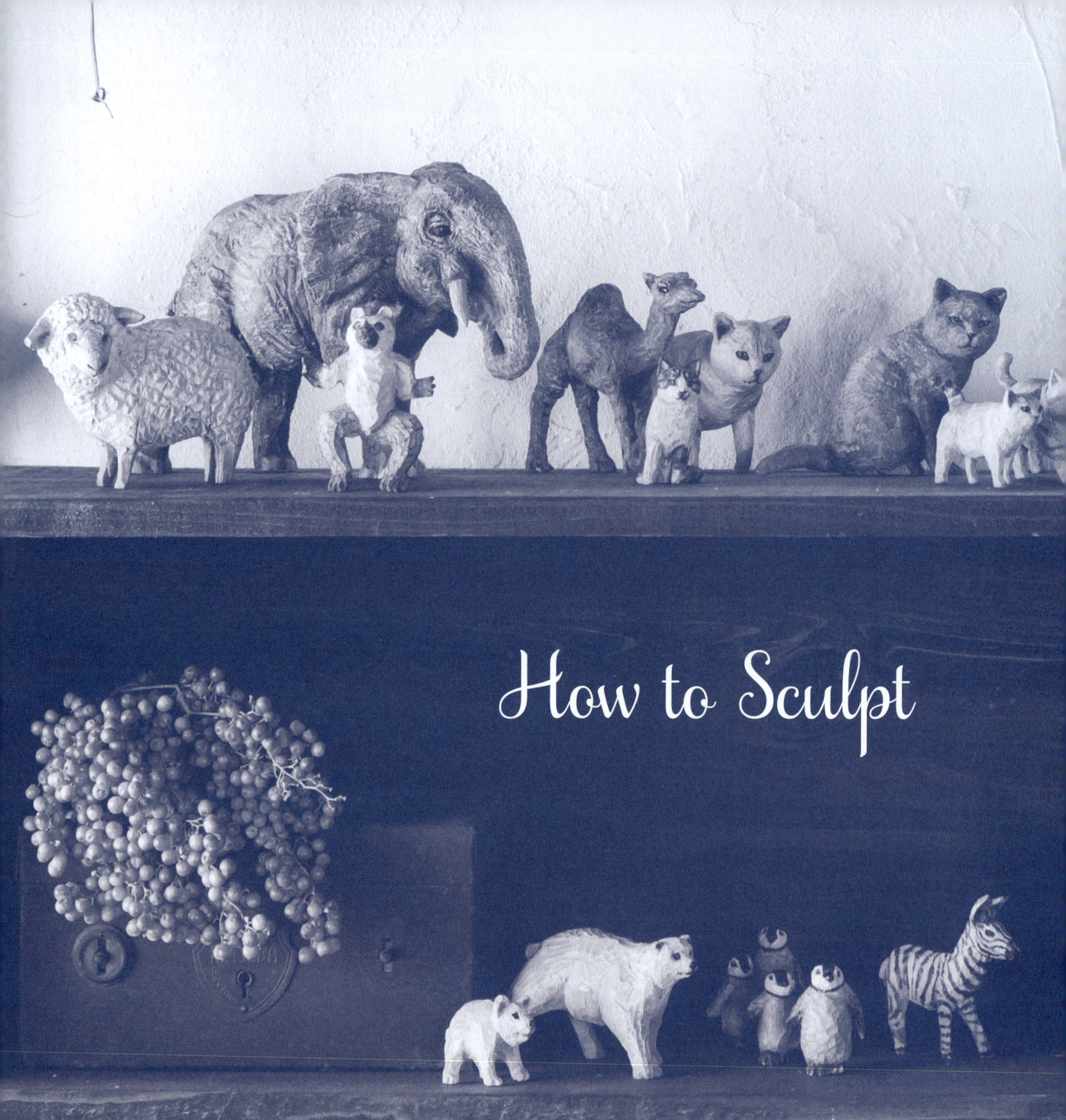
How to Sculpt

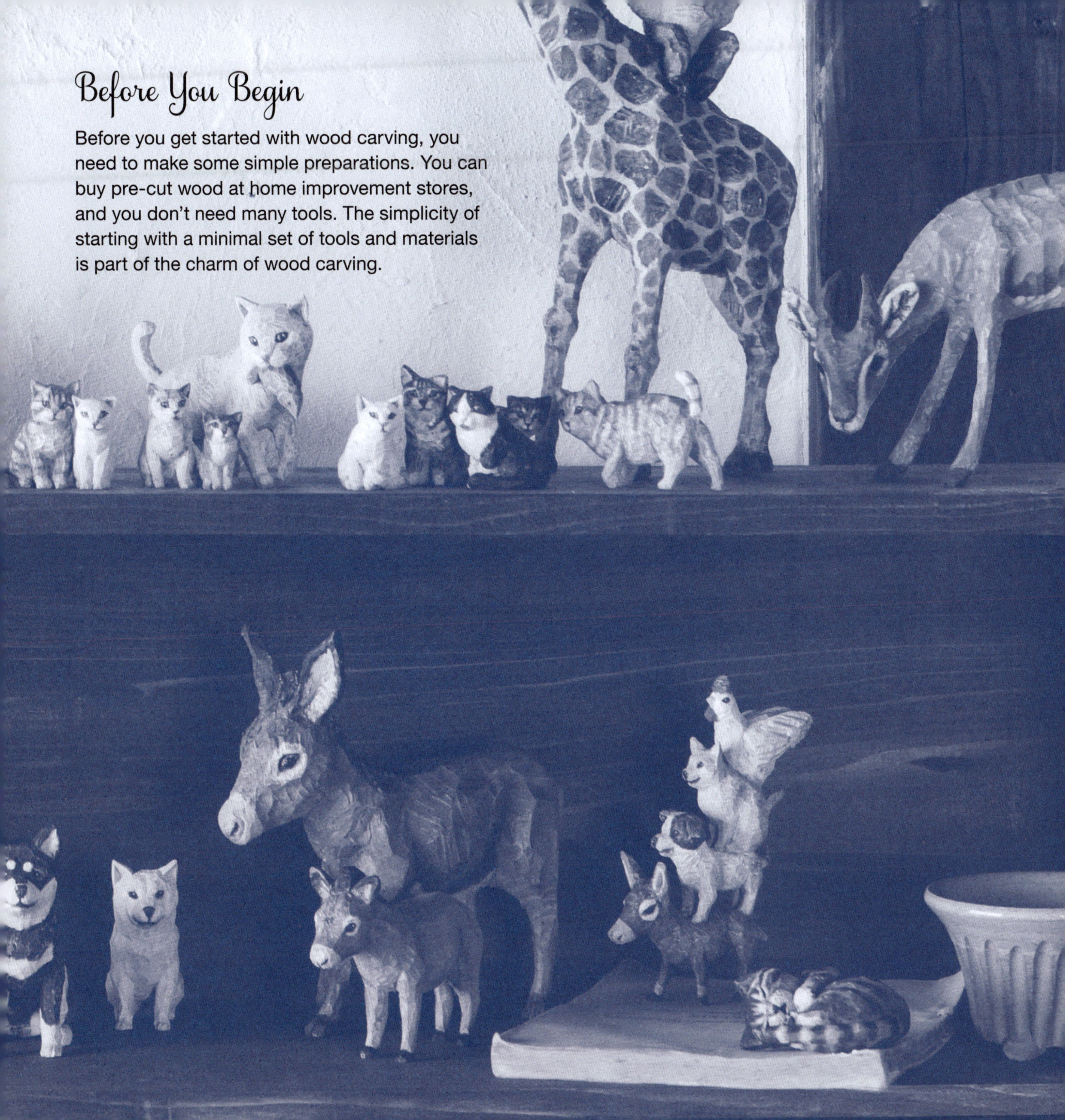

Before You Begin

Before you get started with wood carving, you need to make some simple preparations. You can buy pre-cut wood at home improvement stores, and you don't need many tools. The simplicity of starting with a minimal set of tools and materials is part of the charm of wood carving.

Types of wood

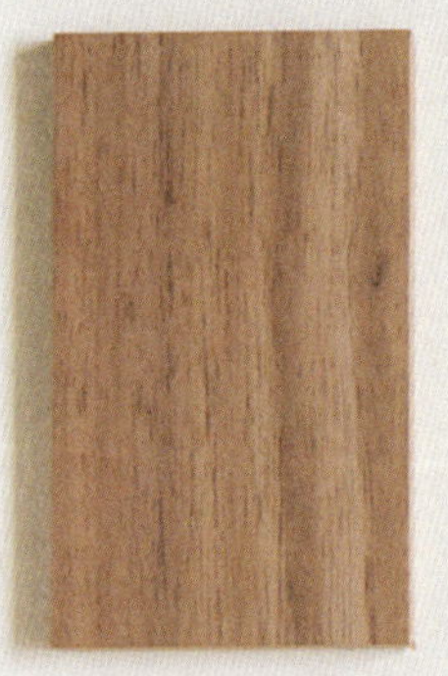

Walnut

A medium-hard wood that carves smoothly and is known for its beautiful reddish-brown color. Suitable for wooden products like brooches and spoons.

Camphor

Known in Japan as *kusa*, the author prefers this material for animal sculptures. It allows for free expression, with a moderate hardness and pleasant scent. Most of the wood used in this book is camphor, which is now rarely sold in home improvement stores in sizes suitable for carving, making it generally difficult to obtain. A selection of camphor wood is available to customers in Japan from the book's website: http://tenaraicho.jp/

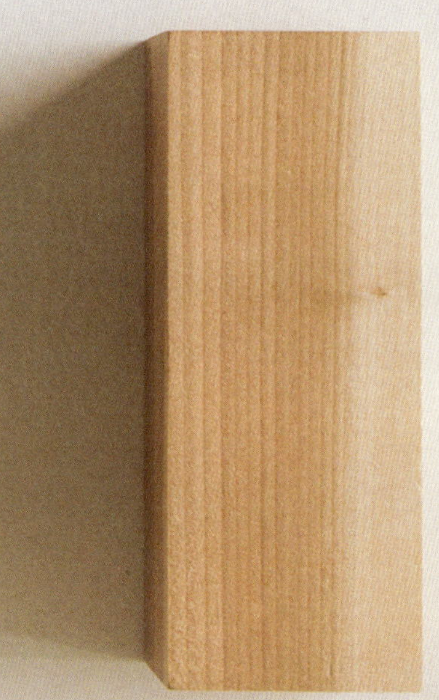

Cherry

Known in Japan as *sakura*, this hardwood allows for detailed depiction but requires a bit of strength for beginners. It smells lovely and is suitable for crafts.

Cypress

Known in Japan as *hinoki*, this wood is easy to carve and has a pleasant scent, making it suitable for crafts.

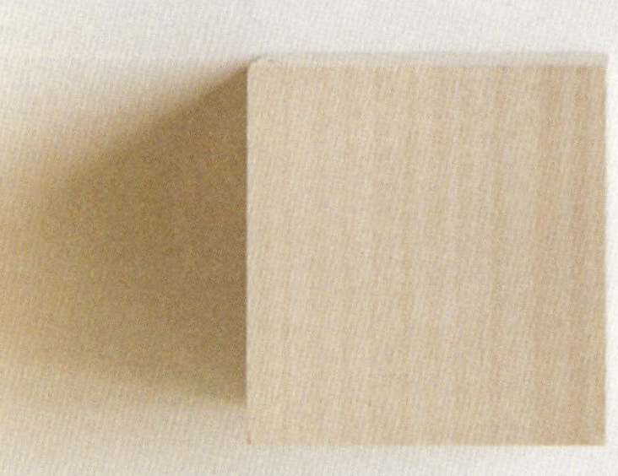

Basswood / Linden

Known in Japan as *hou*, this widely available wood has a slightly dull color, so care is needed when coloring. The hardness is moderate, and the grain is fine.

Redbud / Judas Tree

Known in Japan as *katsura*, this wood has a dense carving feel, suitable for detailed sculpture.

Tools you'll want to have on hand

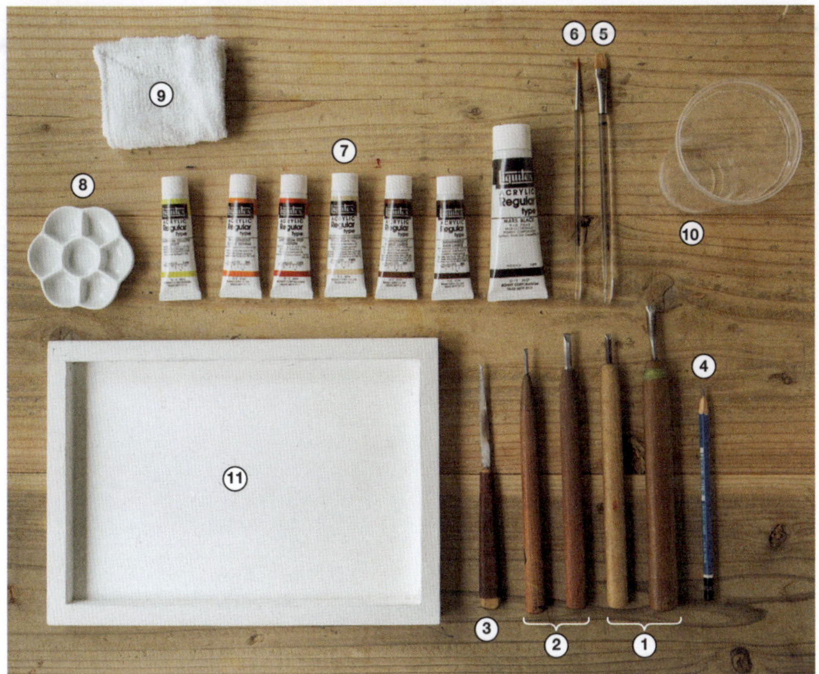

③ **Leather saw (fine-tooth craft saw)**

④ **Pencil (or pen)**

⑤ **Flat brush (No. 4)**

⑥ **Menso (ultra fine) brush (No. 0)**

⑦ **Watercolor paints**

Water-based paints, including acrylics, are fine for coloring. In this book, Liquitex acrylic paints are used.

From left to right: Cadmium Yellow Light, Transparent Burnt Sienna, Cadmium Red Medium, Unbleached Titanium, Transparent Burnt Umber, Transparent Raw Umber, Mars Black

⑧ **Paint palette**

⑨ **Dishcloth**

⑩ **Water container**

⑪ **Chip collection tray**

Use trays sold at art supply stores. Chips and sawdust stay inside, making cleanup easier. Also, the tray's lip helps secure the sculpture and provides a useful surface for sawing.

① Gouges

Scoop-shaped gouges are ideal for creating a soft surface finish on animal carvings. It does not require much force to use a gouge for carving, but sharpening one can be challenging if the blade dulls. Be careful not to overuse a gouge at the outset.

② Chisels

I recommend using a chisel for most tasks. They allow for precise control and make it easy to carve boldly for expressive work. Fine details can be inscribed using an angled chisel point.

About sharpening a chisel

If the blade chips, it becomes difficult to carve without applying excessive force, which can be dangerous. An inexpensive whetstone from a home-improvement store can be used for sharpening, but it may not sharpen well, resulting in a duller blade. For beginners, it might be an option to rely on a specialist for sharpening. Consider picking up a book about DIY sharpening.

For those starting out on a budget

Basic tools like these Tombow chisels and fine-tooth craft saw are affordable and widely available.

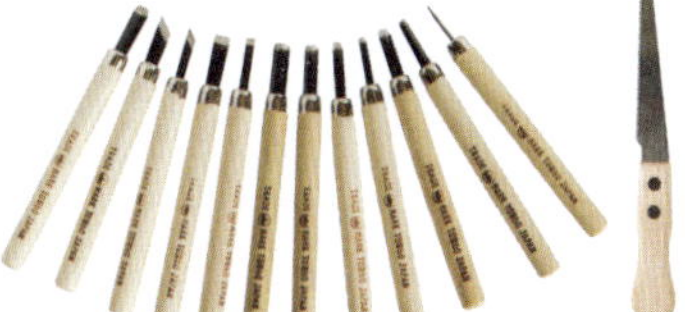

For those diving in with both feet

There are premium chisels available from Japanese artisan tool makers. Start with the minimum necessary number of chisels and add more as needed.

Other useful tools

Chip collection tray

A wooden tray under the work area keeps the chips and dust from scattering.

Woodworking vise

When working on larger pieces, it's safer if you secure the wood.

Learn about wood grain

As shown in the diagram, it's easier to carve when the grain of the wood runs vertically, and the model is positioned either sitting or standing sideways. The end grain, visible on the cross-cut surface of a log, is composed of fibers arranged end-on, making it difficult to carve directly across. As you continue carving, if you encounter a rough angle that is difficult to carve, it's likely because you are going "against the grain." Carving from the opposite direction, "with the grain," will make it easier.

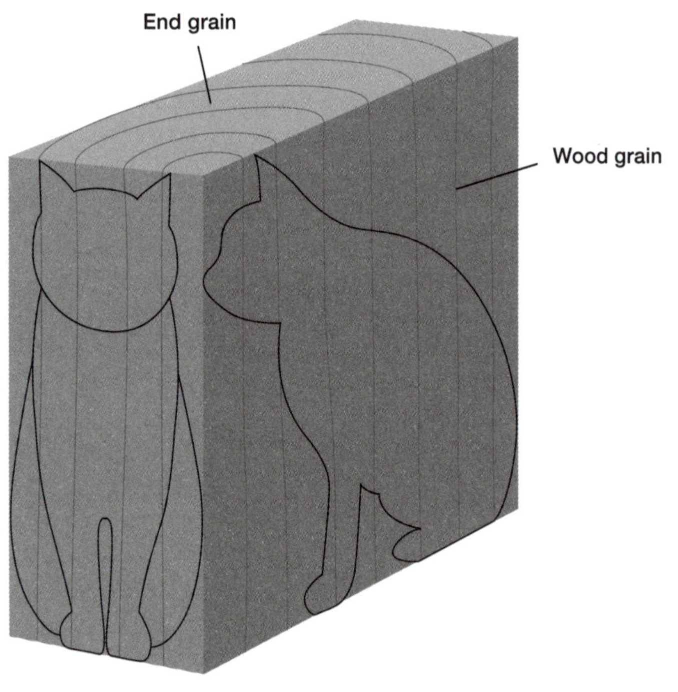

Safety first

The basic rule of wood carving is to never place your hand in the path of the blade. It's best to ensure that your hands are not near the blade in general. The same applies to saws; if your hand isn't in the way of the transit of the teeth, you are unlikely to injure yourself. As the sculpture nears completion, there will be less material to hold onto, making it difficult to stay out of harm's way. In such cases, reduce the force of your strokes, "choke up" on the tool (grasp it closer to the blade) for finer control, and carve while pressing toward the work surface for safety. For beginners, wearing thick leather gloves or synthetic "cut gloves" on the hand that is grasping the wood is also a good precaution.

Kitty Brooch

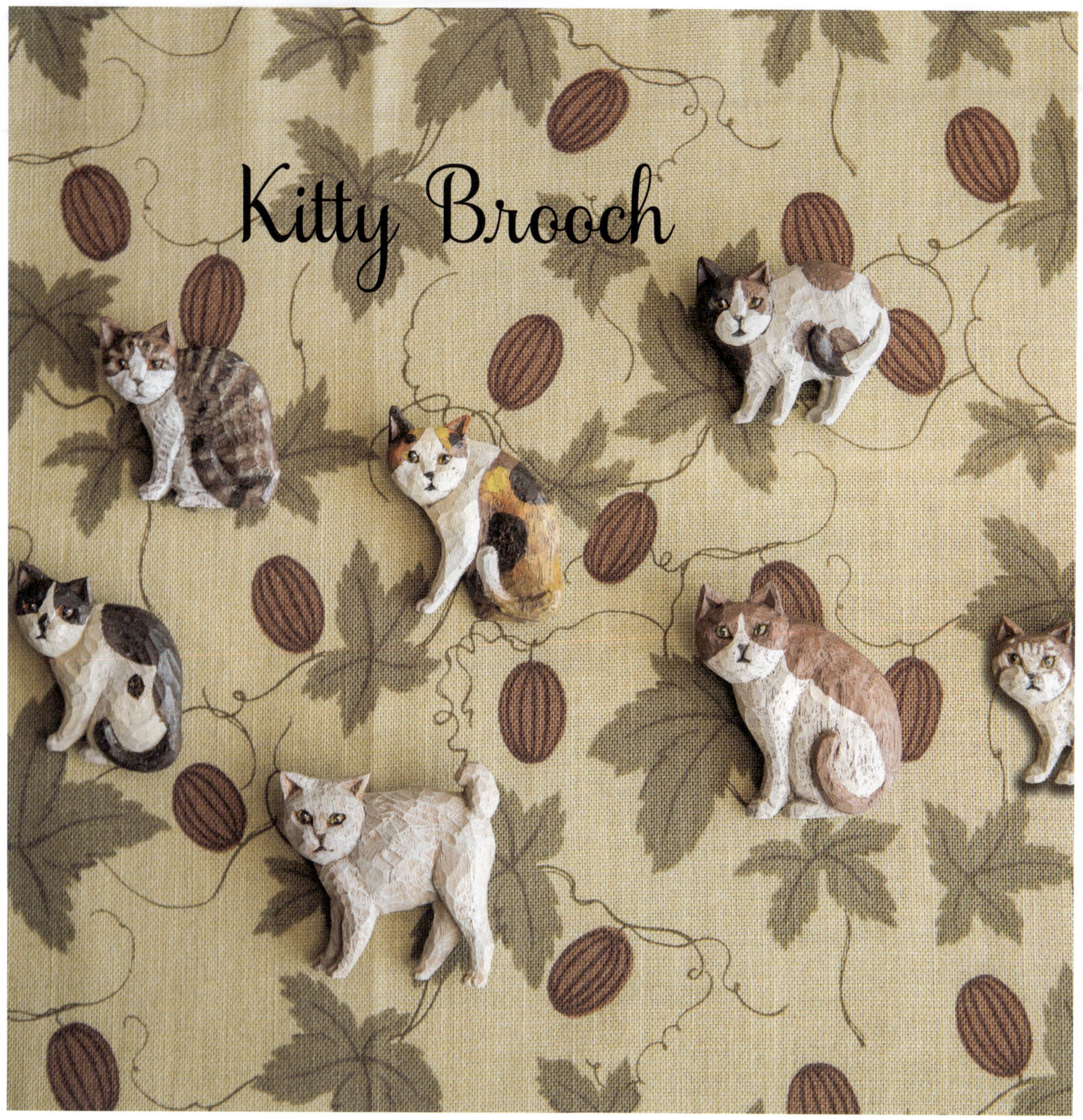

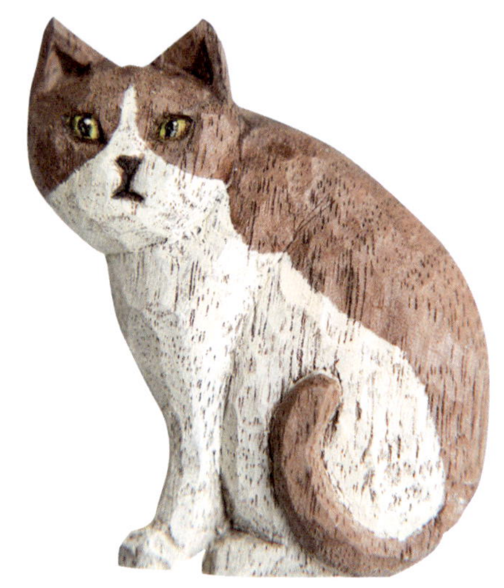

Wearing a cat-shaped accessory can instantly brighten up your usual outfits. Try carving a brooch that looks like your own cat, or make one as a gift for a friend's cat. Because it's a "relief" carving (not fully "in the round"), it's also a great practice project for those new to using carving tools. It's time to take on the challenge of making a cute cat brooch!

Kitty Brooch

Materials:

- Wood block (walnut is used in this example)
- Pen or Pencil
- Saw
- Flat chisel
- Gouge (curved chisel)
- Acrylic paints
- Paint brushes
- Varnish (clear)
- Rag (for varnish application)
- Pin back hardware (1-in / 25-mm safety pin)
- Attachment screws (pin back screws—M2.5x4mm or similar)
- Screwdriver

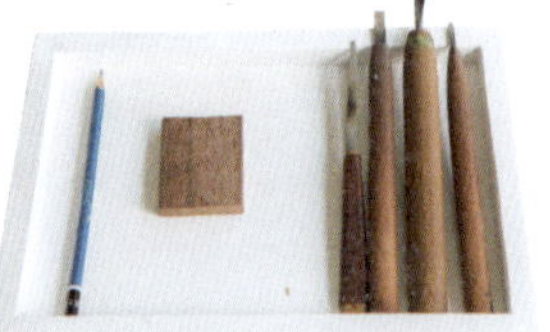

Which wood should you use?

The wood used for brooches can include easy-to-carve types like magnolia and camphor, as well as slightly harder woods like walnut and cherry, which are more challenging to work with but recommended. If possible, choose wood in a color that closely matches the cat you want to carve.

1 Sketch

Start by sketching the shape of the cat you want to carve. Let's try drawing a cat in a sitting pose. Because the outline will fade as you carve, draw it roughly. If the pencil lines are hard to see, consider using a permanent marker for the outline.

Let's think about the grain of the wood.

It's easier to carve with the grain running vertically. Be careful when extending thin parts like tails or limbs horizontally in your sketch, as wood splits more easily vertically (along the grain), which can cause it to break during carving.

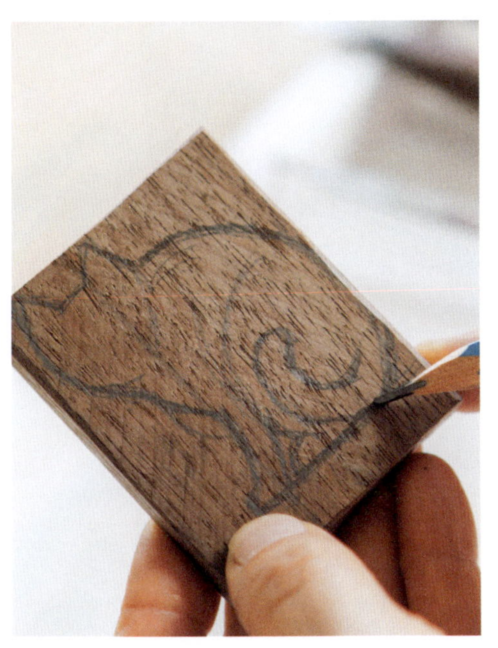

Roughly sketch your favorite pose of the cat for the brooch. Draw with the grain of the wood running vertically.

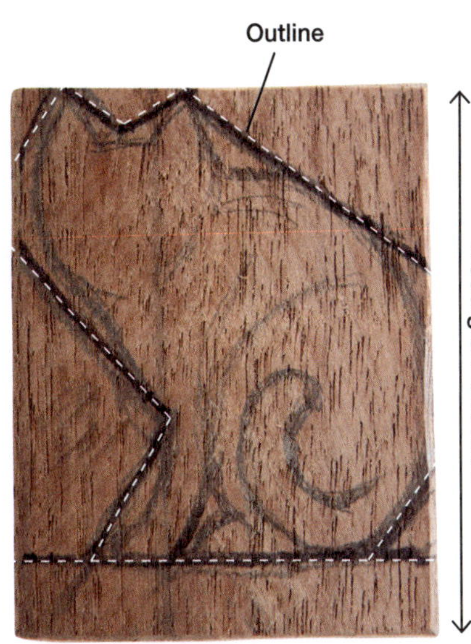

Determine and then draw the outline where you will trim away excess wood. For areas with large curves, plan to cut in stages.

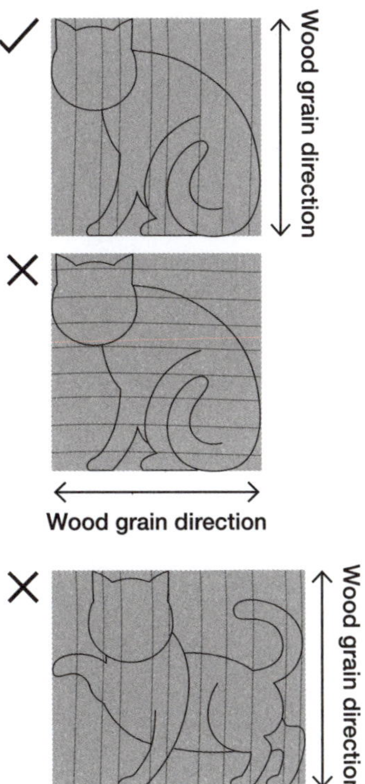

2 Saw

The process involves using a saw to cut off the
excess wood outside the sketch outline. This is
done to minimize the amount of carving necessary
using the chisel afterward. Be very cautious to
avoid injuries.

Using a saw

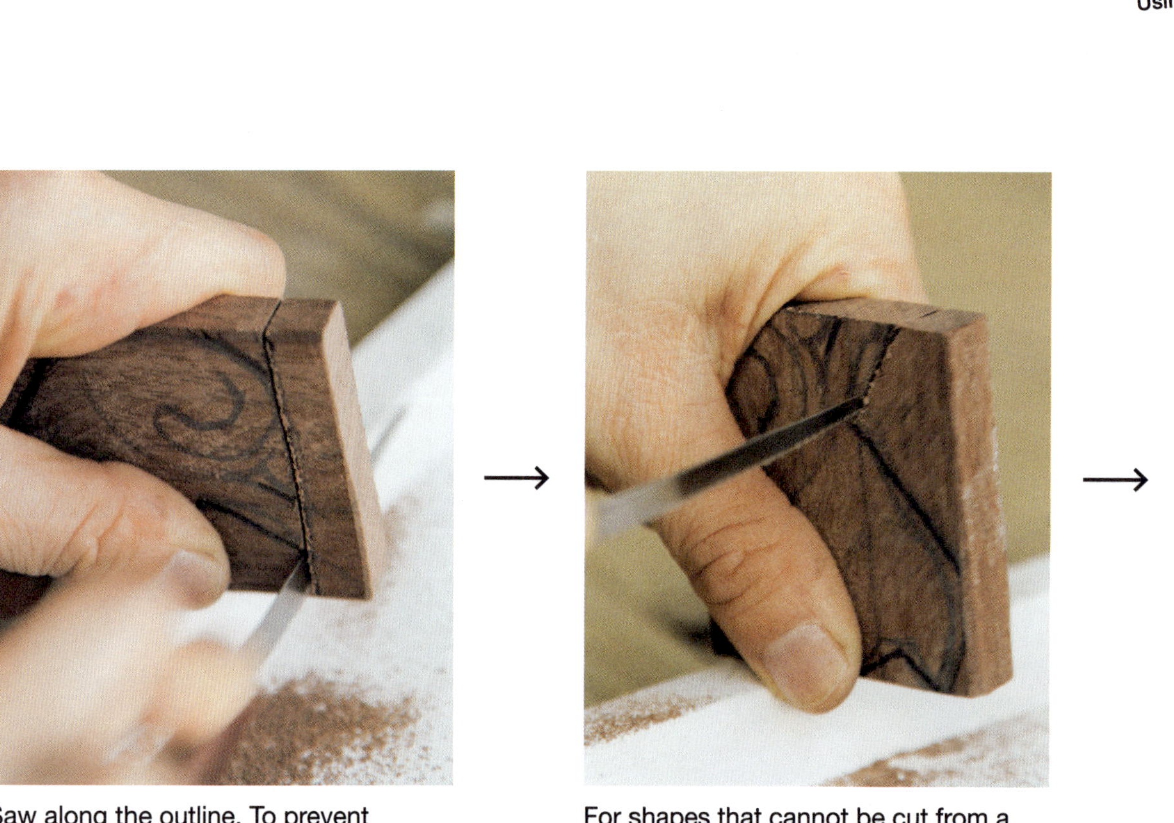

Saw along the outline. To prevent
splitting at the end, hold both pieces
of wood firmly and cut slowly when
finishing the cut.

For shapes that cannot be cut from a
single direction, rotate the wood and cut
from two directions.

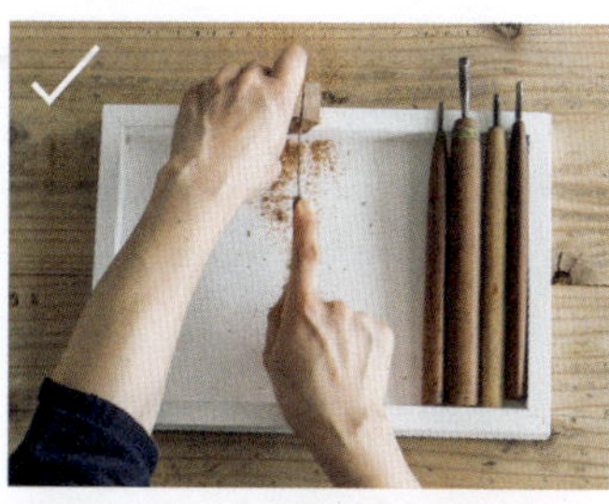

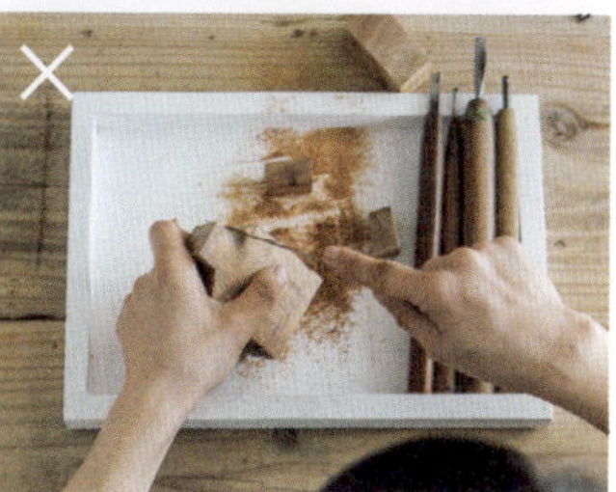

Note

Starting the cut

Extend the hand holding the wood as much as possible and insert the saw straight in relation to your body. Hold the saw with four fingers, and place the index finger along the blade. Tighten the muscles of your chest and pull with your shoulder to make the initial cut easier.

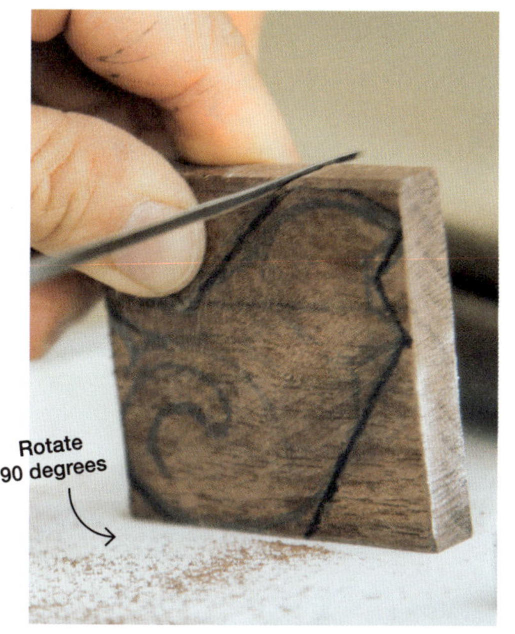

Make sure the saw does not wander toward the hand that is holding the wood.

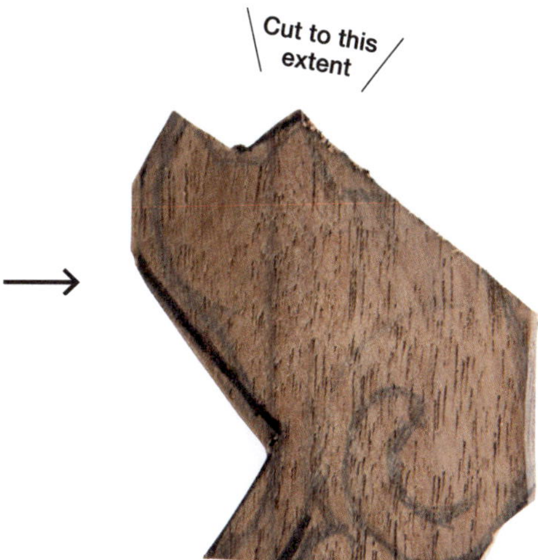

Note

How to use the chip collection tray

Place the tray on a stable table and work within it. For those with less strength, pressing the wood against the edge of the frame with your thumb while carving can make it easier to apply force. Once you get the hang of it, you can also try carving with the wood simply pressed against the surface of the tray.

3 Rough out

The first step using a chisel is roughing out. After cutting out the outline, continue to carve the overall shape to bring it closer to the envisioned image, focusing on boldly and broadly carving to enhance the three-dimensionality of the piece.

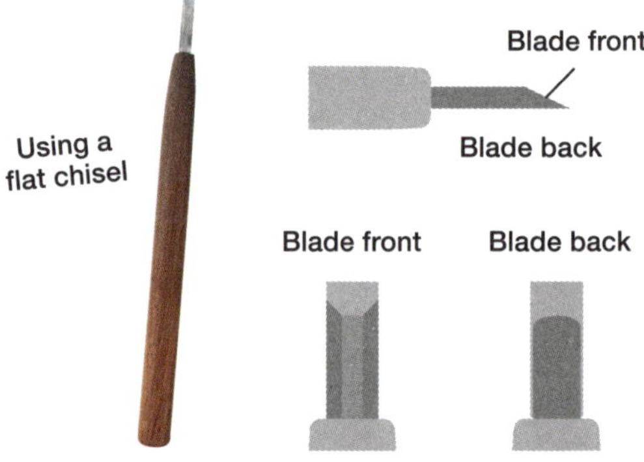

3-1

Smooth

Refine the lumps and bumps along the outline with the chisel.

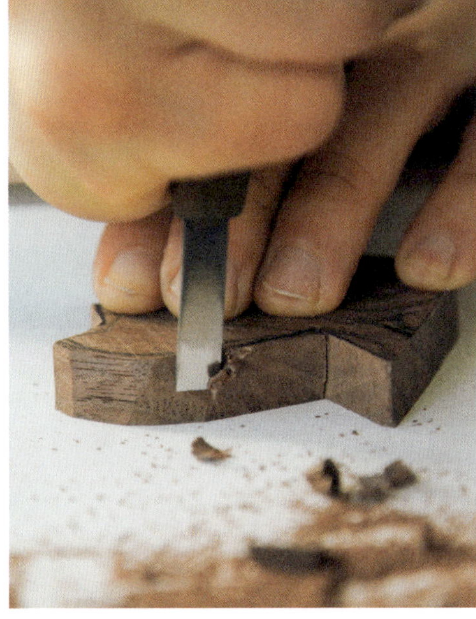

Work the chisel vertically from above following the sketch. Orient the blade front inside, toward the sculpture.

3-2

Carve into a three-dimensional shape

To enhance the three-dimensionality, shave down surface of the body part.

The body is a part that is shaved down one level lower than the face! Draw diagonal lines to make it visually clear

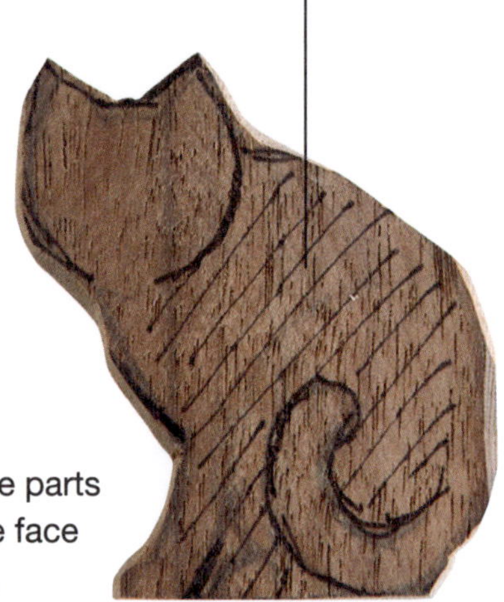

It's okay to sketch lightly on the parts that will protrude most, like the face and tail, to keep them in mind.

Let's make a notch

Preemptively inserting the chisel vertically along the jawline and tail ensures you don't accidentally carve into the face or tail. Make defining cuts to prevent over-carving or accidentally carving off delicate parts.

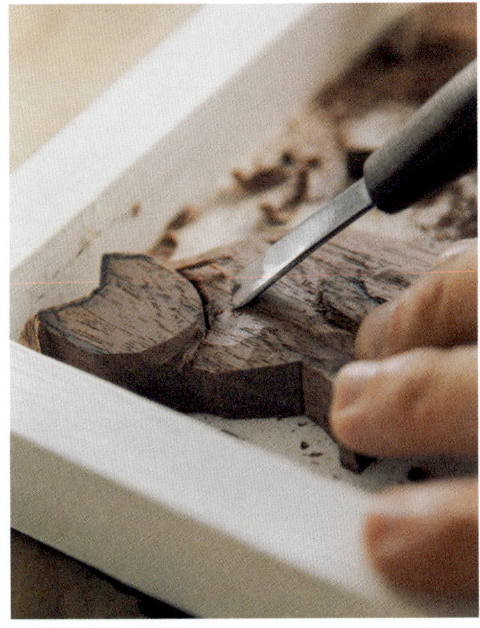

Carve out all areas where diagonal lines are drawn. Make firm cuts to create clear steps.

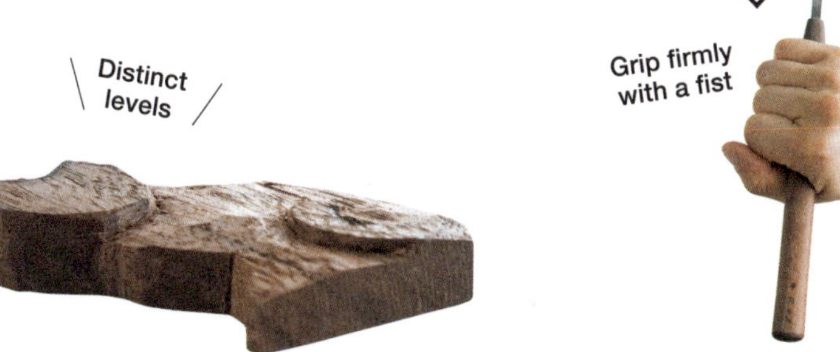

How to hold the chisel

Use a grip that's comfortable for you, whether holding it like a pencil or firmly with a fist. When carving downward, a fist-grip is useful; when pushing to carve, a pencil-like grip makes it easier.

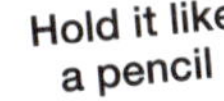
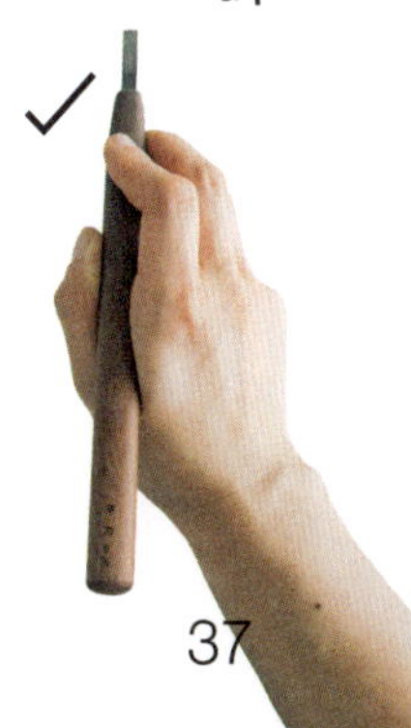

3-3

Add contrast to the face

Let's give the face a three-dimensional look, imagining it in three layers: ears, forehead, and tip of the nose.

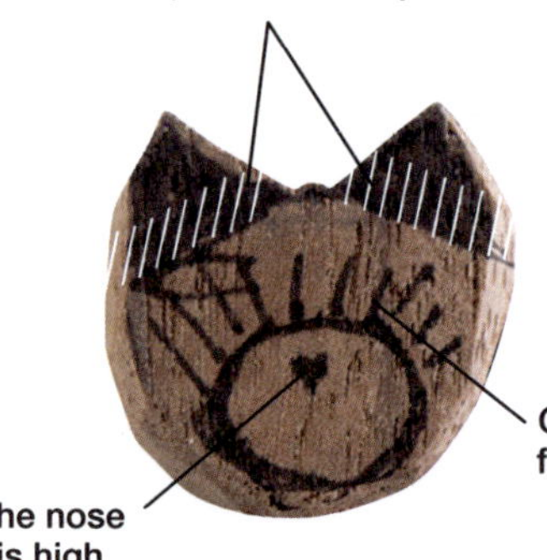

The tip of the nose protrudes the most on the face, so make a substantial change in elevation between the bottom of the jaw and the nose. The ears are set back farther than the forehead, so carve them even lower.

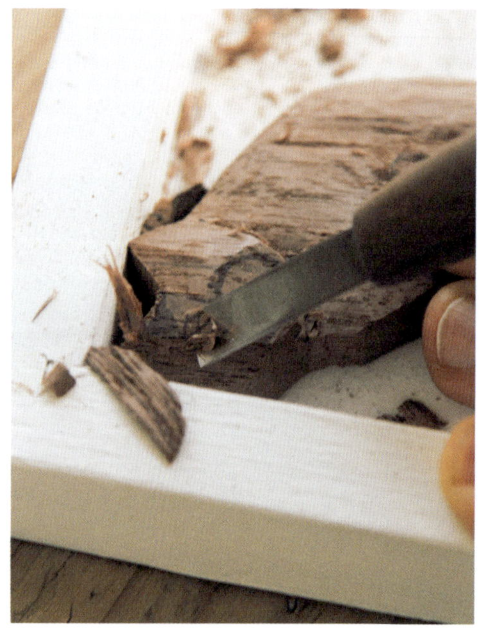

Make incisions at the boundary of the ears and carve them down a level. Carve the face to give it a gentle roundness.

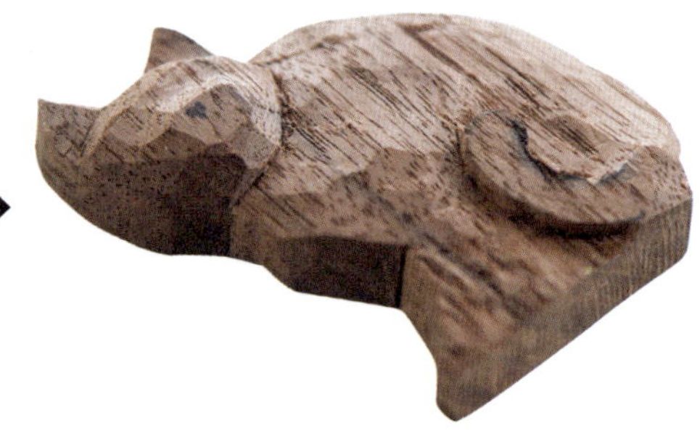

Holding the chisel near the blade-end of the handle and not applying too much force allows for safe and accurate work

3-4

Give shape to the body

Next, add definition to the body. Because a cat's thighs protrude forward, carve a valley between the thighs and the torso to make it three-dimensional.

Sketch the shape. The shaded boundary between the front and back legs will be the deepest valley.

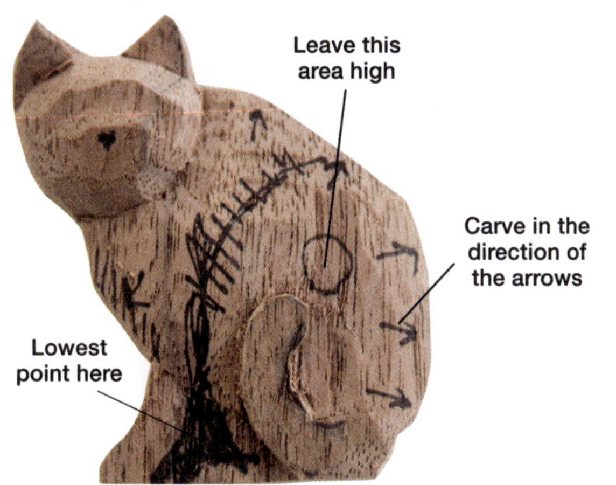

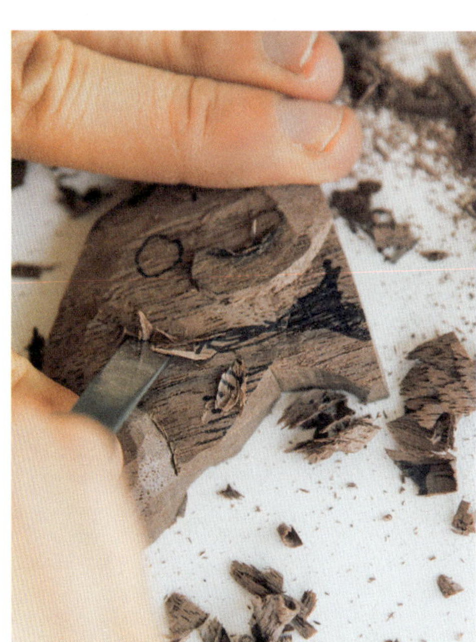

Carve deep valleys at the space between the front legs, back legs and torso, forming a triangular shape.

4 Refine

Chamfer to round angular surfaces. Once you have roughed out a three-dimensional shape, proceed to carve the entire piece to refine the curves. Work carefully and take your time.

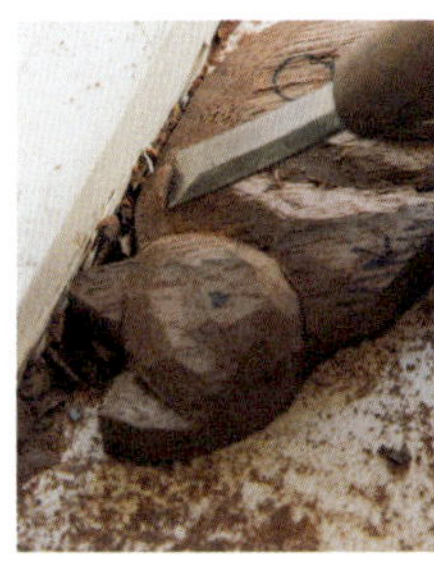

How to carve corners

When shaving off corners, if you place the piece against the tray's edge, you can apply force safely, as the chisel will stop at the lip of the tray.

4-1

Tighten up the entire carving

Check for any areas that have not been carved and adjust to maintain a consistent look.

For curves, use a thin flat chisel and make multiple cuts to smoothly carve them

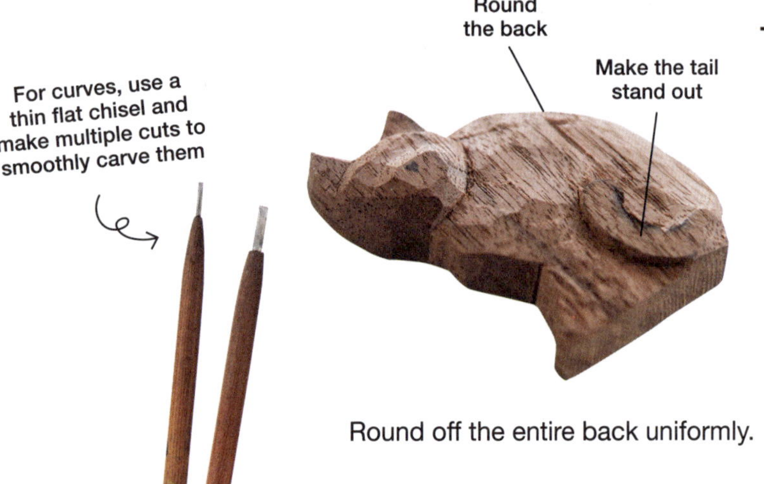

Round off the entire back uniformly.

→

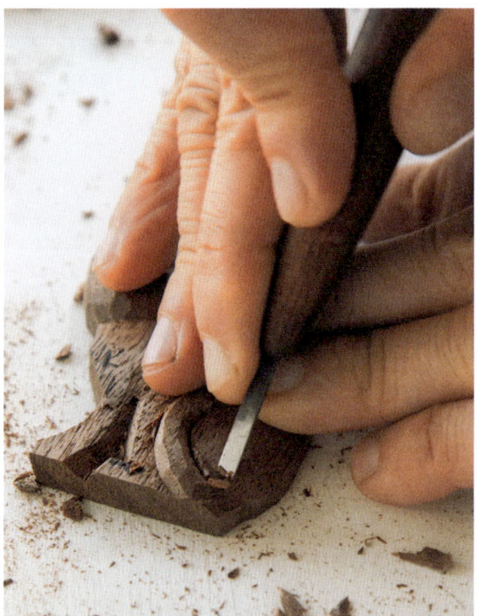

Tail details. Follow the shape of the tail with deep cuts to create sharp definition.

→

Hold the chisel near the blade and avoid applying too much force

4-2

Make the ears fully three-dimensional

Carve the back side of the model as well, to give the brooch a lighter impression. The back of the ears is particularly important. Because cat ears are angled forward, carve diagonally from the back to the front to make them three-dimensional.

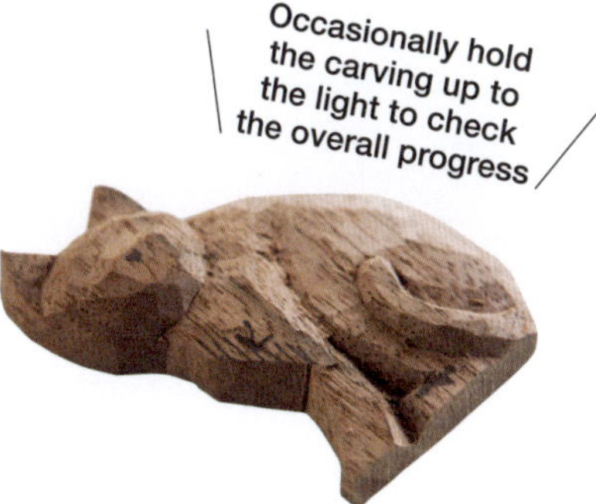

Occasionally hold the carving up to the light to check the overall progress

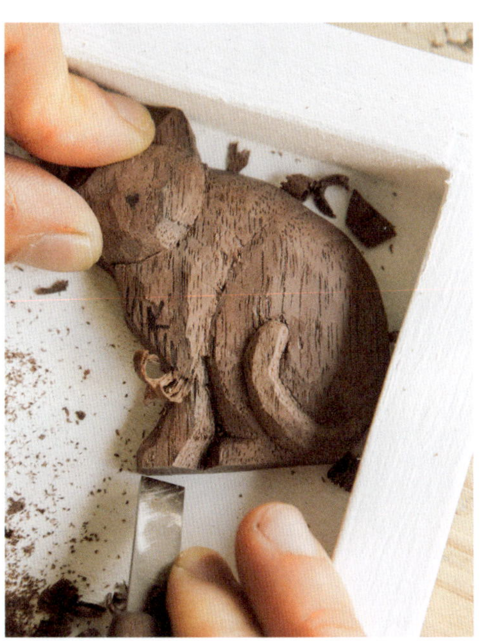

Make the toes three-dimensional too. Finish the spaces between the front and back legs neatly.

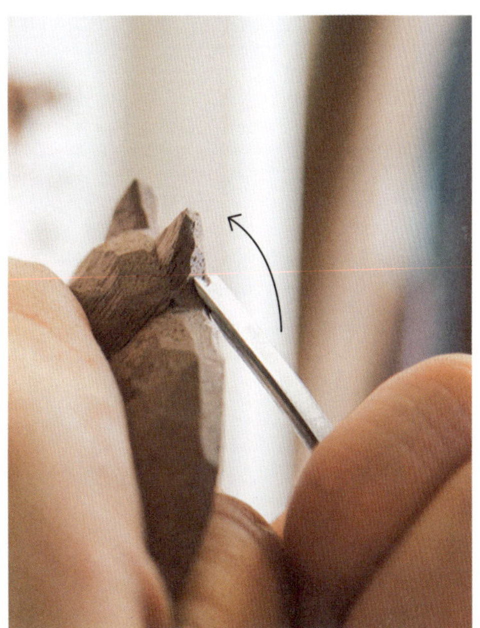

Smooth out any rough edges that could catch on things. Leave a flat area on the back for attaching the clasp at the end.

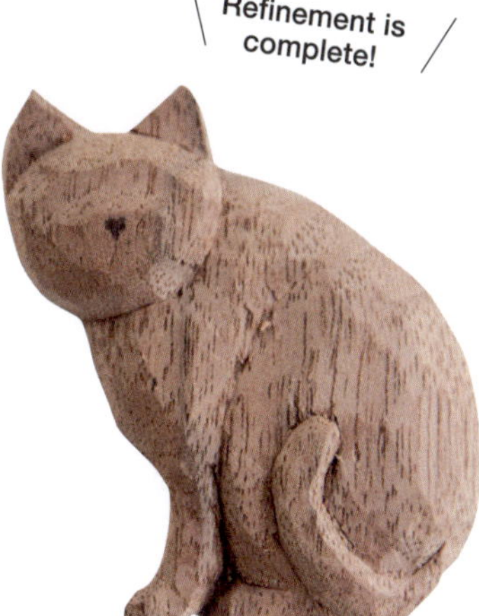

Refinement is complete!

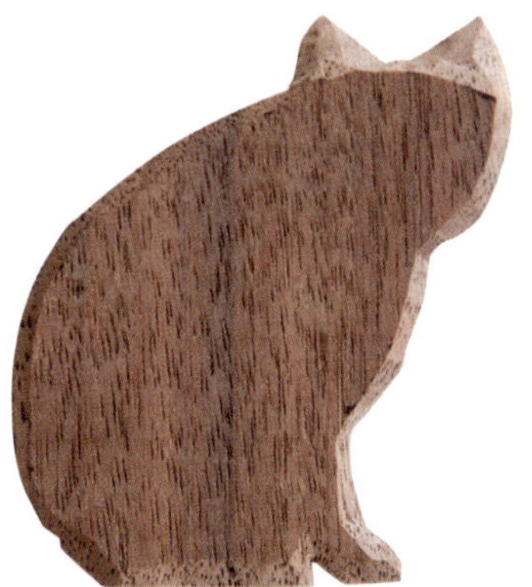

5 Finishing touches

Before painting, it is important to carve the fine details such as the parts of the face and the texture of the body to project a more lifelike look. However, carving too finely can sometimes result in a cold impression of the wood carving, so it's crucial to finish by carving boldly and roughly, and knowing when to stop.

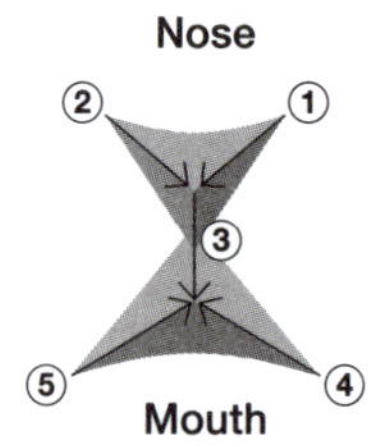

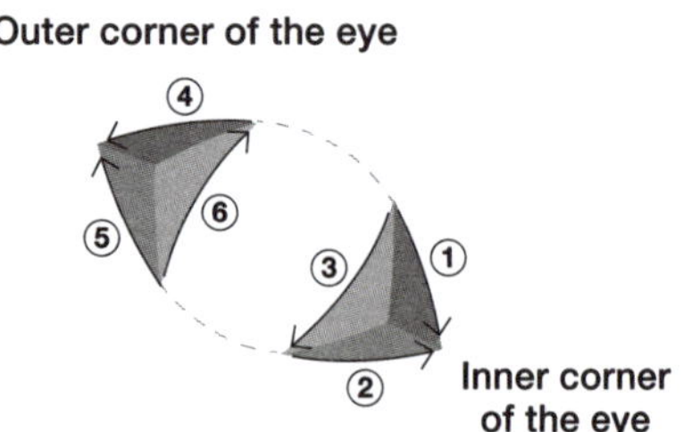

5-1

Finish the face

The face makes the model. Carefully and firmly carve each part: the eyes, nose and mouth.

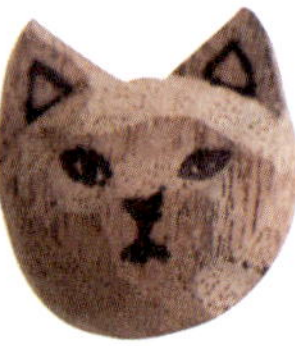

Lightly sketch the parts of the face

Tips for carving a cat's face

Imagine the nose as a small inverted triangle, and the mouth as a small triangle, and carve accordingly. Because a small chin is characteristic of a cat, carve around the chin to make it round.

Nose and mouth

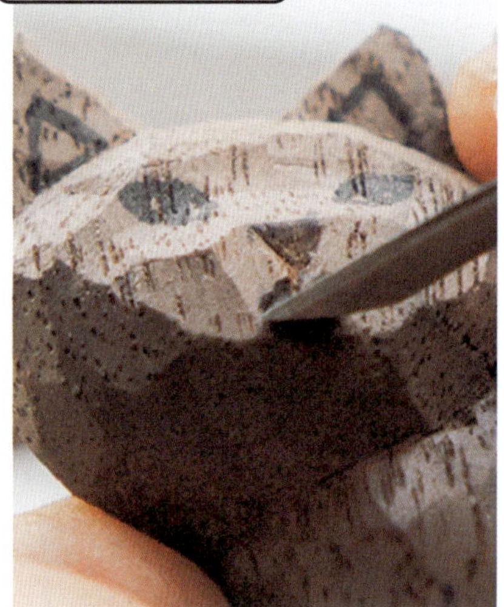

As shown in the diagram, make cuts in the shapes of the nose and mouth, and carefully carve around them in stages.

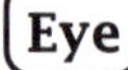
Use a thin flat chisel held like a pencil to lightly shave off the wood

Eye

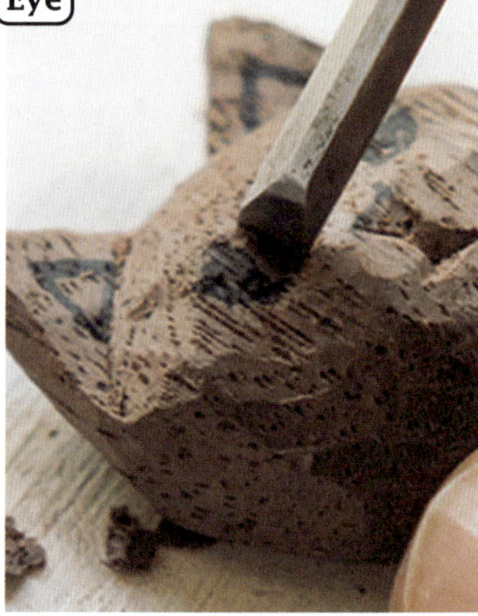

Start carving at the inner and outer corners of the eyes by making triangular cuts. Do not apply too much force, and visualize removing the wood inside the triangles.

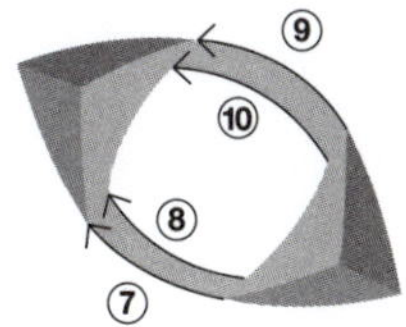

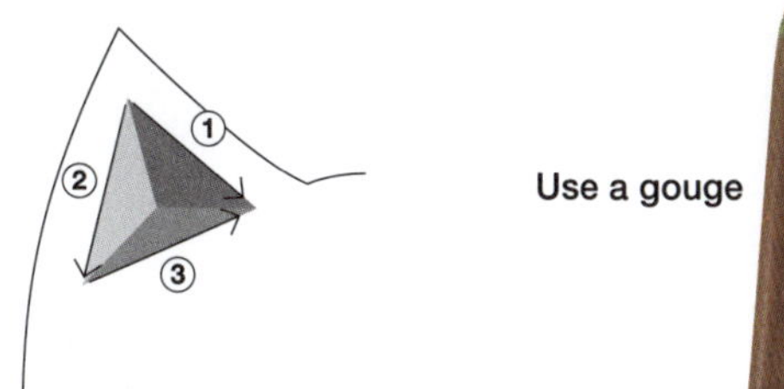

Use a gouge

5-2

Finish the body

Finally, use a gouge to create a sense of three-dimensionality and softness in the body. As you work, envision each part of the body like the thighs, shoulders and belly of the cat.

Ear

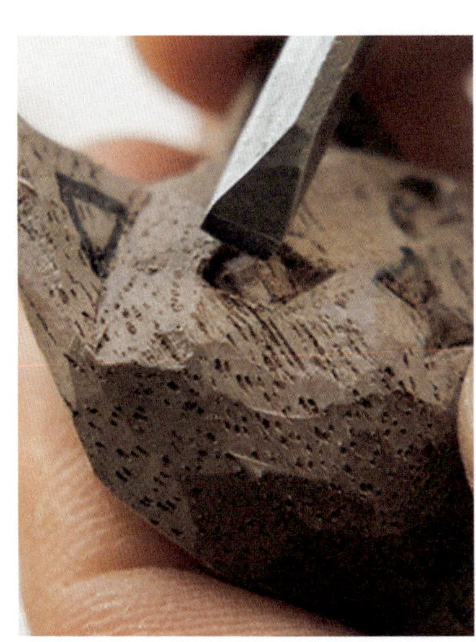

Connect the inner and outer corners of the eyes to form the shape of the eyes. Carve slowly and carefully around the eyes toward the eyelids, as if creating eyeballs.

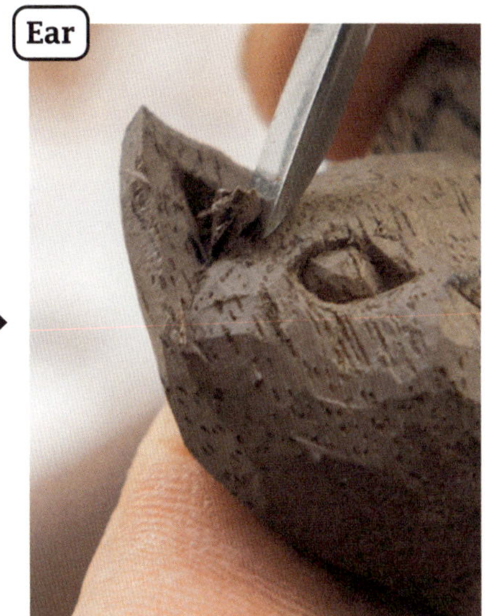

Carve the ears to create triangular recesses, similar to how you carved the eyes, following the steps ①→②→③.

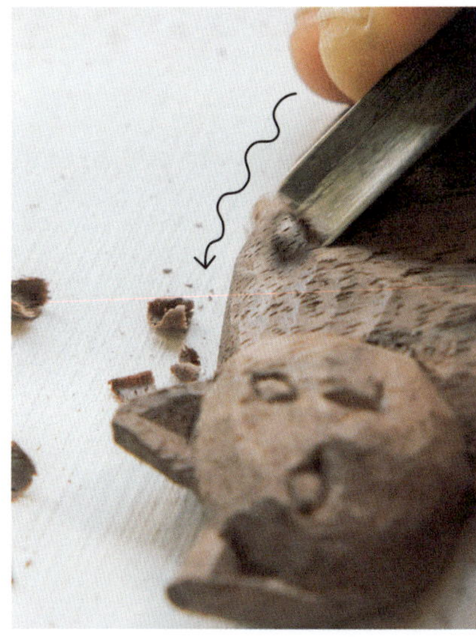

Add texture to simulate the cat's fluffy fur throughout. Imagine the flow of the fluffy fur and carve by wobbling the chisel to the left and right as you work.

6 Adding color

Painting the well-formed sculpture brings it to life through coloration. As you become more experienced, try painting without preliminary sketches for the eyes and patterns. This will produce a beautiful finish without any muddiness.

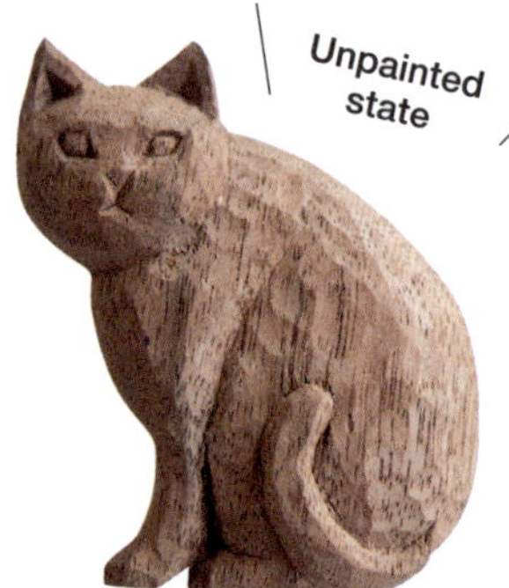

What is dry brushing?

When painting, always dab away any visibly wet paint with a cloth. Thinly coat the entire brush with paint, and use it to lightly apply color in a practically dry state.

6-1

Painting the face

The facial coloring is a crucial part that greatly affects the overall impression. Paint carefully and take your time.

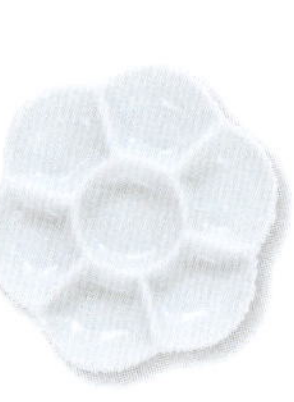

A "plum-dish" palette is easy to use

Fine detail brush

Coloring tips

Use a fine brush for detailed parts like the eyes. Avoid overpainting as it dulls the colors and can obscure the wood's texture. Consider the wood's natural color as one of the colors, and try to enhance it through painting.

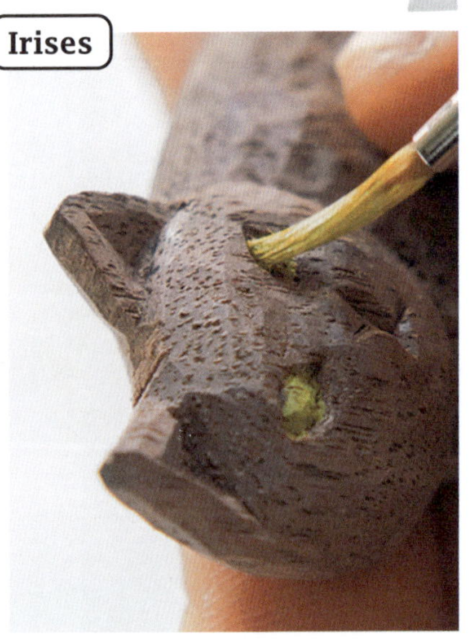

Start painting from the eyes using a fine detail brush. For eyes, choose a brighter shade within the same color family. Be careful not to let the paint spill over.

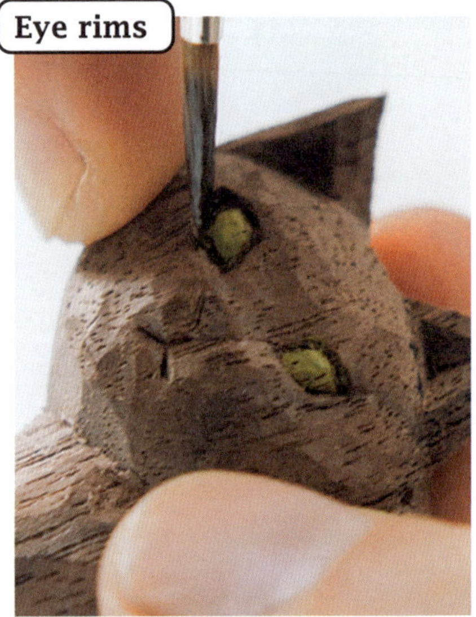

Adding black around the eyes like eyeliner makes it more cat-like. By the way, when carving a dog, "eyeliner" is often not added.

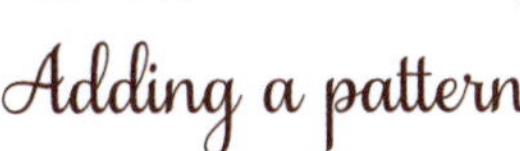

Note

Applying white paint

White color works well with the wood if you use an "unbleached" shade. Apply paint sparingly to create a fluffy fur appearance. Try to blend it well into the wood grain.

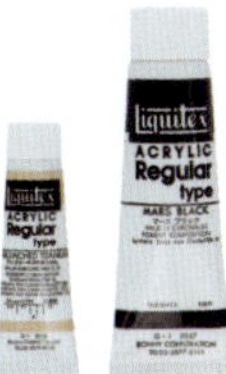

6-2
Adding a pattern

Add favorite patterns to the face and body. Paint whatever patterns you like, whether it's a pet cat or a stray.

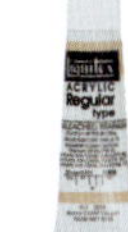

Pupils

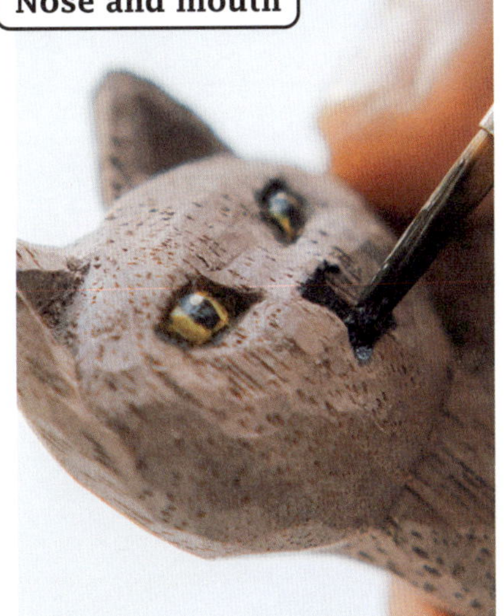

Nose and mouth

Carefully paint the pupils black. Cats look cuter with large black pupils, but paint the eyes as you like them. Adding a small white highlight makes them look more lively.

Paint the nose and mouth. Add your favorite colors to the carved areas. If you want sharp lines, shave off the excess paint with a chisel after painting to refine it.

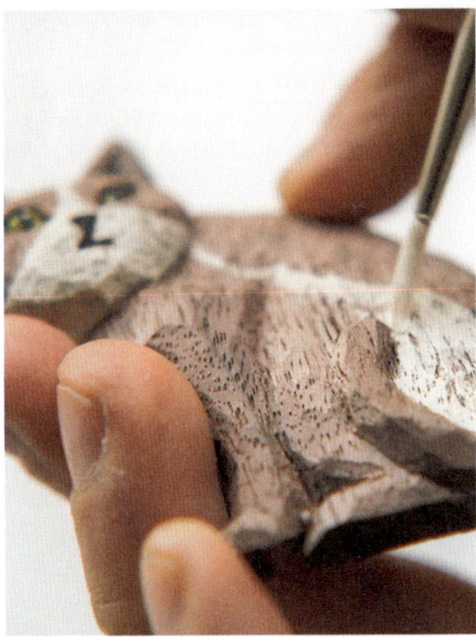

Feel free to add any patterns you like to the body, just like the face. Use a larger brush for large areas and frequently reload the brush with paint.

7 Seal and complete

Note

Varnish

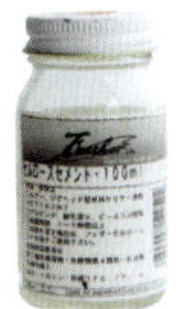

Soak a portion of a rag in varnish and apply it evenly over the entire surface by dabbing it. One complete application should be sufficient.

Note

Hardware installation

For pins, screws will be more durable than glue. Right-handed people should choose a clasp that opens to the right, as shown in the photo, for ease of use.

Application

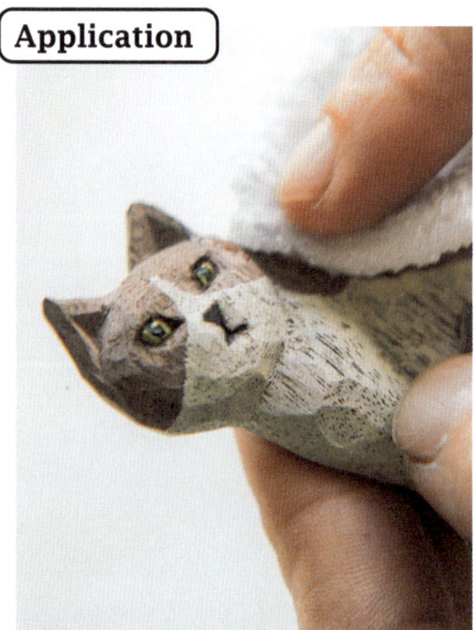

Apply a protective varnish to the surface to protect the paint against dirt and moisture. Do not apply varnish to the back, as it may stain clothes.

Affix the pin

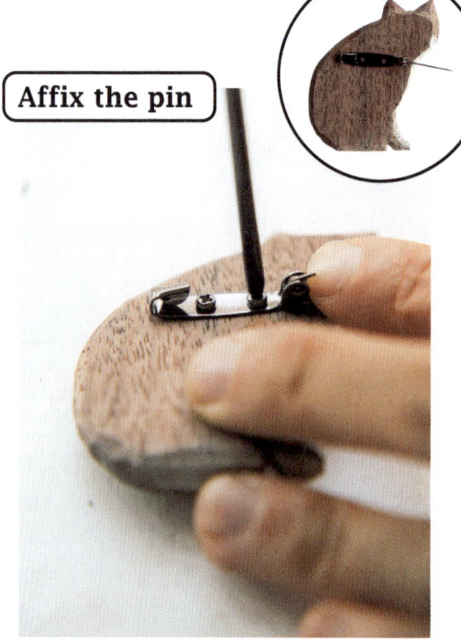

Attach the hardware slightly above the center of the brooch, being careful not to extend beyond the edges of the brooch.

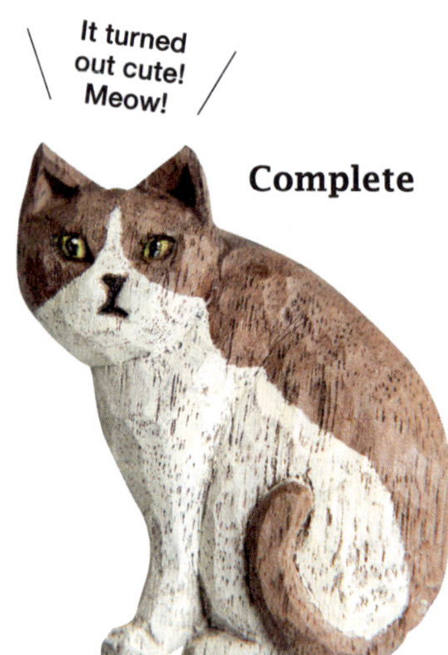

Complete

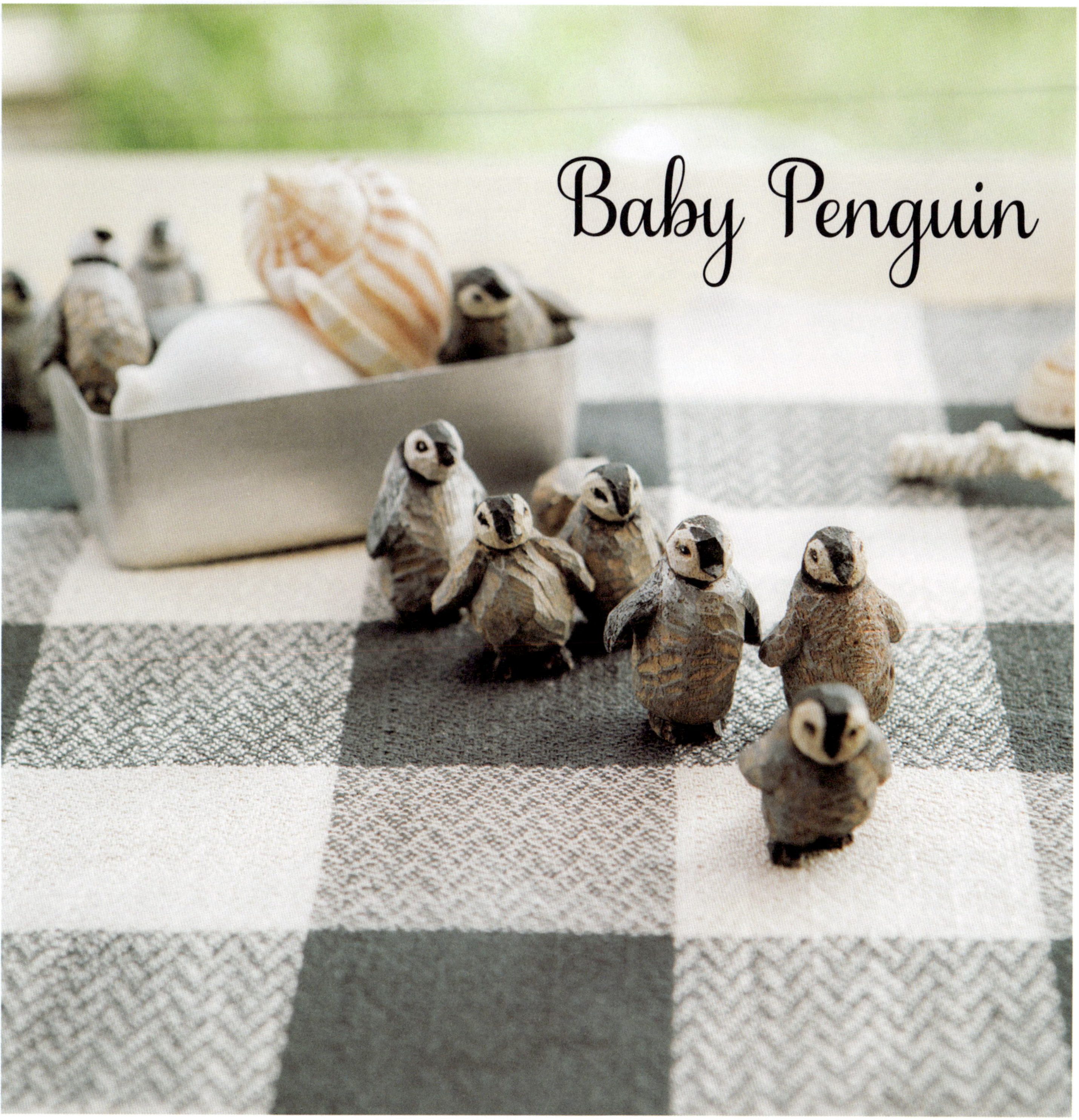

Baby Penguin

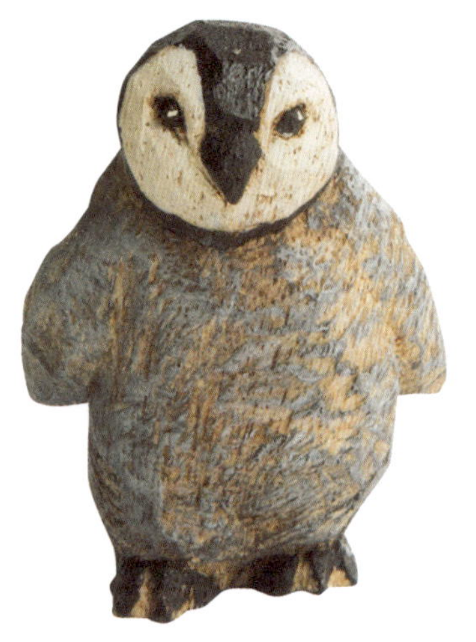

Here is a small and cute wooden carving of a baby penguin. Its charm can add a playful feel to any room. This is perfect for your first in-the-round three-dimensional project as it provides a good opportunity to learn about the flow of sculpting. Because it requires few materials, try making several chicks to display in a group.

Baby Penguin

Materials:

- Wood block
- Pen or pencil
- Saw
- Flat chisel
- Acrylic paints
- Paint brushes

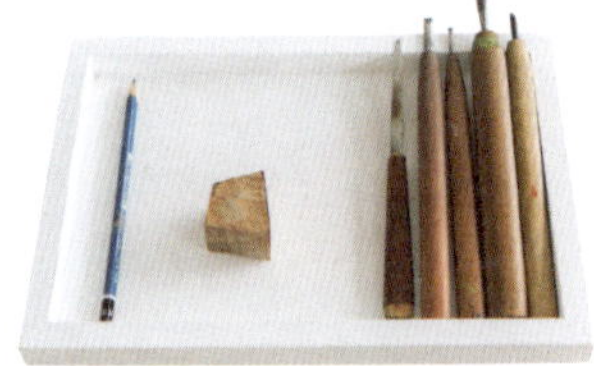

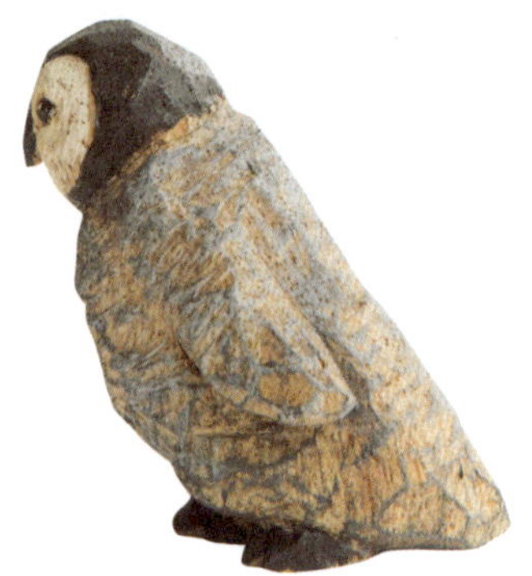

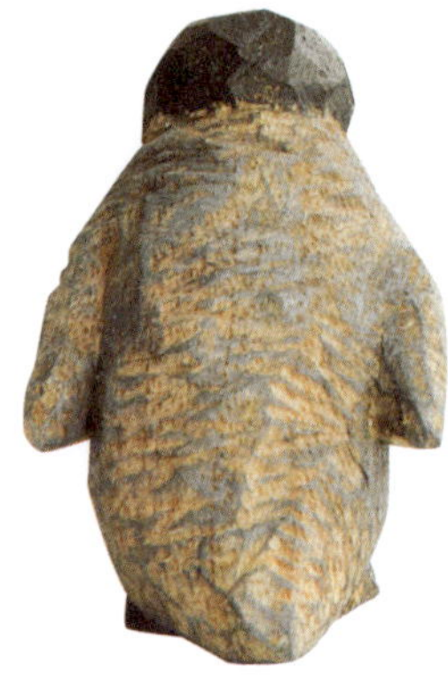

1 Sketch

Start with the side view

For three-dimensional carvings, start by sketching the side view. I find it's easier to grasp the overall form of the sculpture this way than by starting with the front view.

Follow the sketch to determine the outline to be cut with the saw.

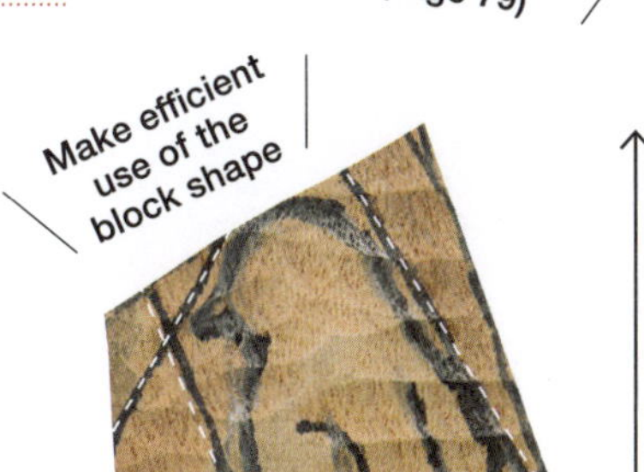

2 Saw

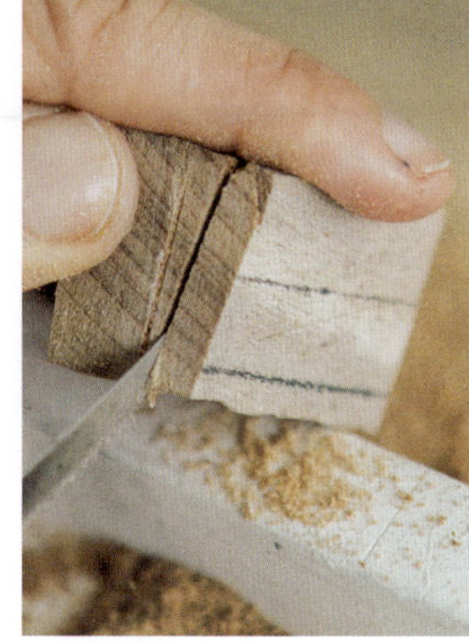

Cut along the outline with the saw. Be meticulous, as the block used for the penguin is small and tolerances are tight.

3 Rough out

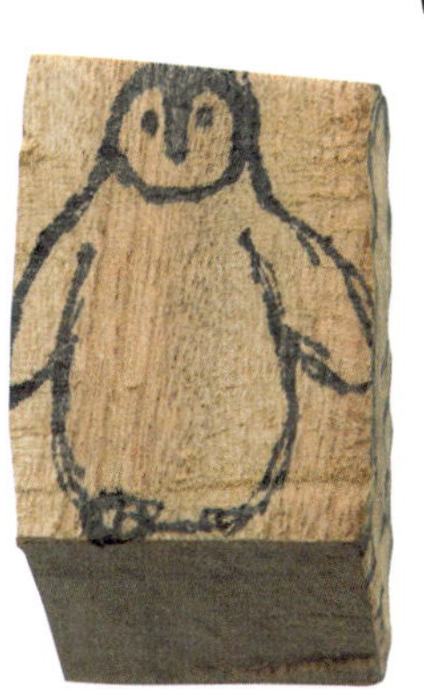

Define the structure

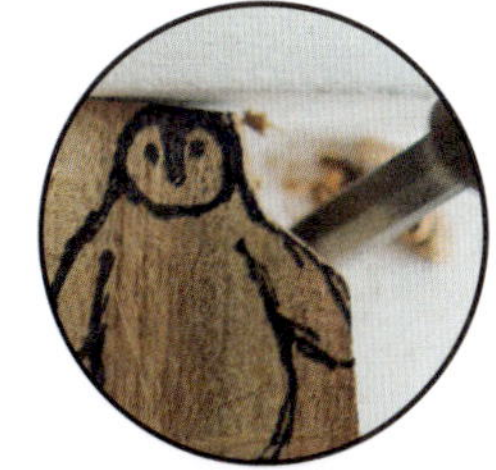

Following the front sketch, carve down from above along the outline. Be very careful to avoid injury.

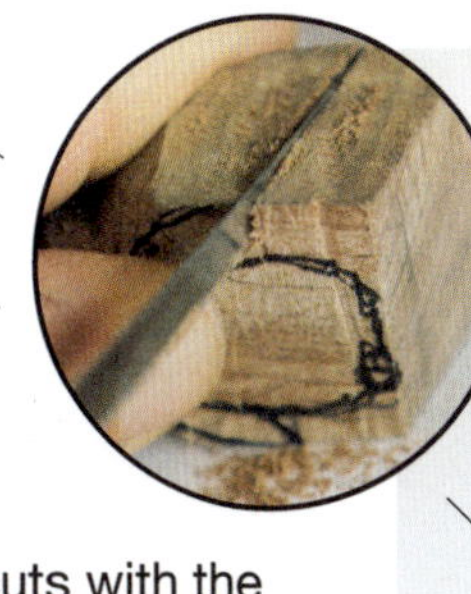

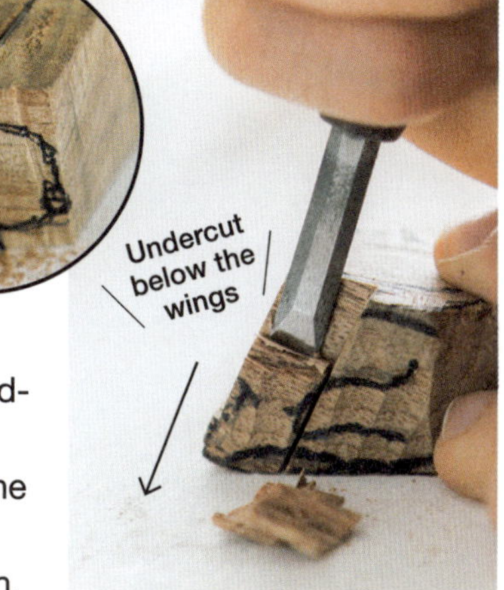

Make cuts with the saw along the spread-out wings. Use the chisel to carve out the area under the saw cuts in one operation, taking advantage of the wood grain.

Carve into a three-dimensional shape

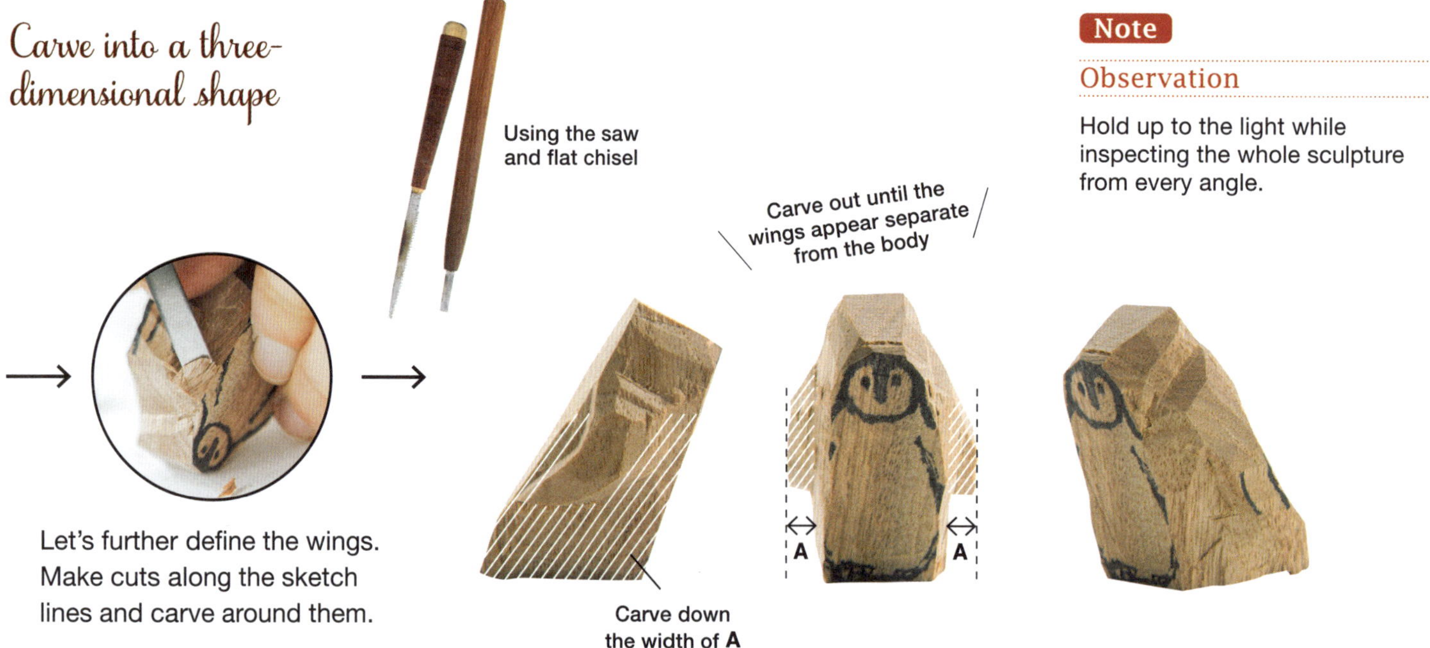

Note

Observation

Hold up to the light while inspecting the whole sculpture from every angle.

Let's further define the wings. Make cuts along the sketch lines and carve around them.

Add some definition

The beak, belly, and feet protrude in that order: ① beak, ② belly, ③ feet

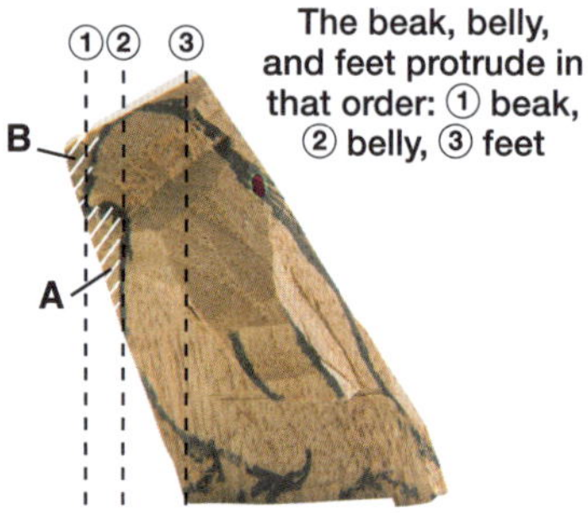

You can further sketch out the image, focusing on protruding areas such as the beak and toes.

Face

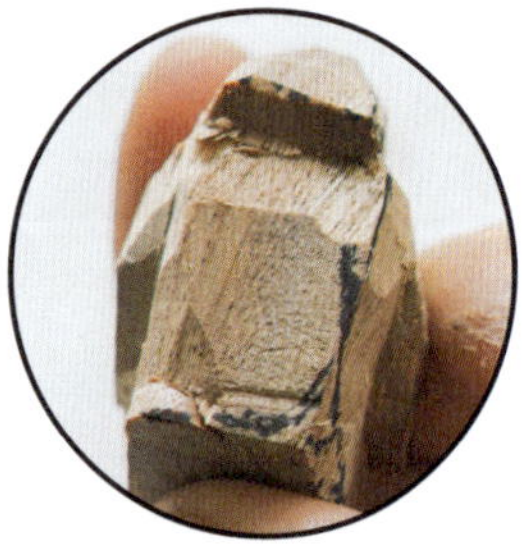

Starting at the tip of the beak, carve away a significant amount of material toward the base of the neck (A) and the top of the head (B).

Beak

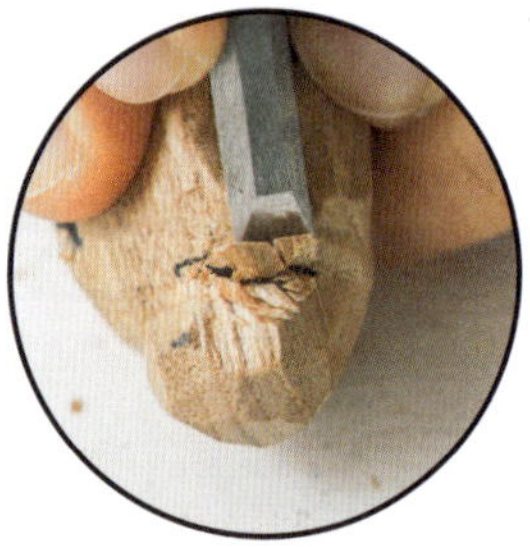

Carve around the sides of the beak to make it pointy. It's okay if the beak protrudes a bit.

Toes

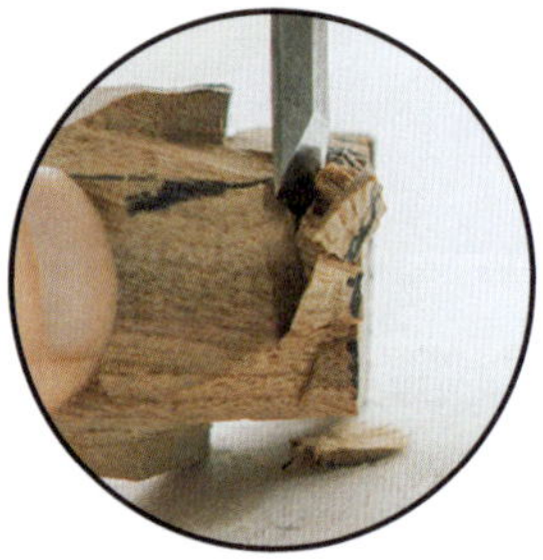

Now, chisel the undercut of the belly to reveal the toes of the left and right feet.

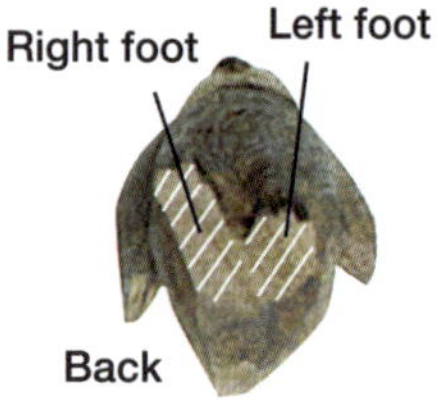

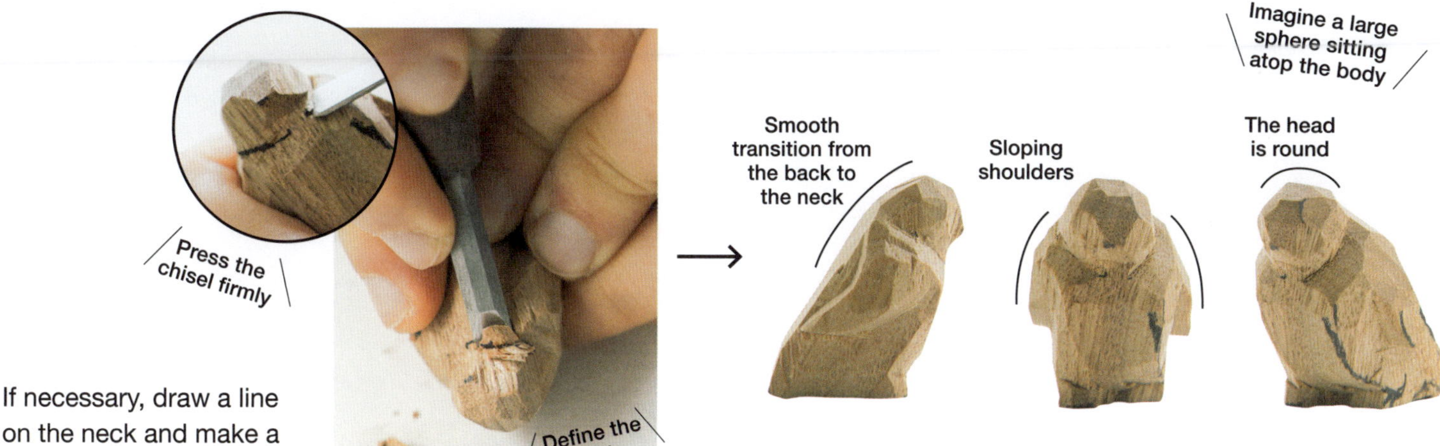

If necessary, draw a line on the neck and make a cut. By differentiating the face and body, a sense of three-dimensionality emerges.

Tail

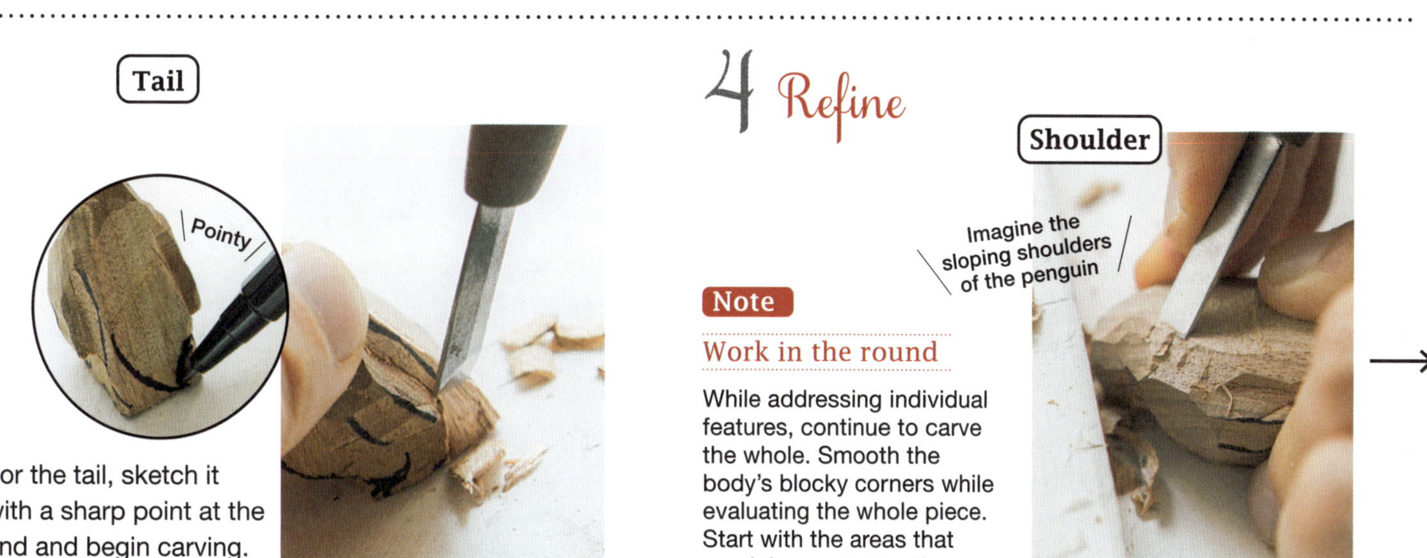

For the tail, sketch it with a sharp point at the end and begin carving.

4 Refine

Note

Work in the round

While addressing individual features, continue to carve the whole. Smooth the body's blocky corners while evaluating the whole piece. Start with the areas that need the most attention.

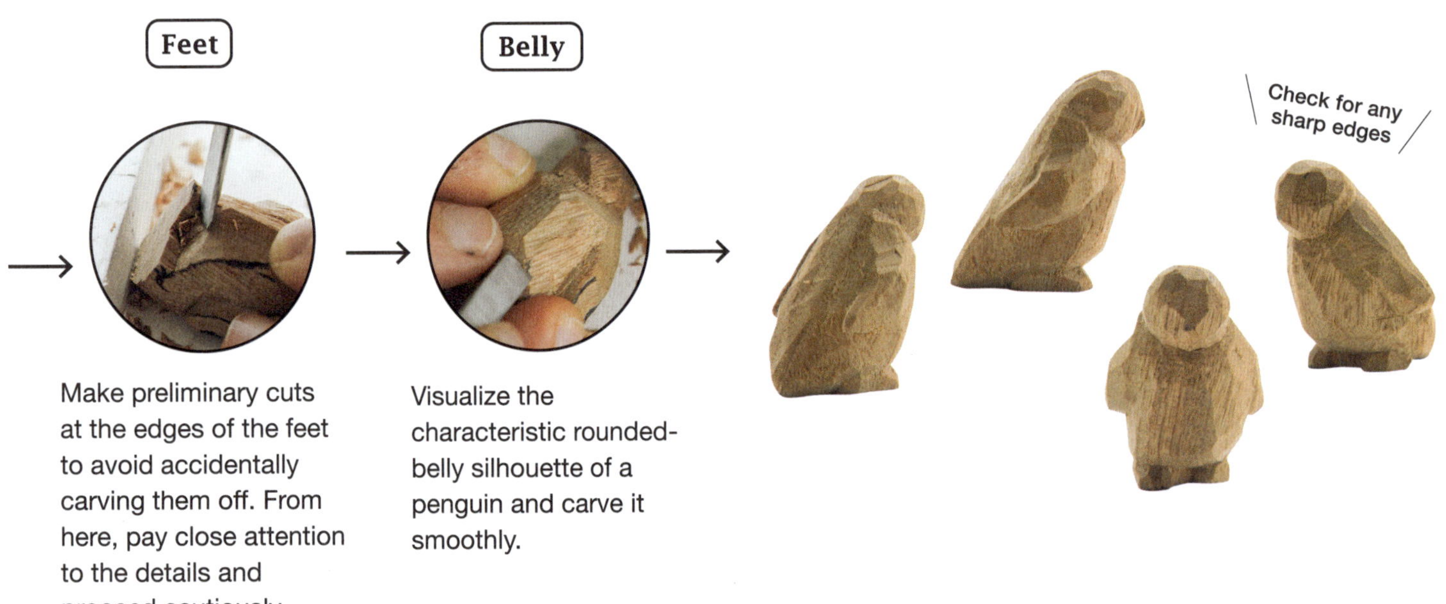

Make preliminary cuts at the edges of the feet to avoid accidentally carving them off. From here, pay close attention to the details and proceed cautiously.

Visualize the characteristic rounded-belly silhouette of a penguin and carve it smoothly.

5 Finishing touches

Beak

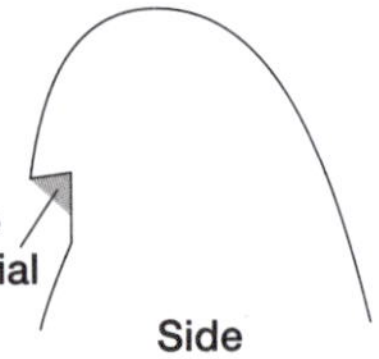

Remove this material

Side

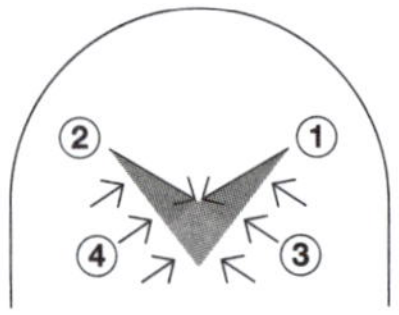

Front

Carve the sides of the beak to a point, creating the characteristic silhouette with realistic shadows.

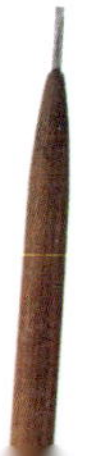

Use a thin flat chisel

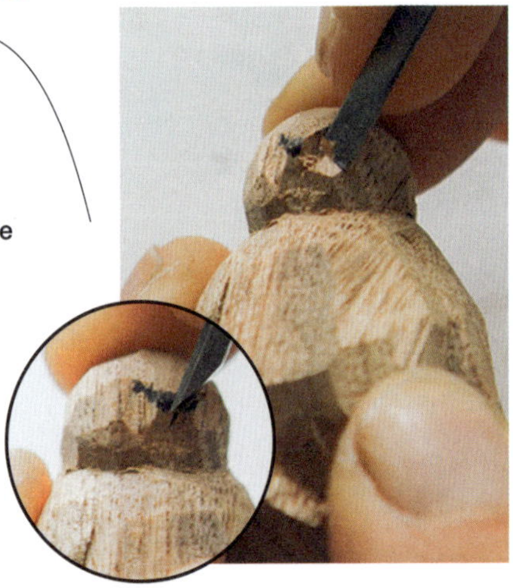

Inner and outer corners of the eyes

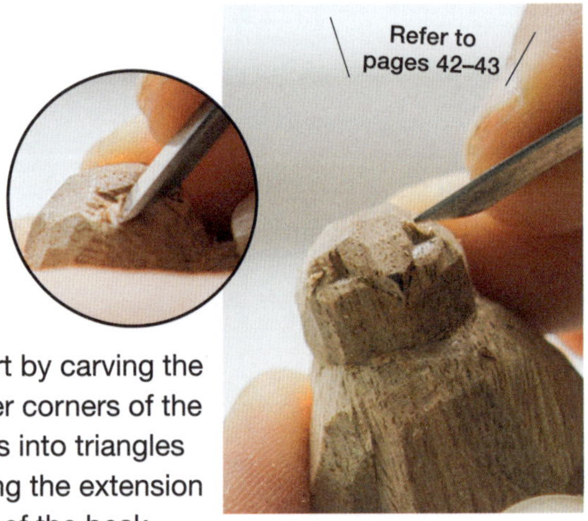

Refer to pages 42–43

Start by carving the inner corners of the eyes into triangles along the extension line of the beak. Then, carve the outer corners. Do not apply too much force.

Eyeball

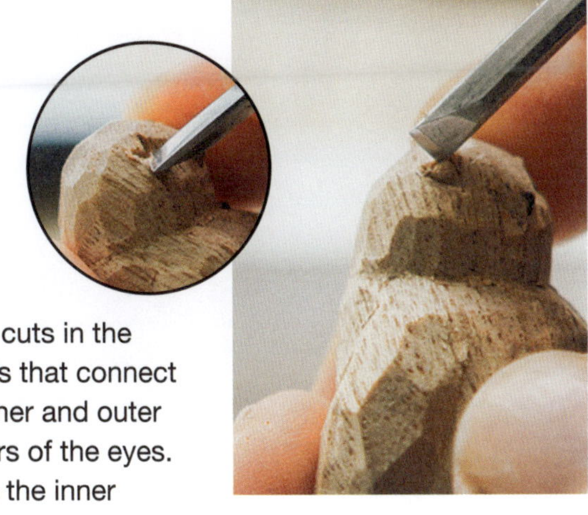

Make cuts in the eyelids that connect the inner and outer corners of the eyes. Carve the inner surface of the eyes to create the appearance of eyeballs.

Webbed feet

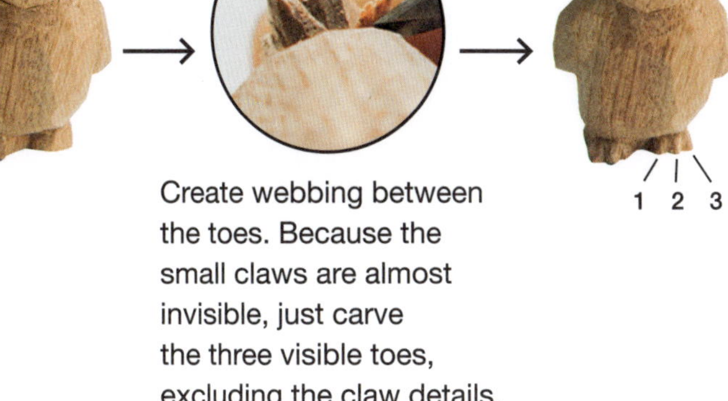

Create webbing between the toes. Because the small claws are almost invisible, just carve the three visible toes, excluding the claw details.

Adding texture

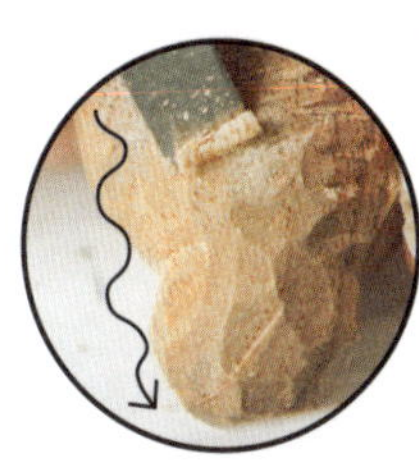

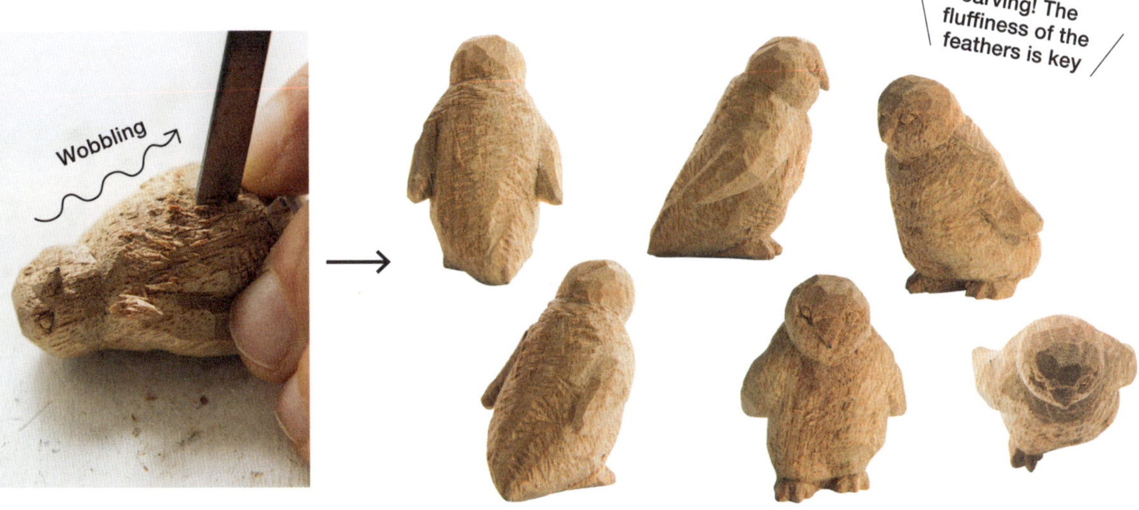

Express the feathers from the neck downward. Carving with the chisel slightly wobbling or wandering left and right while being mindful of the flow will make the figure come alive once it's painted.

6 Adding color

Black

Thin detail brush

Eyes

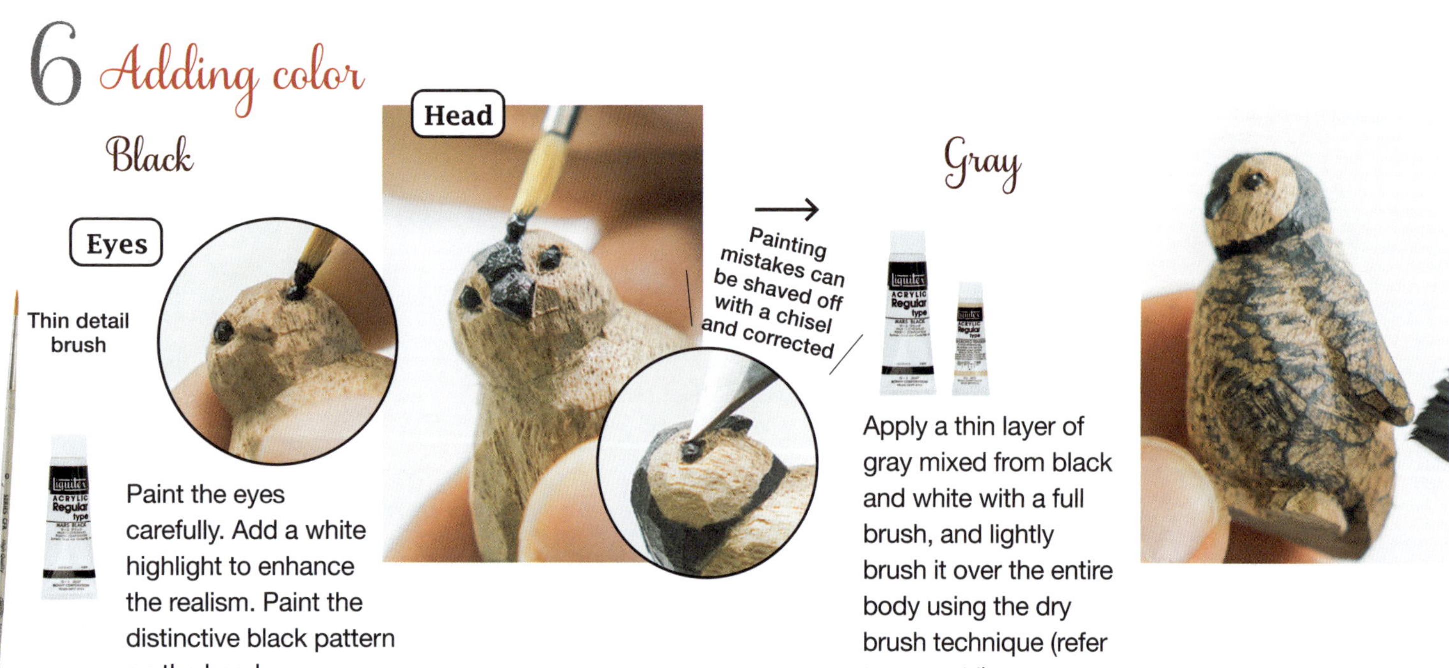

Paint the eyes carefully. Add a white highlight to enhance the realism. Paint the distinctive black pattern on the head.

Gray

Apply a thin layer of gray mixed from black and white with a full brush, and lightly brush it over the entire body using the dry brush technique (refer to page 44).

Black

Webbed feet

White

Face

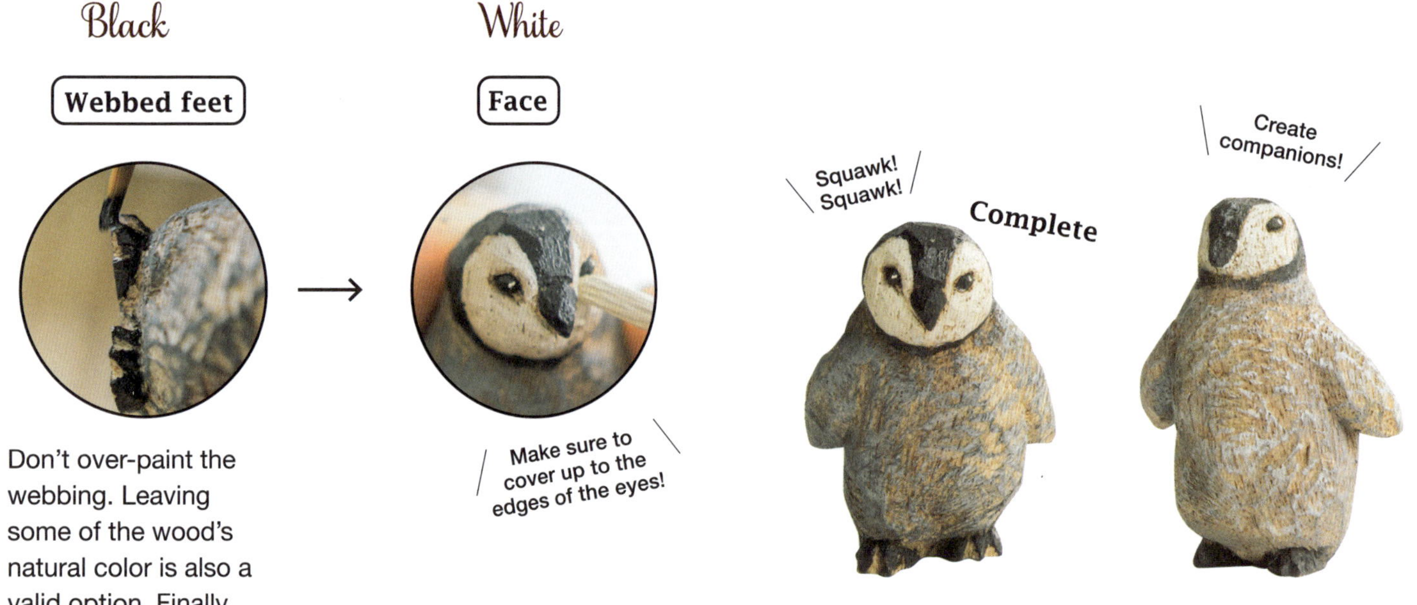

Don't over-paint the webbing. Leaving some of the wood's natural color is also a valid option. Finally, paint the face white.

Make sure to cover up to the edges of the eyes!

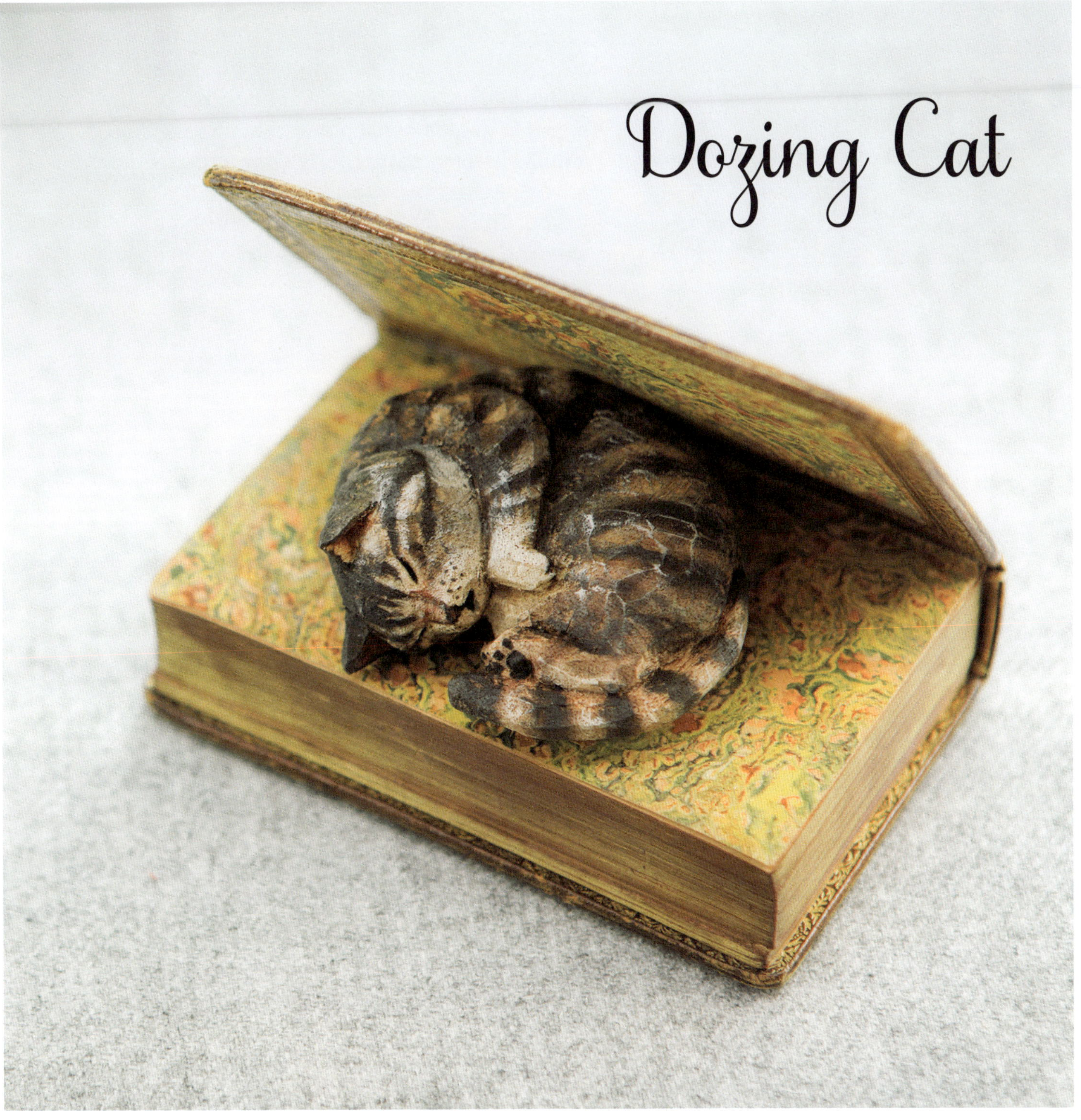

Dozing Cat

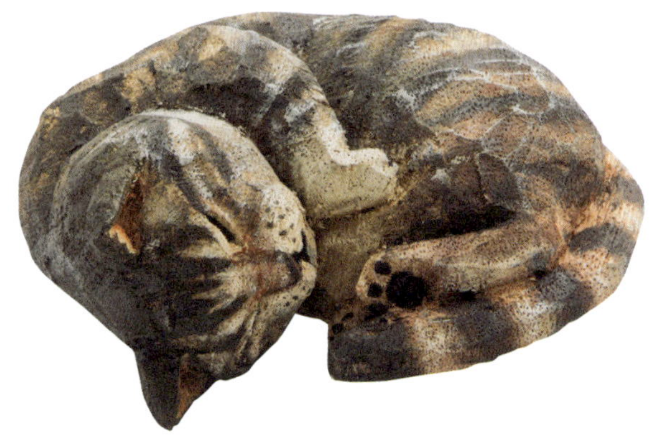

In this lesson, we'll carve a curled-up, soundly sleeping cat. Observing and sketching an actual sleeping cat is pretty easy to do, so take advantage of the opportunity if it's available to you. The techniques used for carving a sleeping cat can also be applied to a sleeping dog. Let's begin!

Dozing Cat

Materials:

- Wood
- Pen or Pencil
- Saw
- Flat chisel
- Gouge (curved chisel)
- Acrylic paint

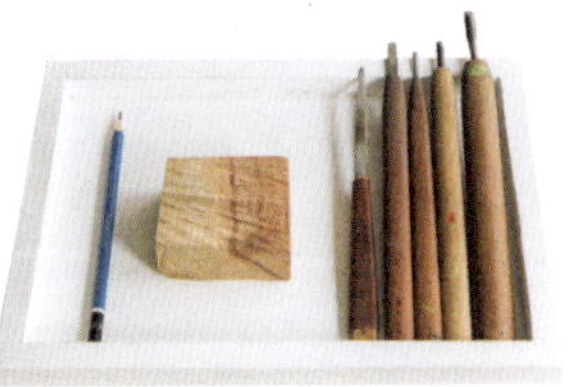

1 Sketch

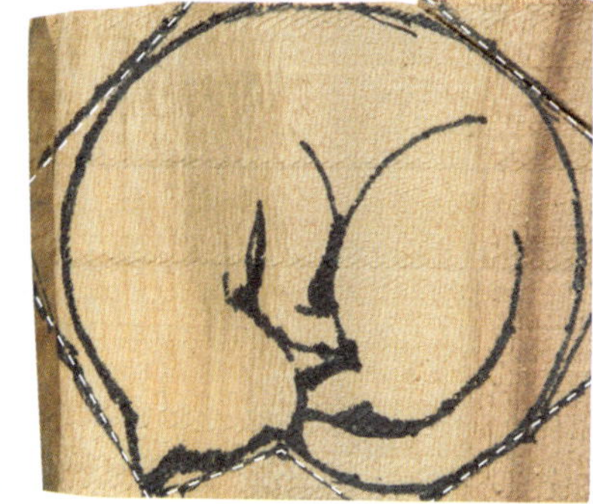

A sketch of a sleeping cat viewed from above. The drawing should fill most of the area of the block. Draw sawing guides around the form.

2 Saw

Use the
saw

The shape will
drop away in the
direction of the
arrows

Sketchy lines
indicate the
plane one
step below
the level of the
head

The highest
point

Sleeping cats

The curled-up sleeping position, characterized by overlapping parts like the front legs, hind legs and face, adds complexity. Be cognizant of final three-dimensional form while carving.

Leave only the plane of the face portion untouched, and give roundness to the body, significantly sloping the perimeter away in the direction of the arrows.

3 Rough out

Hold the flat chisel tightly like making a fist

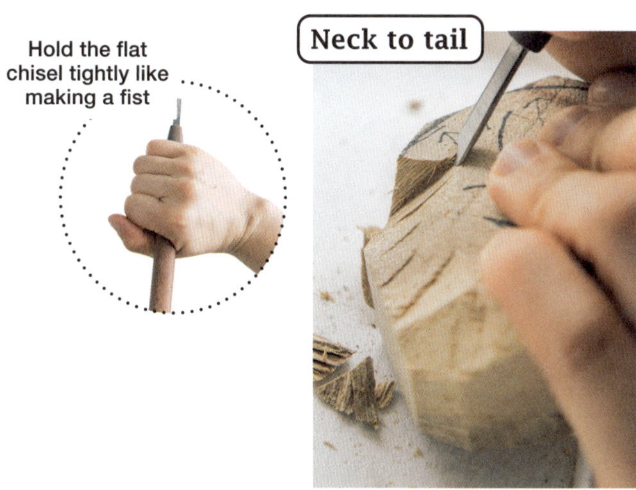

Neck to tail

Grip the flat chisel firmly and make powerful carving strokes. Be bold and carve vigorously.

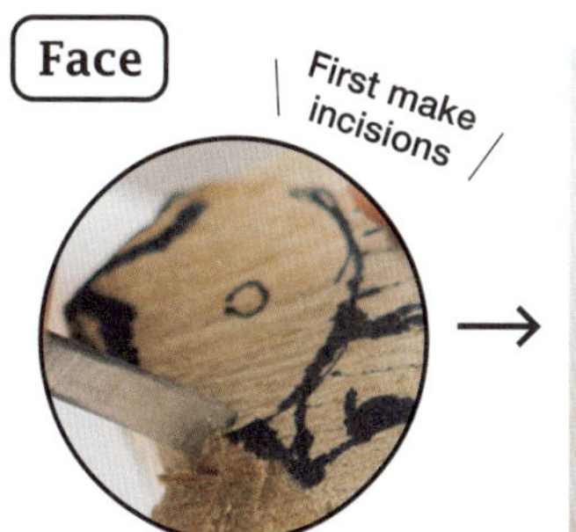

Face

Make cuts along the outline of the face. Similar to making the brooch (see page 37), carve to reduce the height of the area around the face.

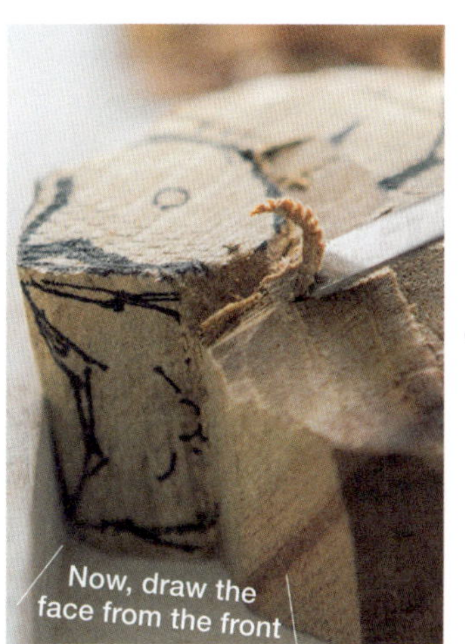

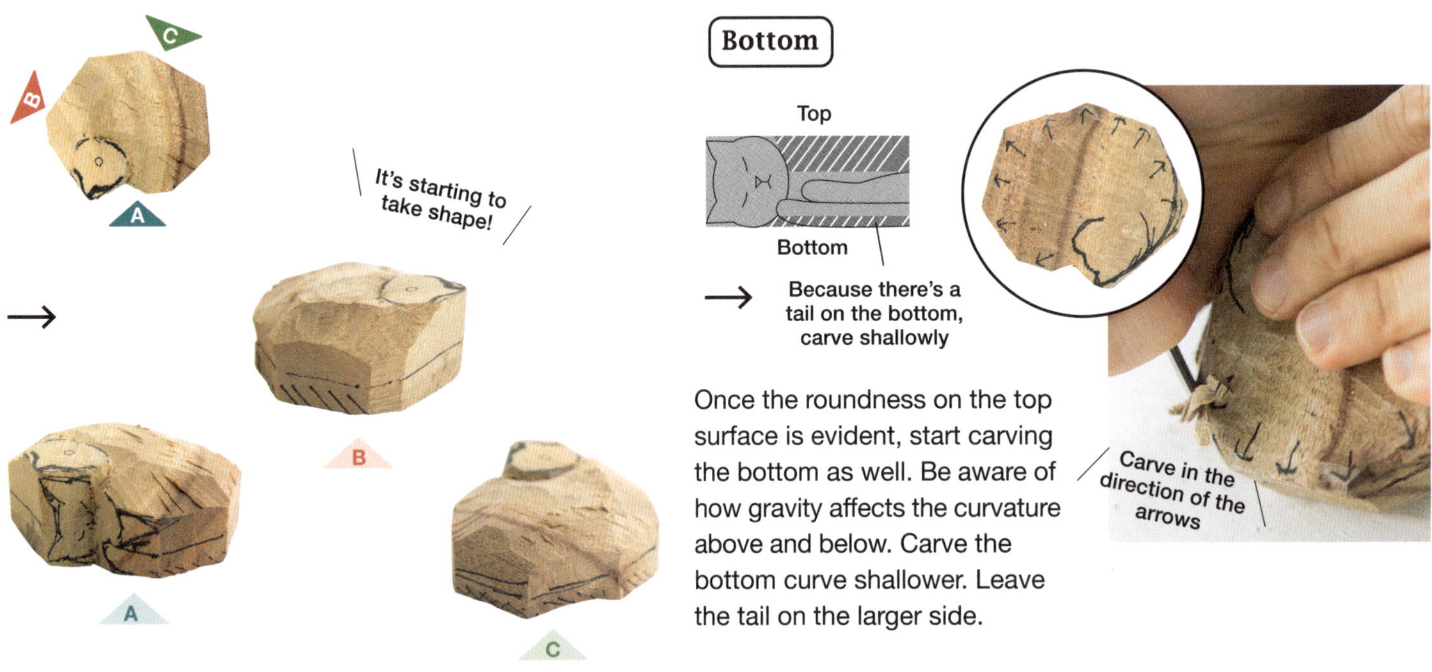

Bottom

Once the roundness on the top surface is evident, start carving the bottom as well. Be aware of how gravity affects the curvature above and below. Carve the bottom curve shallower. Leave the tail on the larger side.

Side

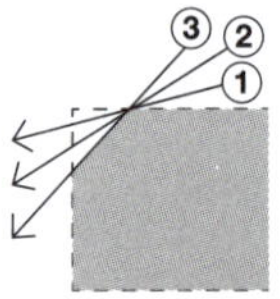

Do not plunge the chisel into the corners too aggressively— gradually deepen the angle

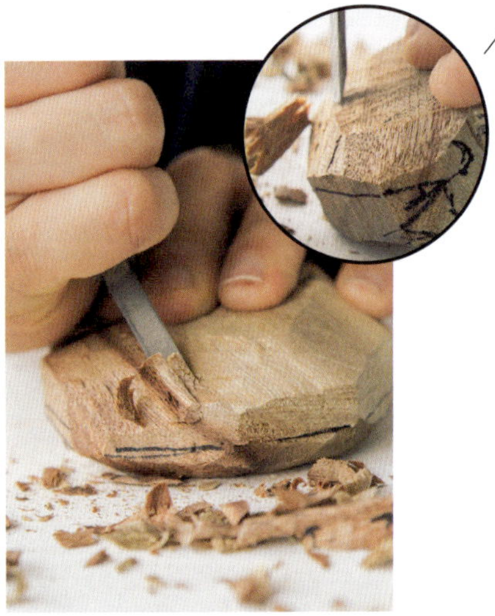

When refining the outline, grasp the chisel firmly in your fist and carve vertically. To create roundness, hold the chisel close to the blade and push it forward at an angle.

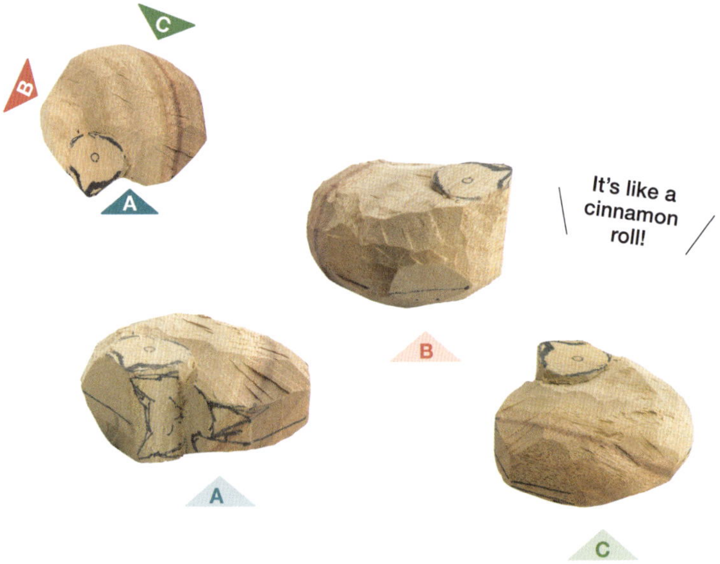

4 Refine

Ears

Start cutting from A to B up to C

B
A

Do the same on the opposite side

Top surface

C
B
A Carve here

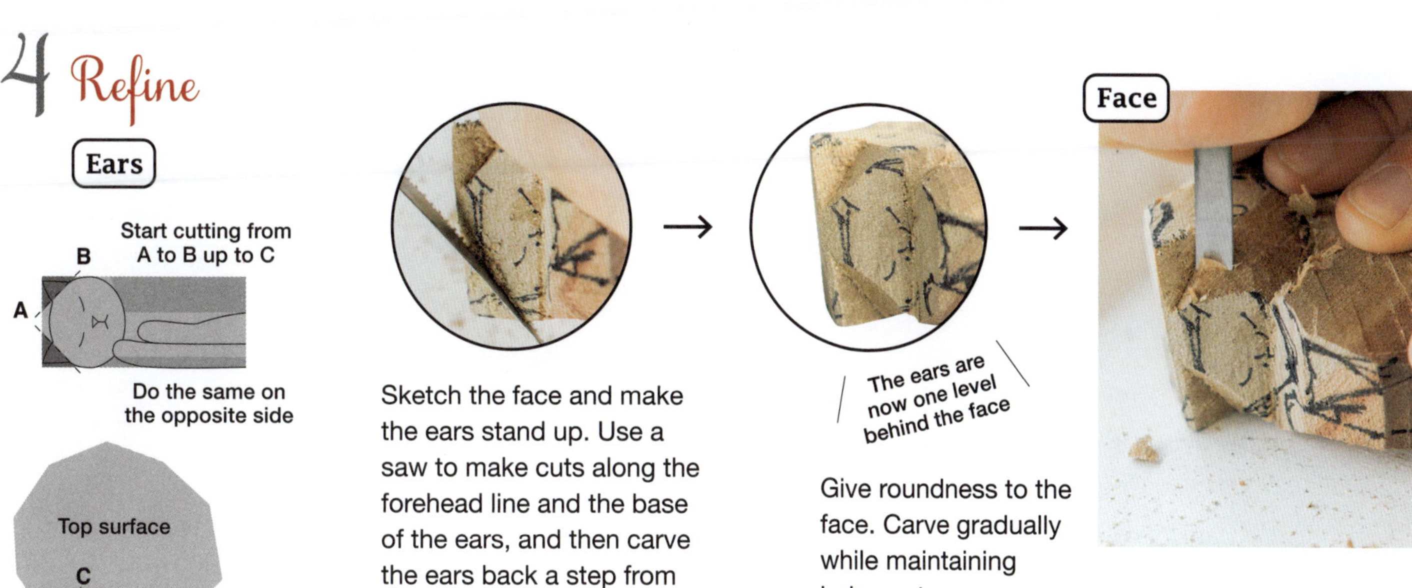

Sketch the face and make the ears stand up. Use a saw to make cuts along the forehead line and the base of the ears, and then carve the ears back a step from the plane of the face.

The ears are now one level behind the face

Give roundness to the face. Carve gradually while maintaining balance to ensure symmetry.

Face

Tail

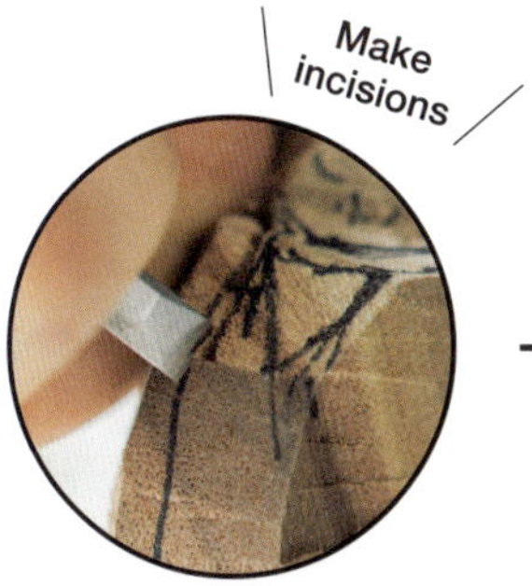

Make incisions

Make preliminary cuts around the outline of the tail to avoid accidentally carving it off.

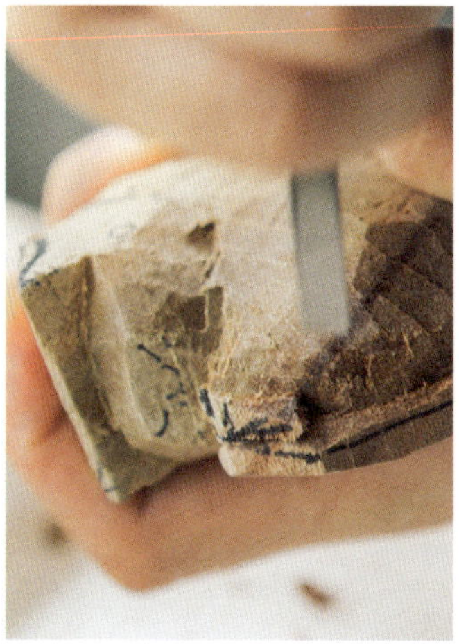

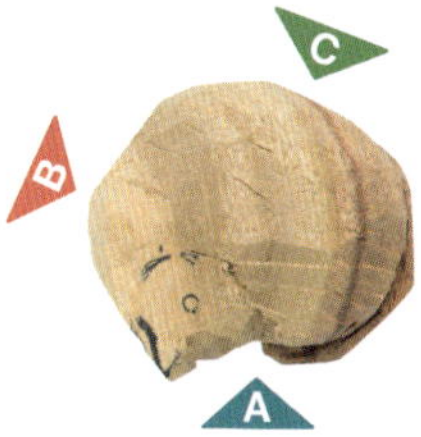

Note

Check your work

The consistency of the chamfering work is revealed by the play of light and shadow across the form as you view it from various angles.

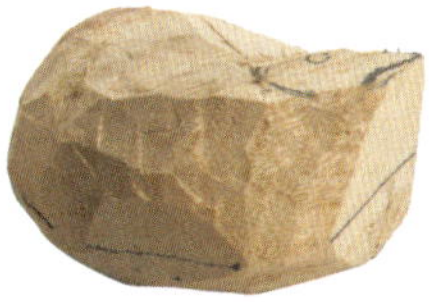

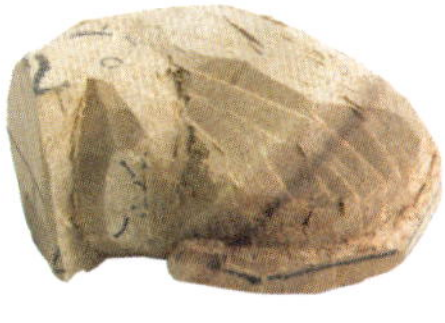

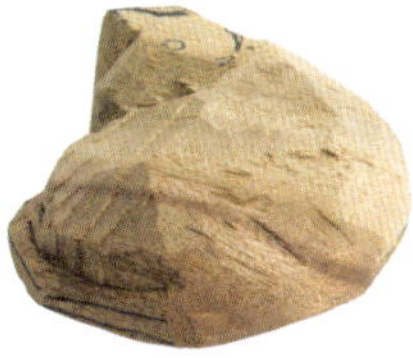

Neck

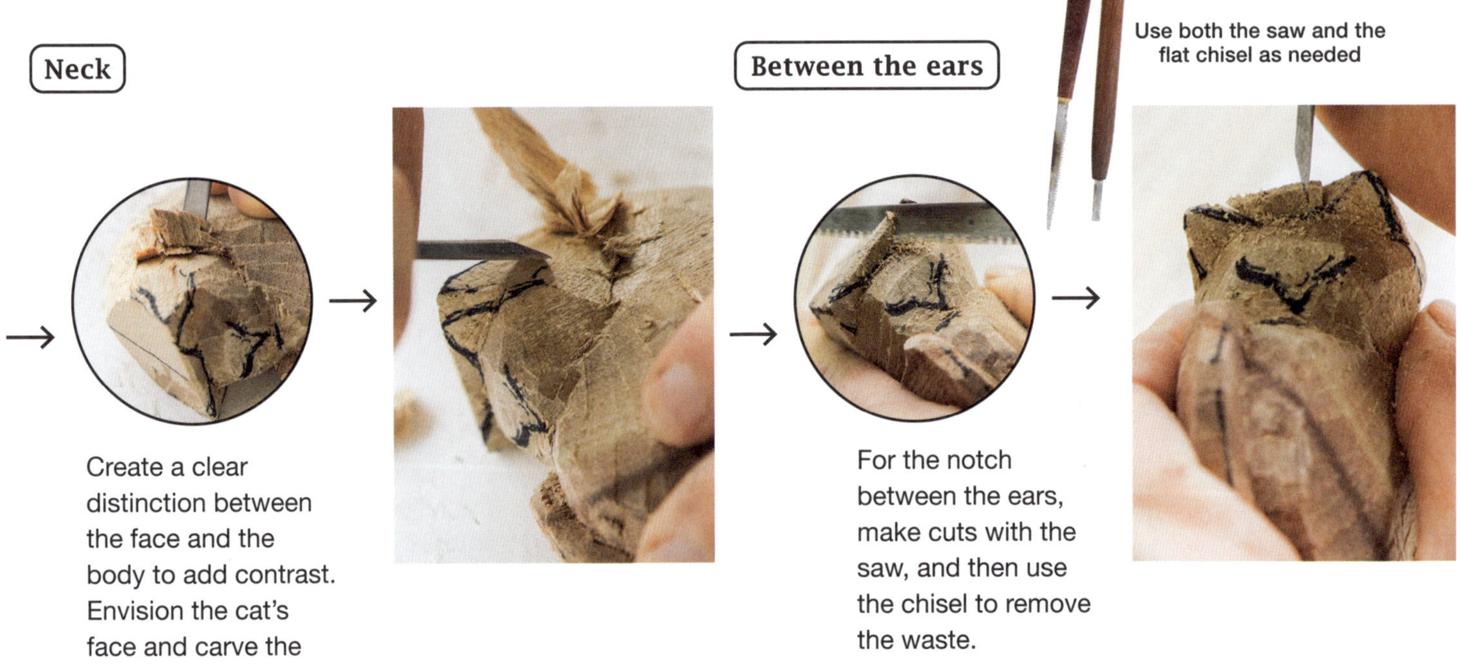

Create a clear distinction between the face and the body to add contrast. Envision the cat's face and carve the outline roundly.

Between the ears

For the notch between the ears, make cuts with the saw, and then use the chisel to remove the waste.

Back of the head

Don't forget to carve the back of the head. Shape it so that it rounds out from the back toward the crest.

Chin

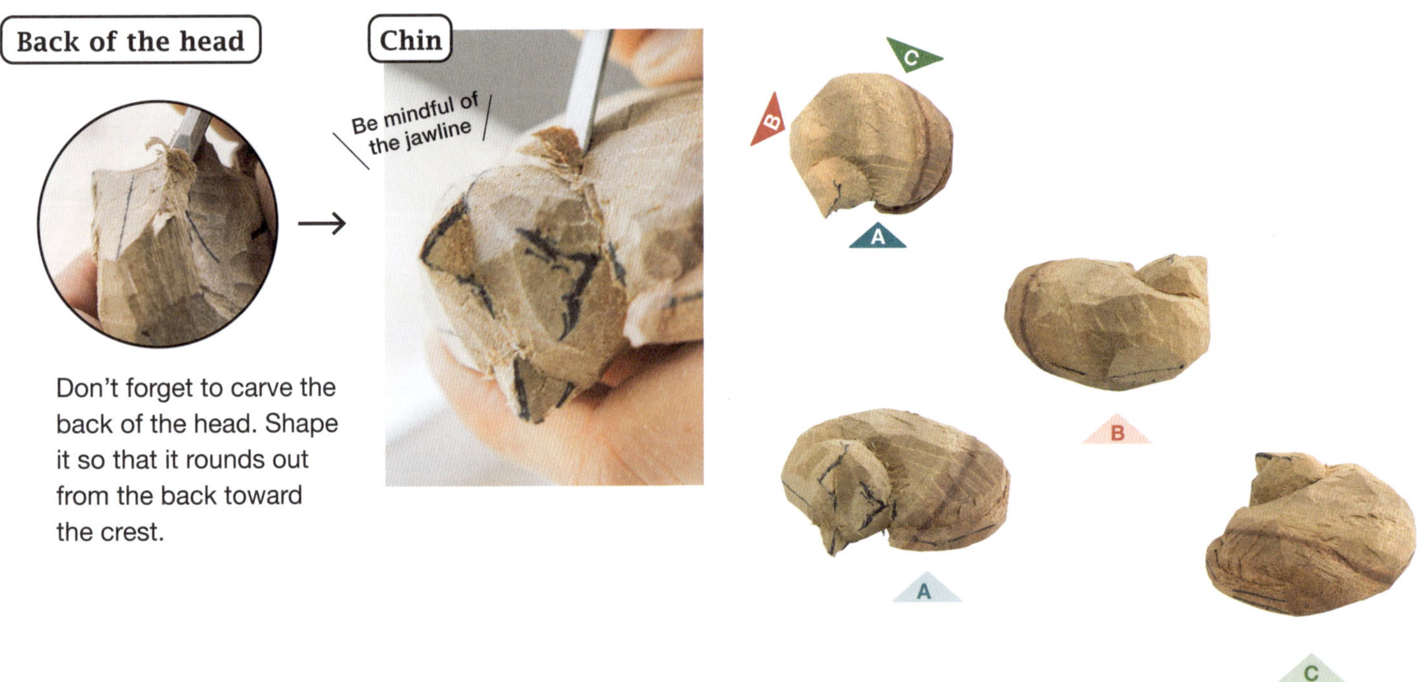

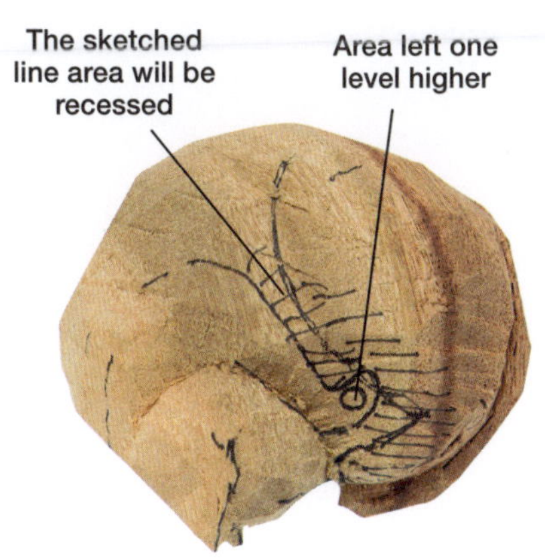

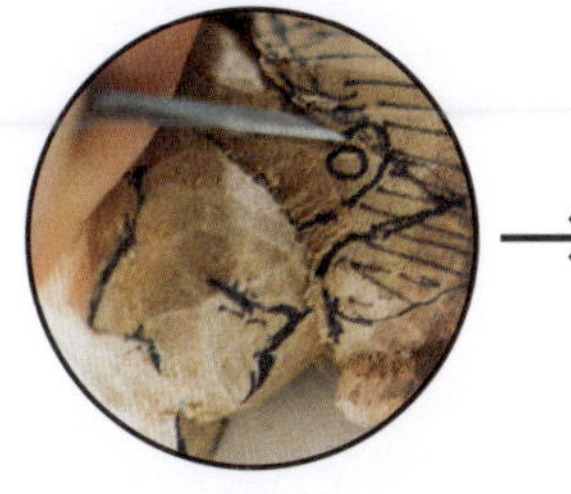

Make cuts along the shoulders, elbows, and wrists, and sculpt the transitions to the recessed parts smoothly. After firmly establishing the boundaries, shape the forelegs.

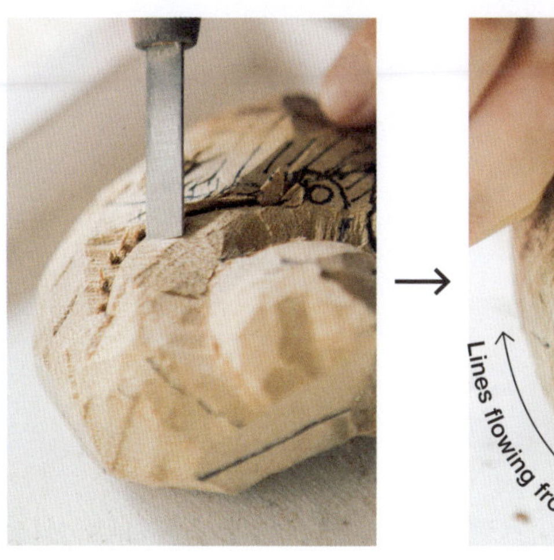

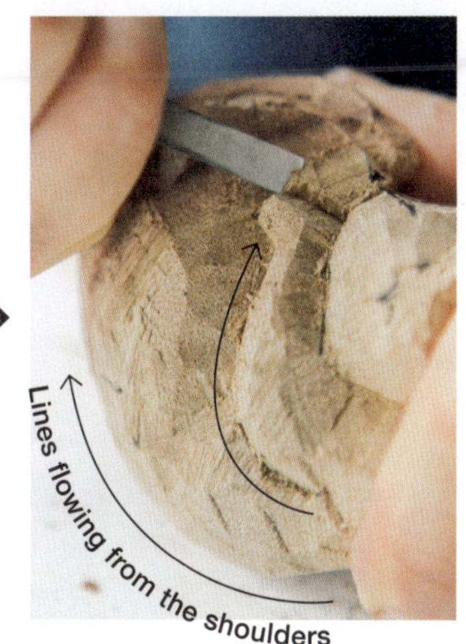

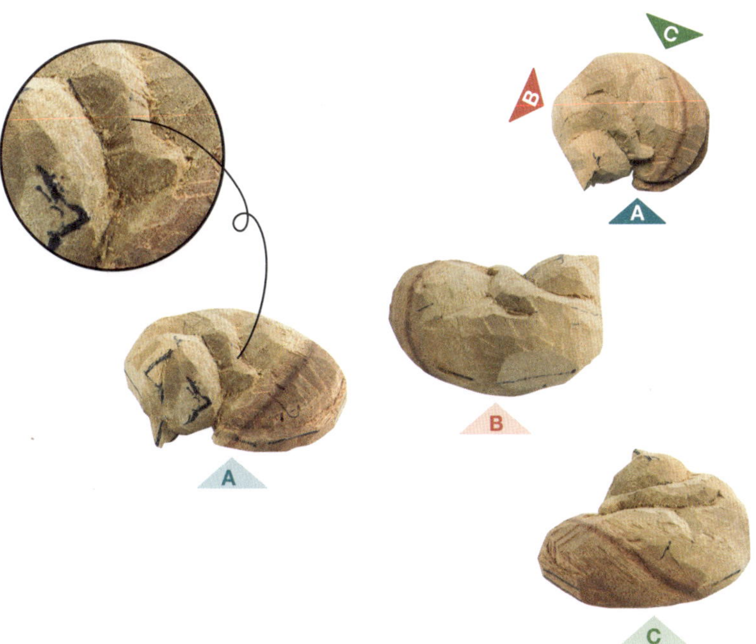

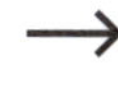

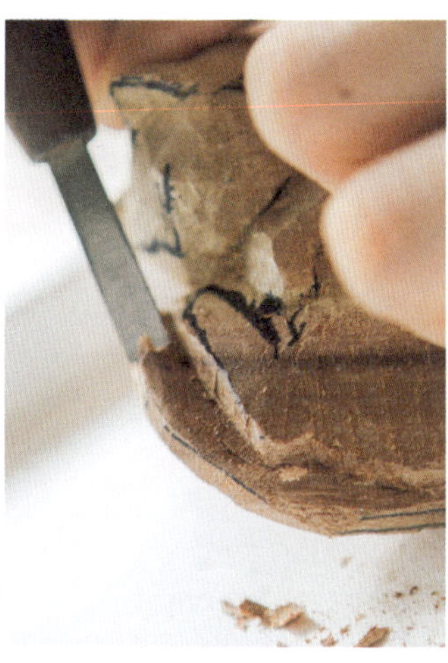

Lightly sketch and then carve the separation between the hind legs' heels and the tail. If carved well, the shadows will fall beautifully.

5 Finishing touches

Sketch the face

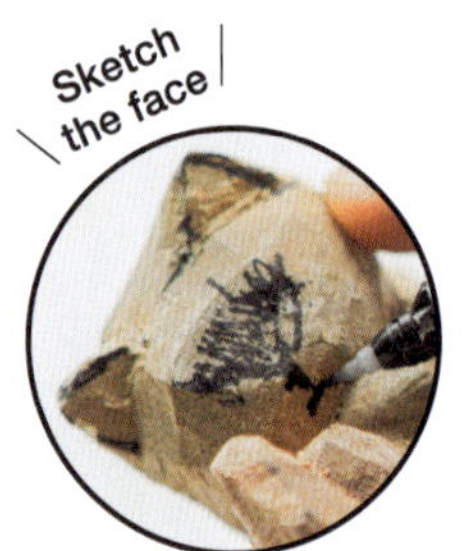

Brow

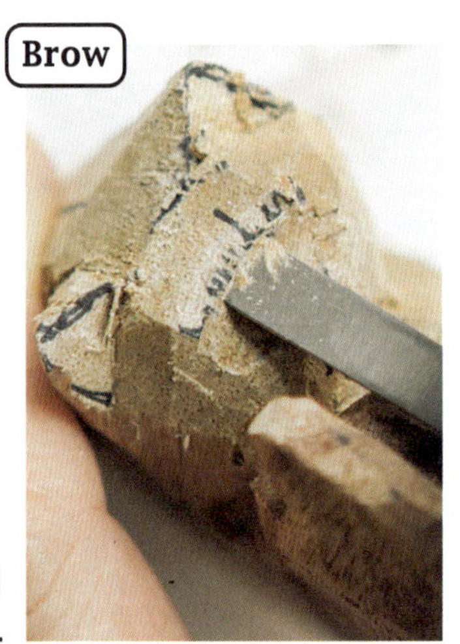

Carve diagonally from the nose to the forehead, creating a step on the forehead to form a brow ridge.

→

Nose and mouth

Refer to page 42

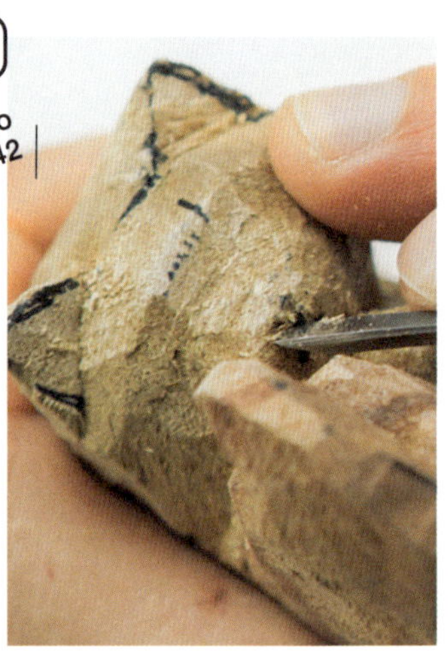

Make deep vertical cuts to open up the nose and mouth, gently carving the inside. Use the corner of the chisel for fine work.

Eyes

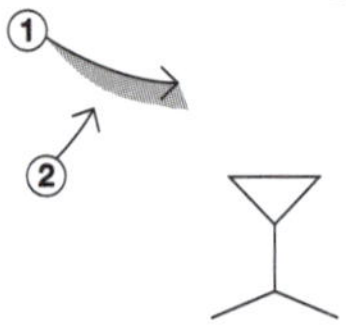

Be mindful of the underlying shape of the eyeballs

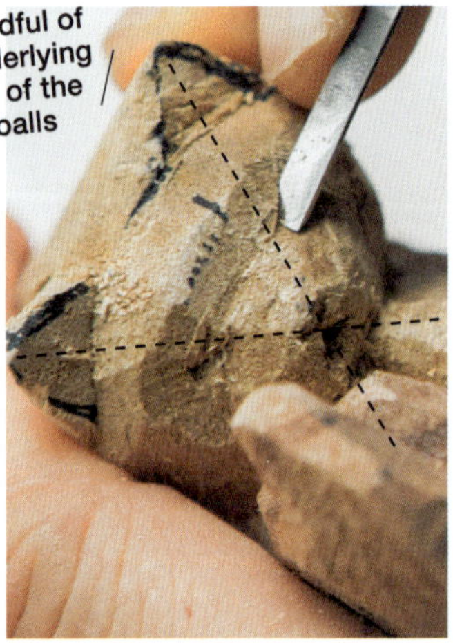

① →

② ↗

Make deep cuts along the eyelid lines and smoothly carve underneath the eyelids.

→

Ears

Refer to page 43

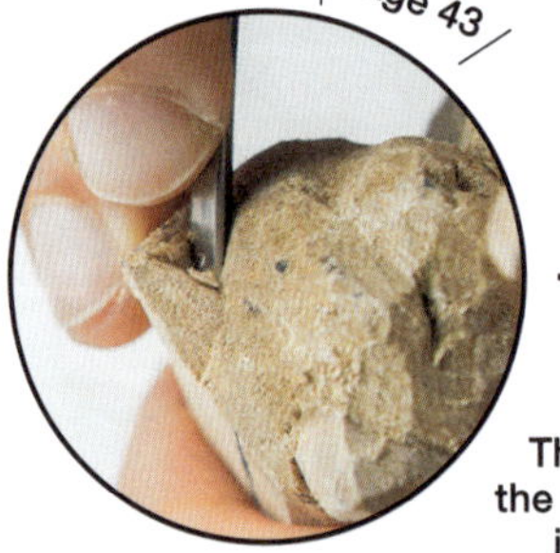

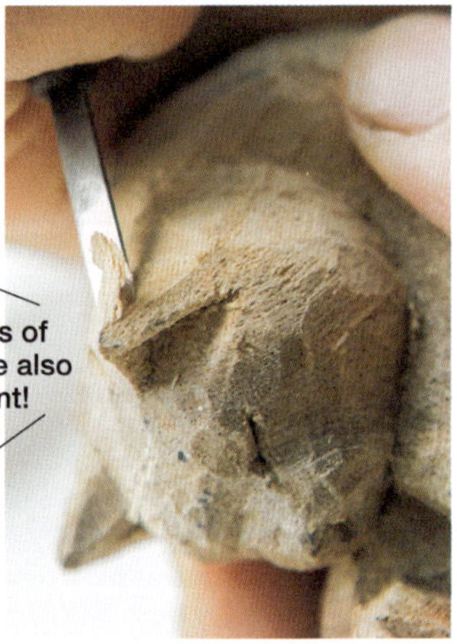

Use the corner of a thin flat chisel

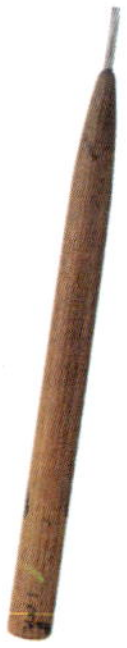

Use the chisel to open up triangular shapes for the ear openings. Carve from behind the ears as well, making the ears thin and three-dimensional.

→

The backs of the ears are also important!

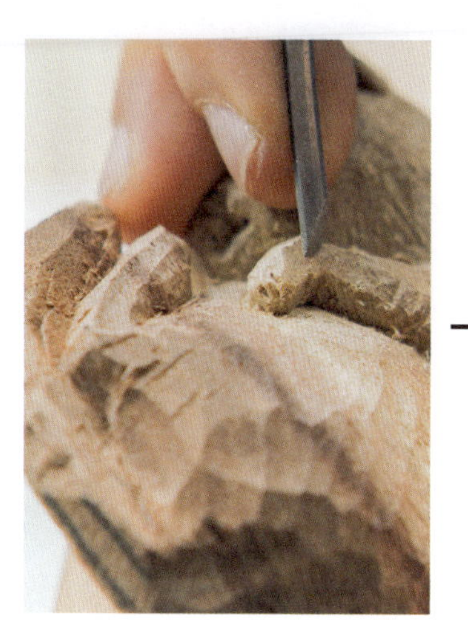

Carve details like the pads and ends of the paws. Round off the tip of the tail.

Pads

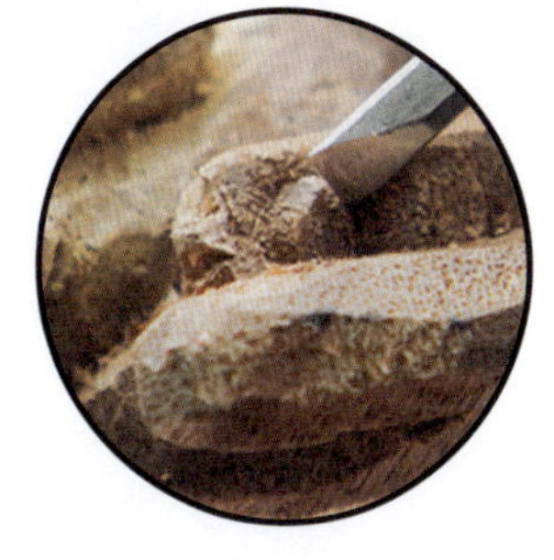

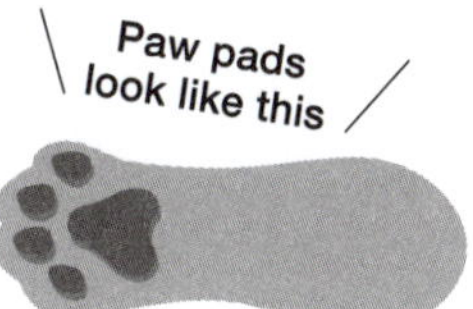

If you can inspect a cat's paw pads, take a look, and then carve—if a cat is unavailable or uncooperative, refer to the diagram first.

Adding texture

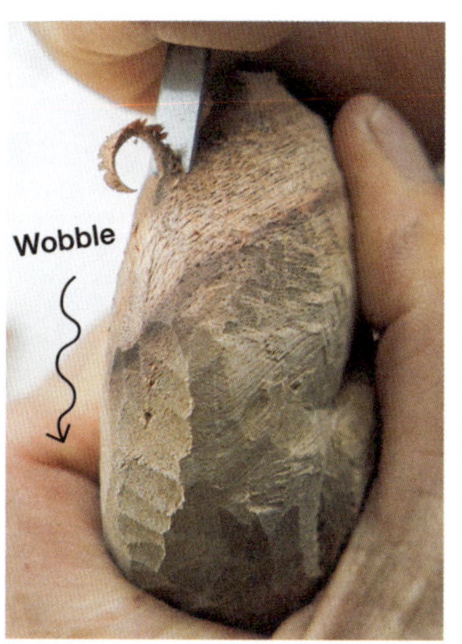

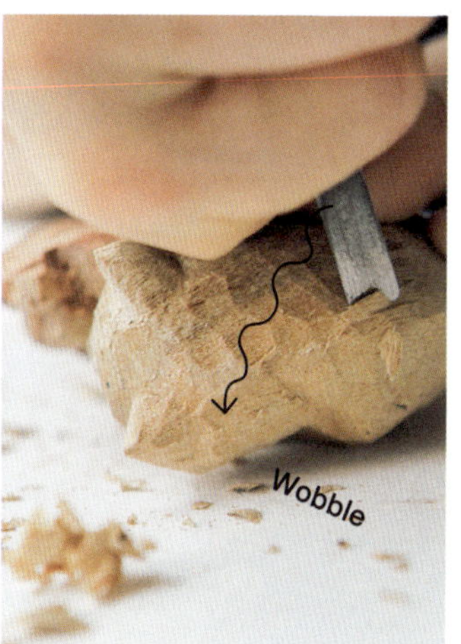

Use various chisels to carve the whole piece. Try carving by wobbling the chisel from side to side.

Note

Finishing tips

Finishing the shape meticulously is a crucial point in carving. Because cats are supple, check the entire sculpture for sharp angles and shave them off if necessary. Work on protruding parts like the tip of the tail last, as they are fragile and require careful handling.

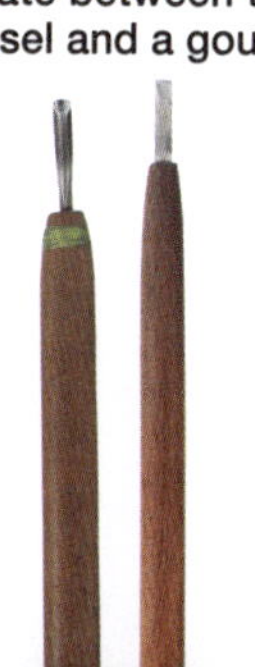

Alternate between the flat chisel and a gouge!

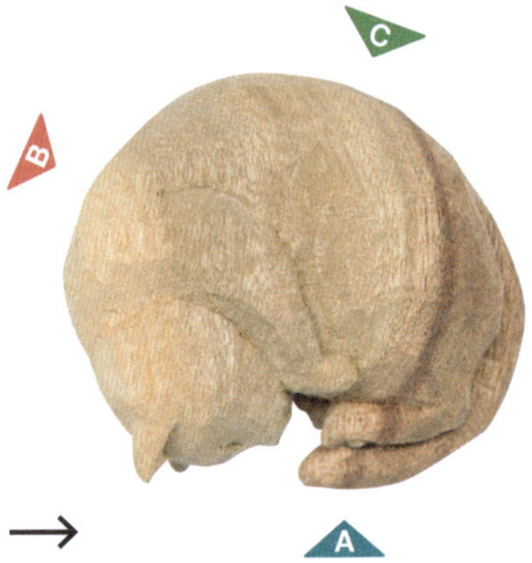

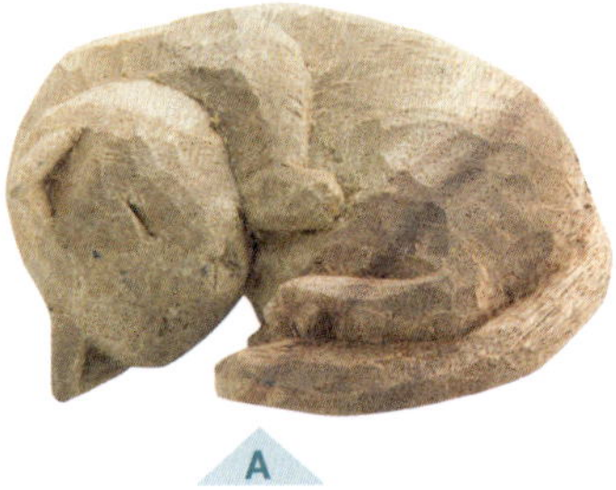

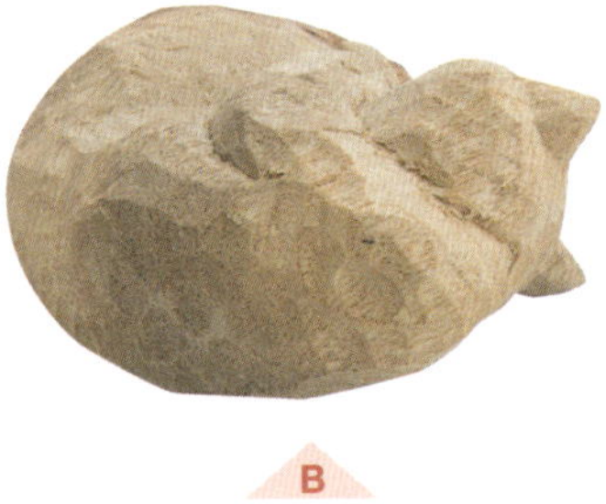

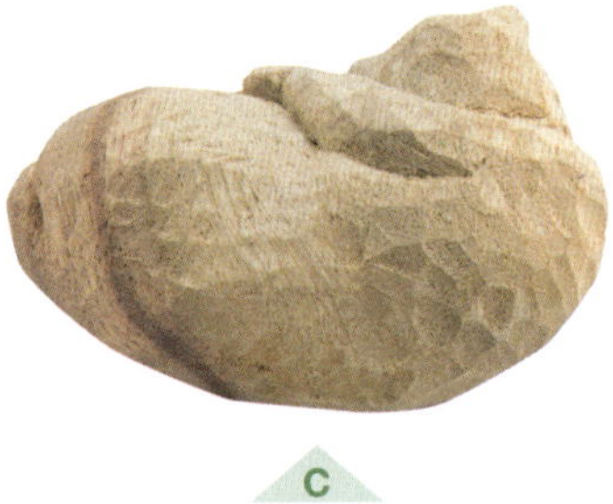

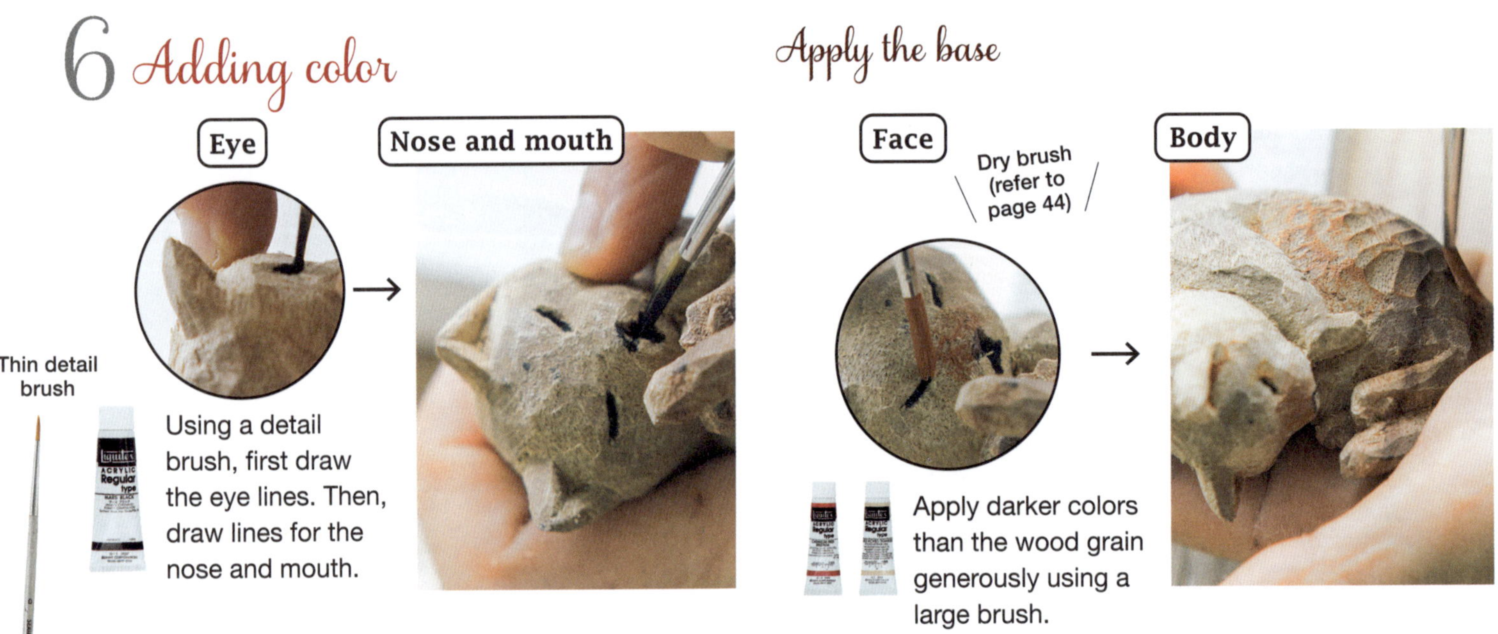

6 Adding color

Apply the base

Eye

Nose and mouth

Thin detail brush

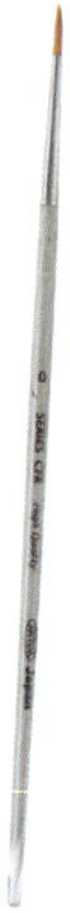

Using a detail brush, first draw the eye lines. Then, draw lines for the nose and mouth.

Face

Dry brush (refer to page 44)

Body

Apply darker colors than the wood grain generously using a large brush.

Applying a pattern

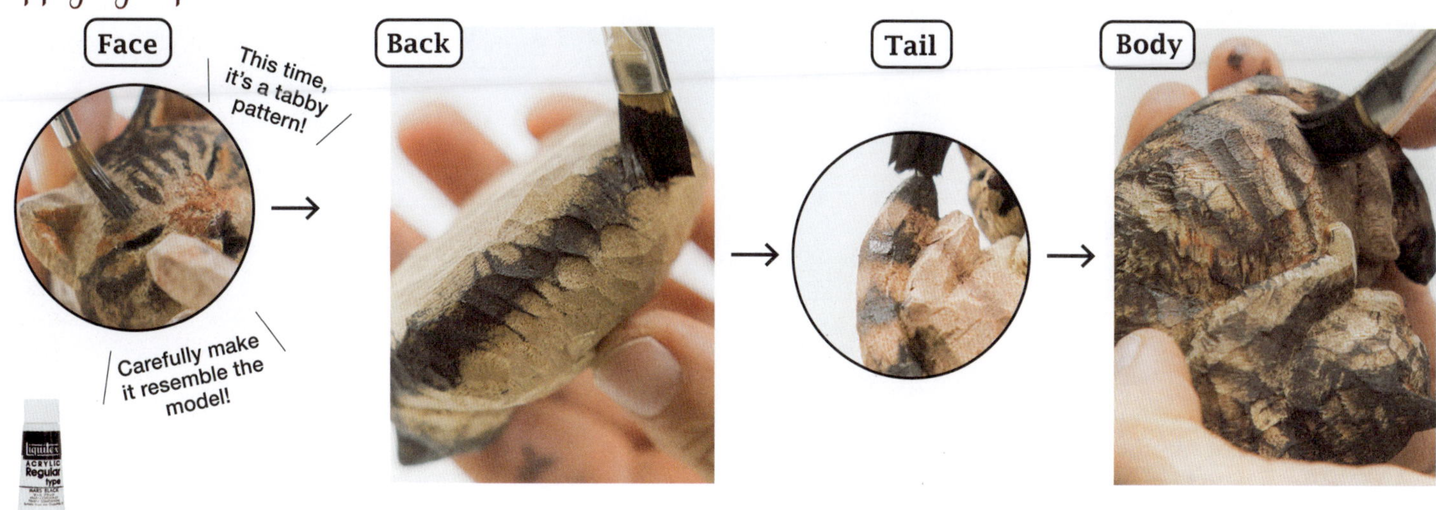

....

Paint the bottom side too

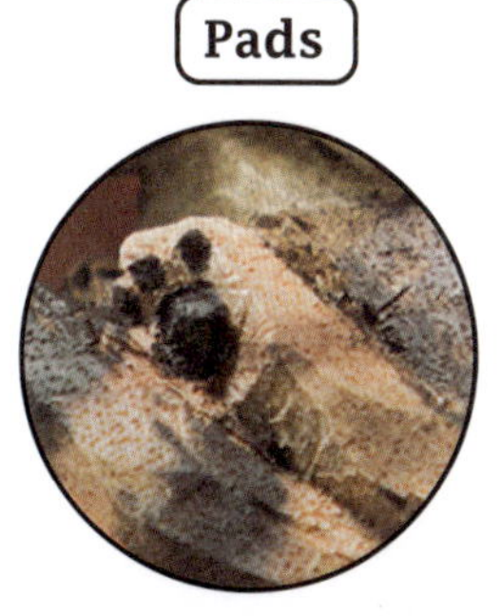

Paint details such as the paw pads on the soles of the feet thoroughly. It will look lifelike when completed.

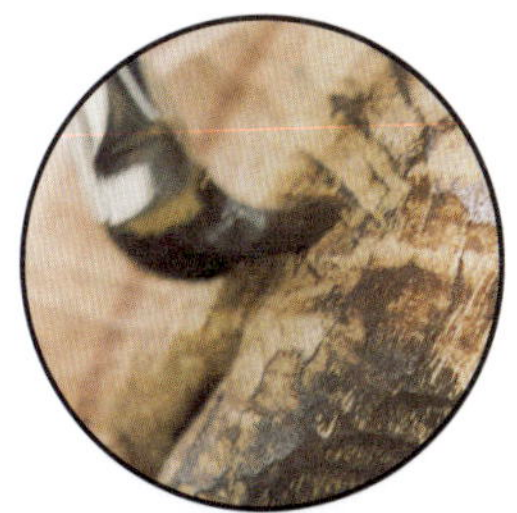

Paint underneath as well. The key is to paint while preserving the natural wood grain. For the darkest parts, like the back and behind the ears, apply multiple coats.

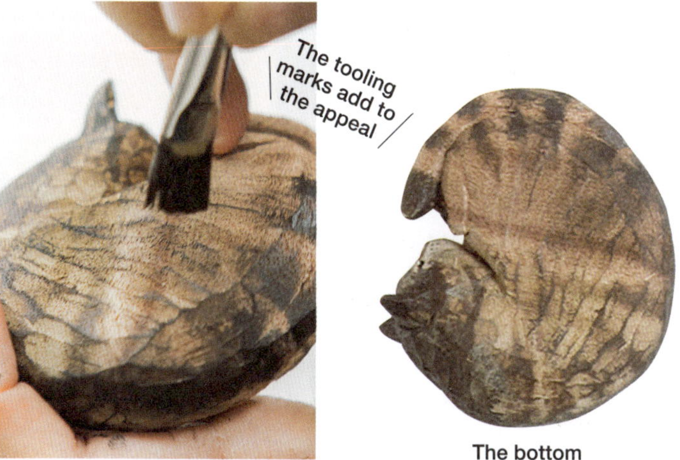

The bottom

Adding highlights

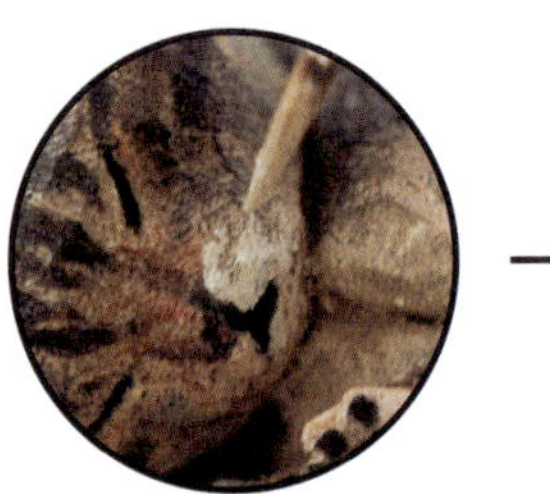

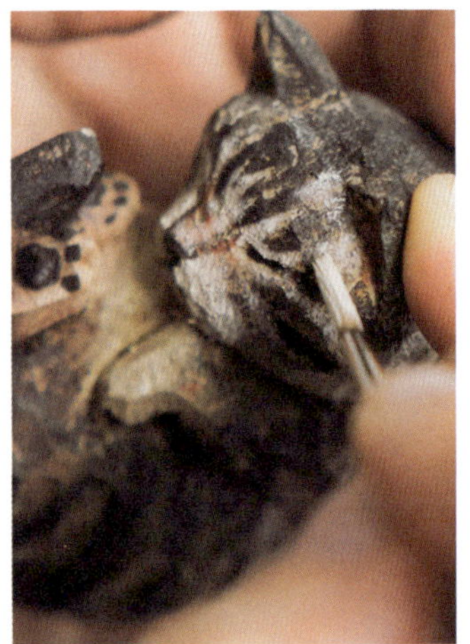

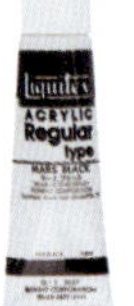

White is used last in coloring. Paint the areas around the mouth and eyes white. Faithfully paint the colors according to the patterns of the pet cat or the model cat.

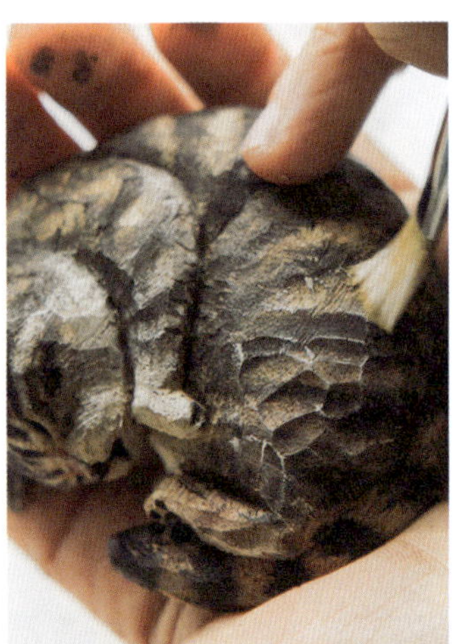

Use white to add highlights across the body, giving the fur a glossy look.

Final details

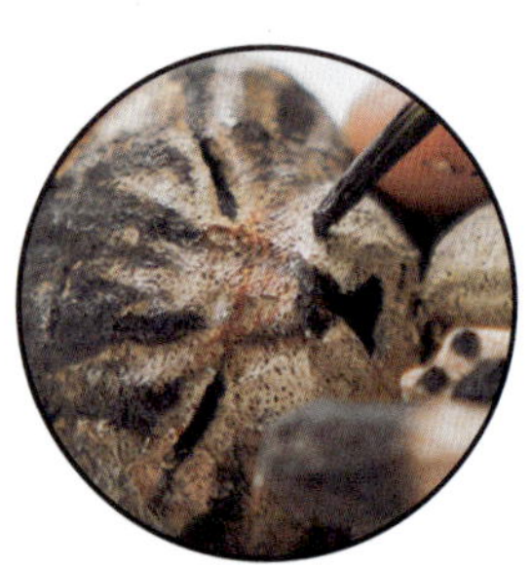

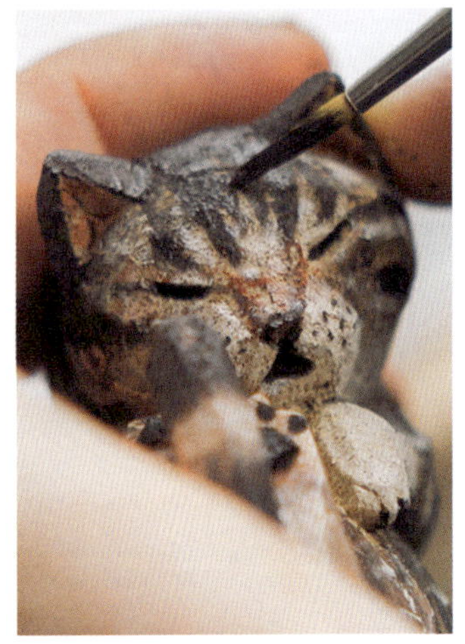

With a detail brush, add small specks at the base of the whiskers. Continue carefully until the details are complete.

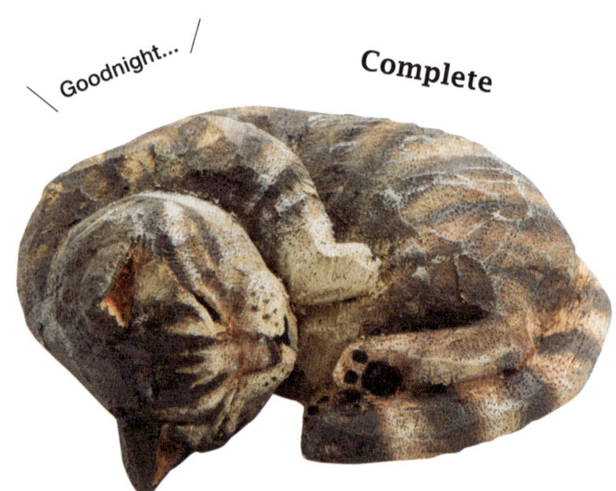

Bear on a Swing

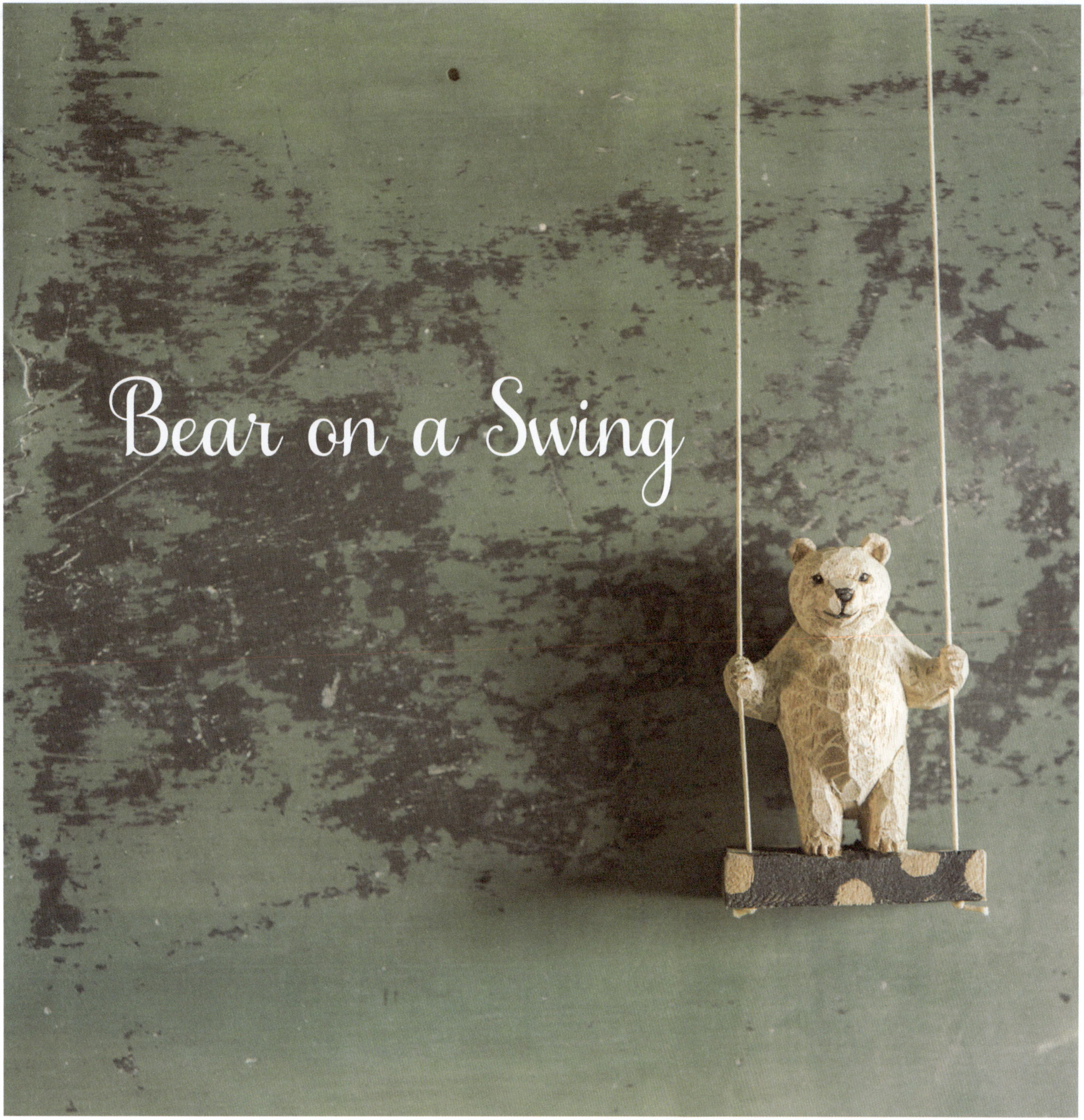

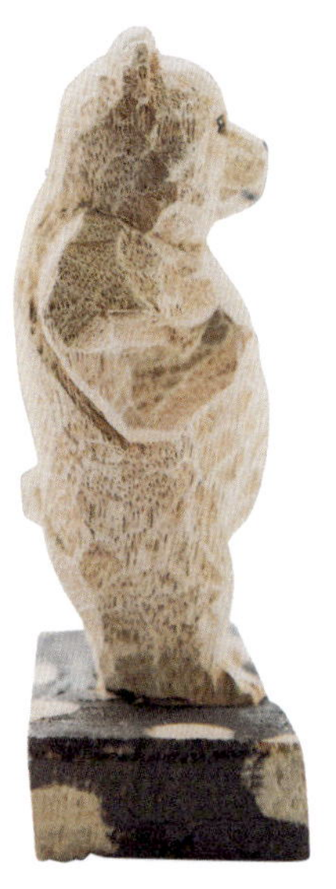
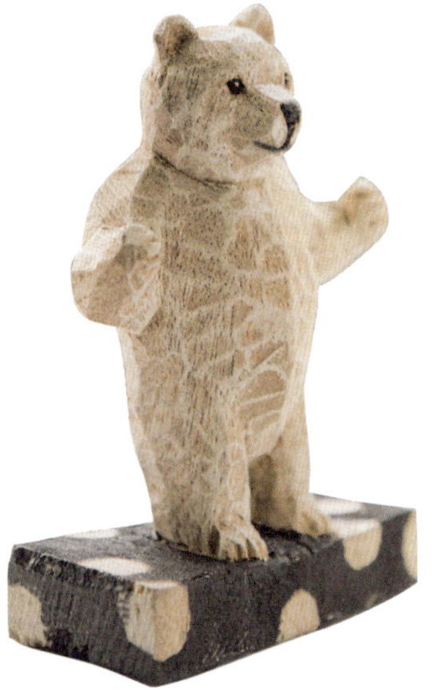

Here's a friendly bear standing on a gently swaying swing. You can hang it on a wall or suspend it like a mobile, allowing for various fun, imaginative uses. It would also make a lovely gift. Give this intermediate project a try!

Bear on a Swing

Materials:

- Wood
- Pen or pencil
- Saw
- Flat chisel
- Gouge (curved chisel)
- Acrylic paint
- Precision drill (1.5–1.6 mm bit diameter)
- Waxed cord (0.5–1.0 mm diameter)

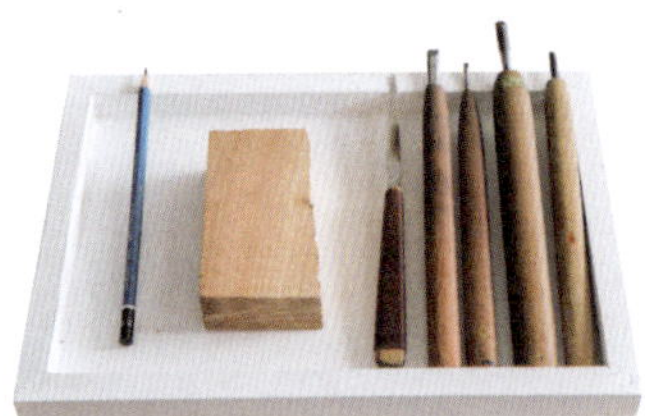

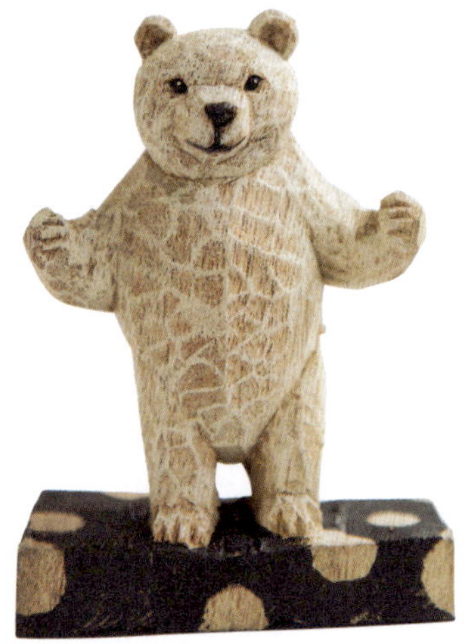

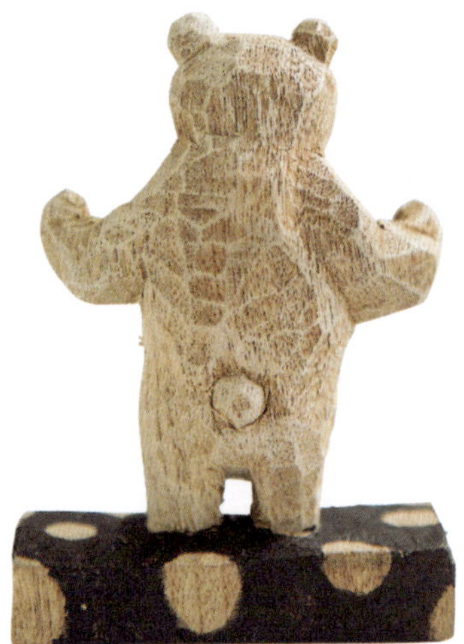

1 Sketch

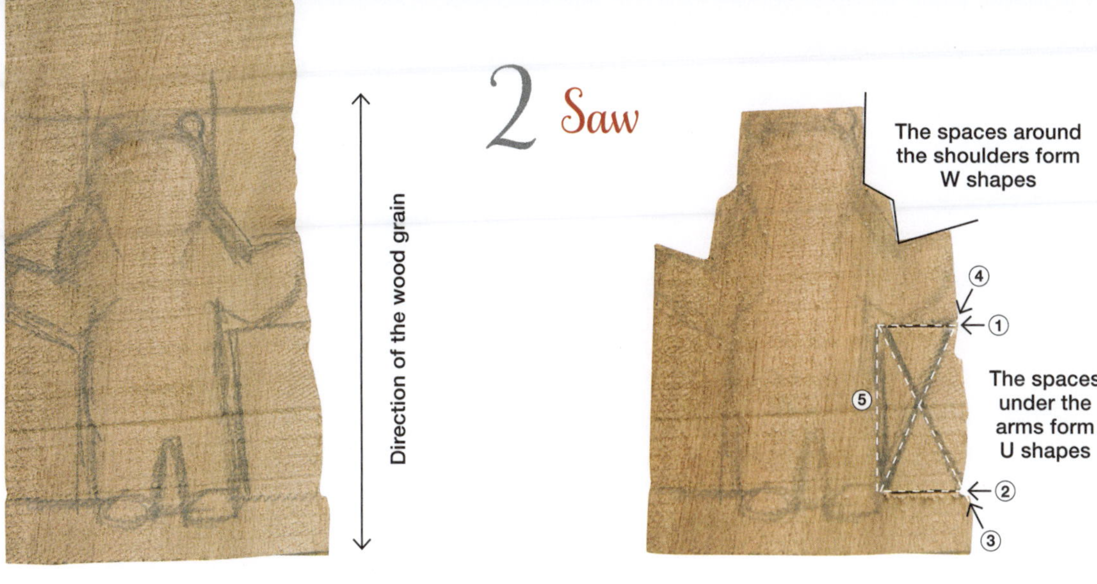

Capture the bear's features by drawing the face and ears small, and the body large and impressive. Here, the ends of the swing go right to the edges of the wood.

2 Saw

Divide the W shape of the shoulders into two L cuts. Remove the remaining waste wood with a chisel.

Make a U-shaped cut

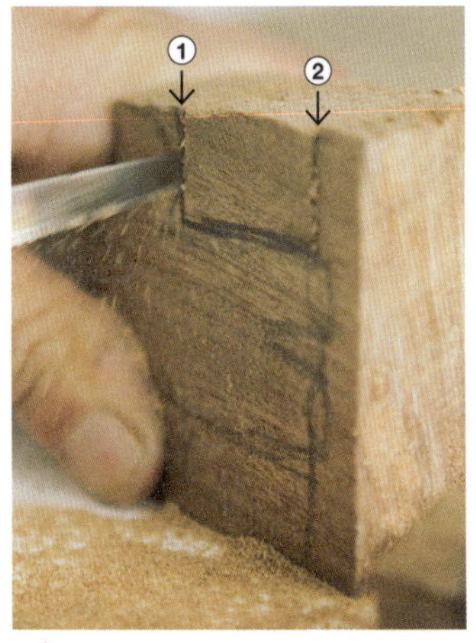

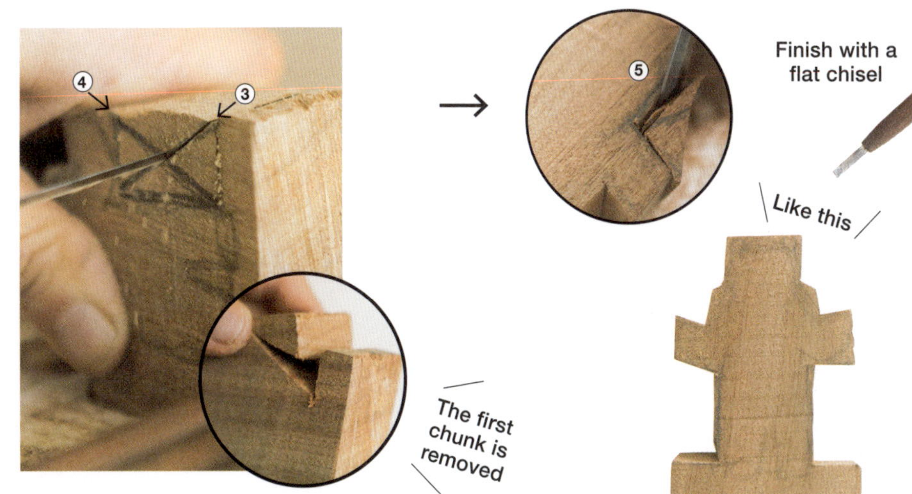

Note

How to make a U-shaped cut

It's easy to plan precise cuts if you draw on lines where you will saw. Use the saw to make the vertical and diagonal cuts to remove triangles of waste wood. Then, set the block down horizontal and use the back of a large flat chisel to vertically carve out the rest along the line.

3 Rough out

Front

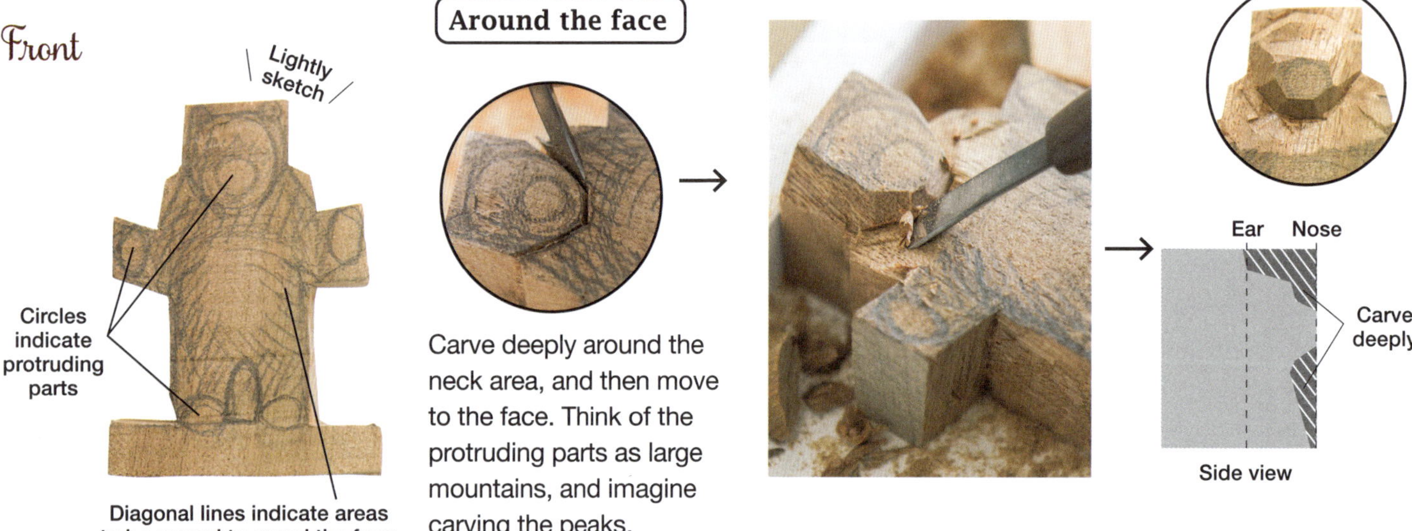

Carve deeply around the neck area, and then move to the face. Think of the protruding parts as large mountains, and imagine carving the peaks.

Body

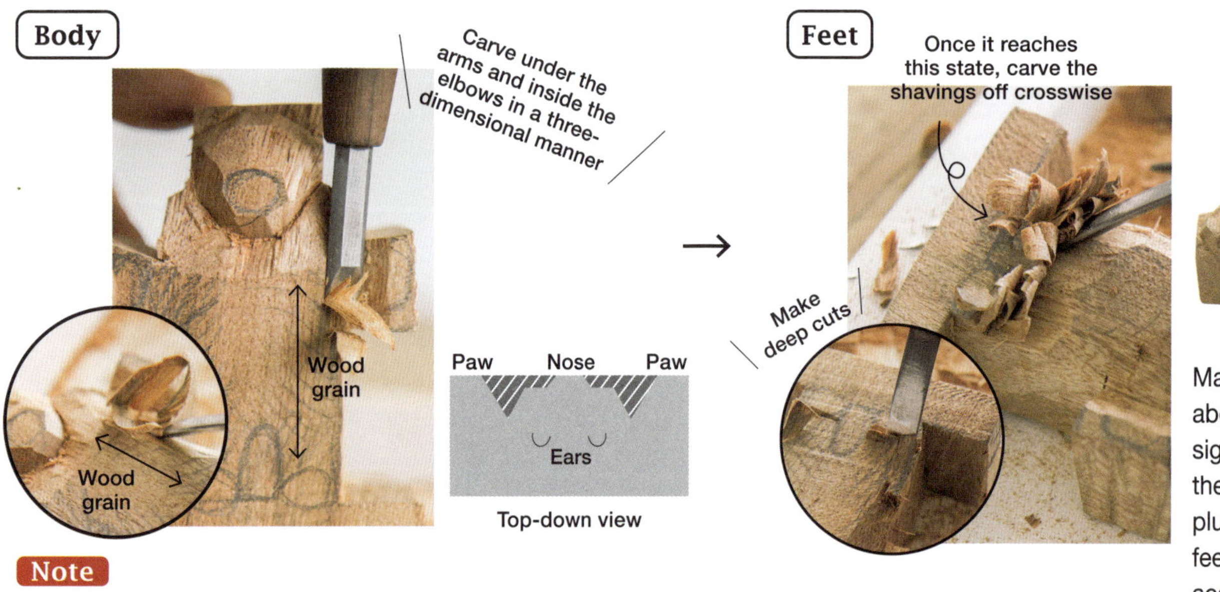

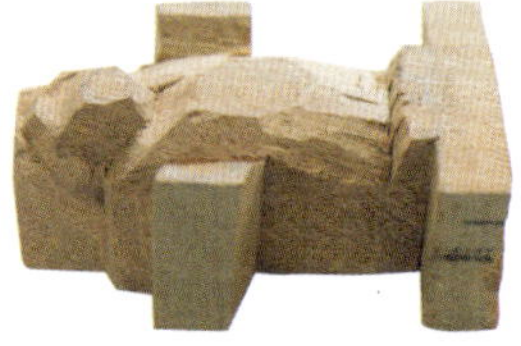

Make deep cuts above the toes, and significantly reduce the material from the plump belly to the feet. Be careful not to accidentally remove the toes.

Note

Carving direction

If you try to carve vertically while the piece is lying down, it can easily chip with disastrous effects. Stand the bear up and run the chisel vertically along the direction of the wood grain. If carving while the piece is horizontal, continue to carve in the direction of the grain.

Back

When carving the back, refer to your profile sketch to determine where to carve on the back surface. Remember to make the arms stand out and shave along the grain of the wood.

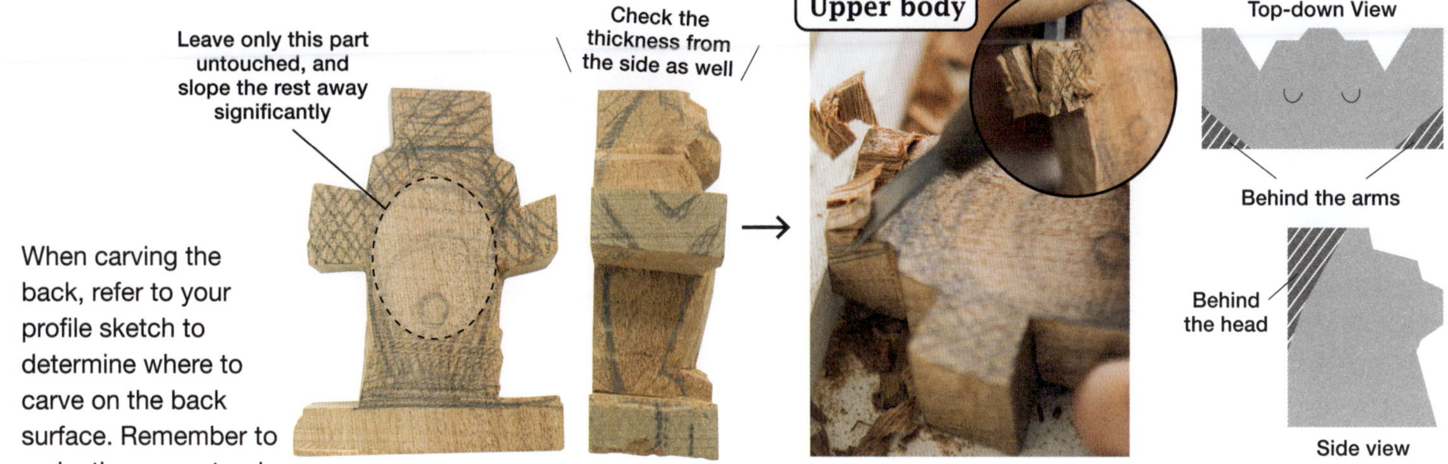

Lower body

For the tail, use a small flat chisel

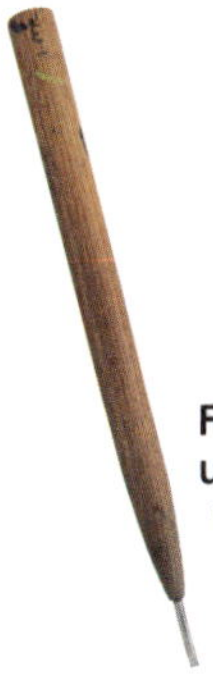

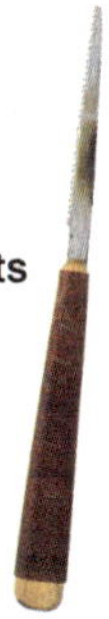

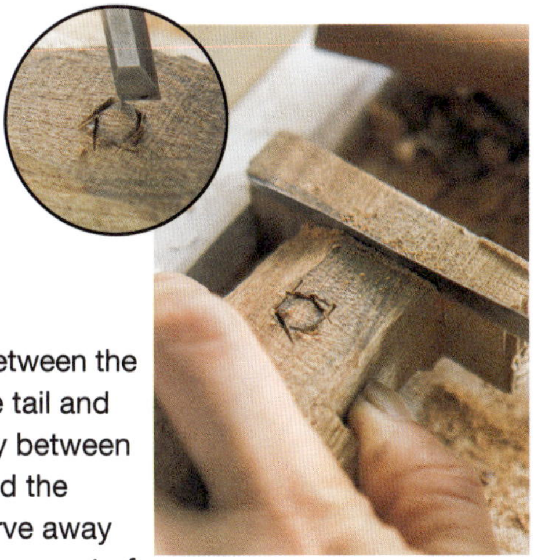

Make cuts between the outline of the tail and the boundary between the swing and the legs, and carve away a significant amount of material in that area.

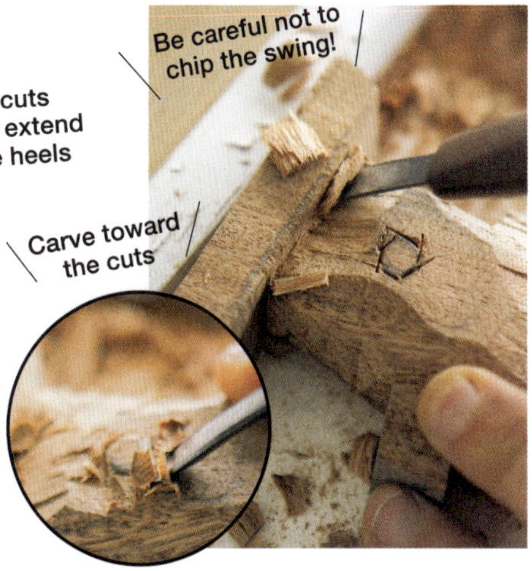

Make the cuts

The cuts should extend to the heels

Be careful not to chip the swing!

Carve toward the cuts

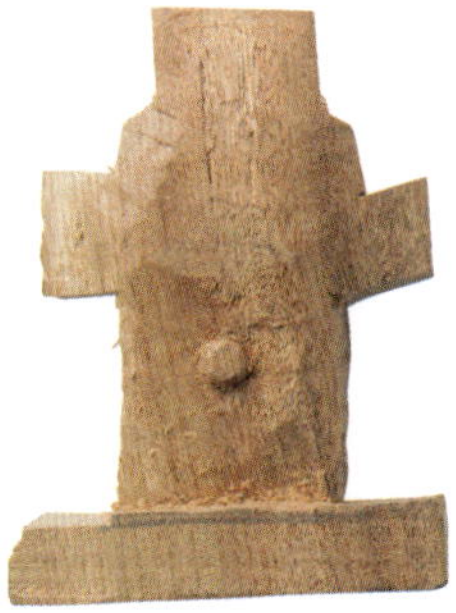

4 Refine

Side

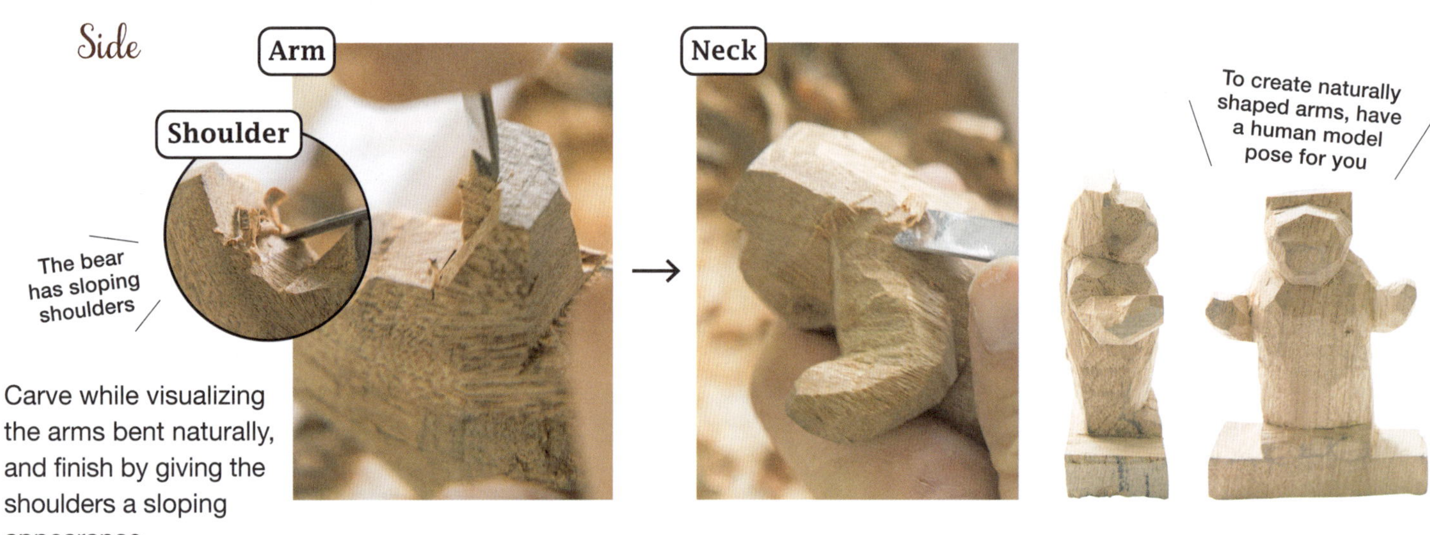

Carve while visualizing the arms bent naturally, and finish by giving the shoulders a sloping appearance.

Front

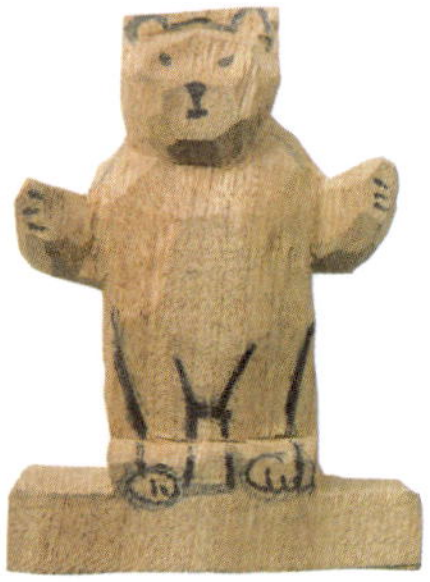

Leg

Between the legs

Before proceeding with carving the lower body, do another quick sketch. Also, draw the ears.

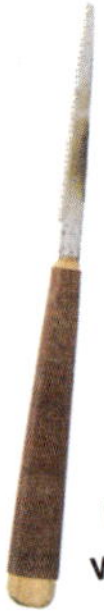

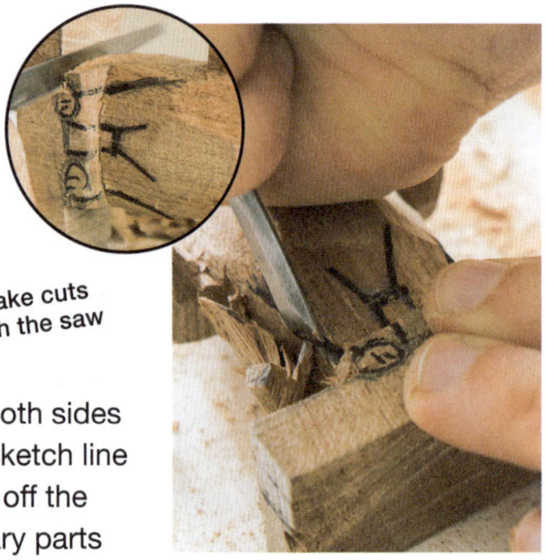

Cut from both sides up to the sketch line and shave off the unnecessary parts along the grain.

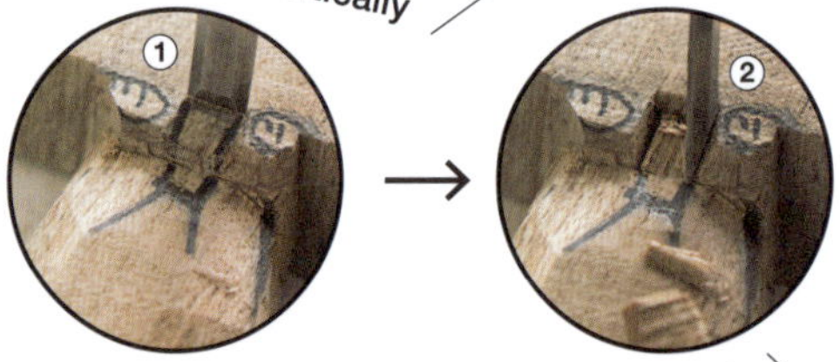

Remove the material between the legs. Work the chisel to create a U-shaped excavation around the swing surface and the sides of the legs, and finally, open up the area between the crotch and the feet.

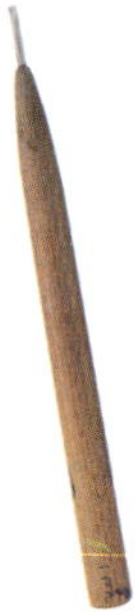

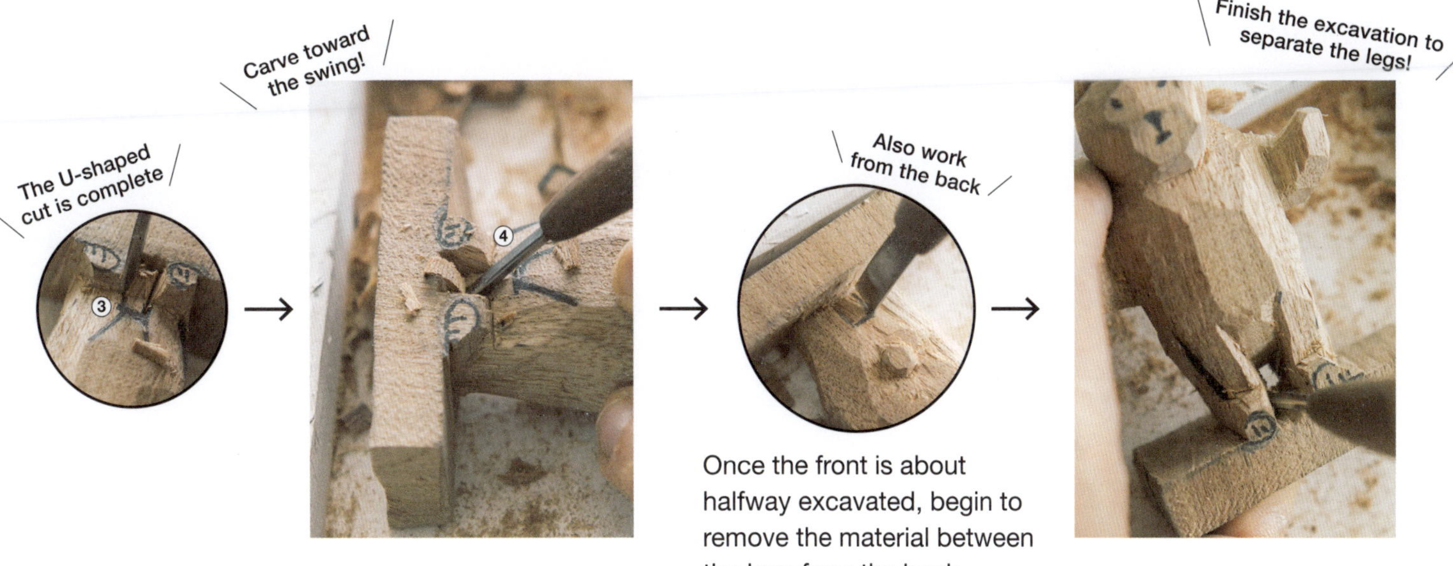

Once the front is about halfway excavated, begin to remove the material between the legs from the back.

....

Ears

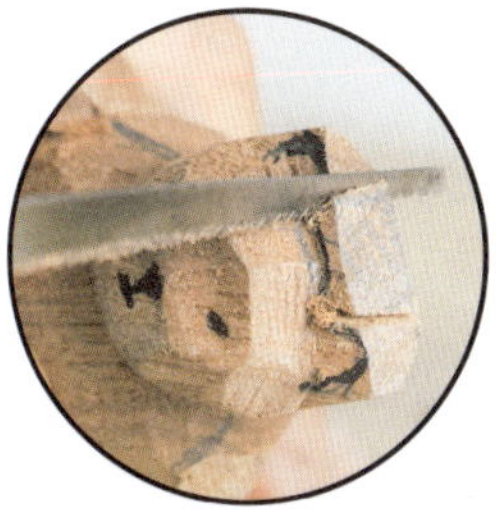

Make cuts with the saw and whittle away the waste with the chisel. Carve the back of the ears to create a rounded appearance.

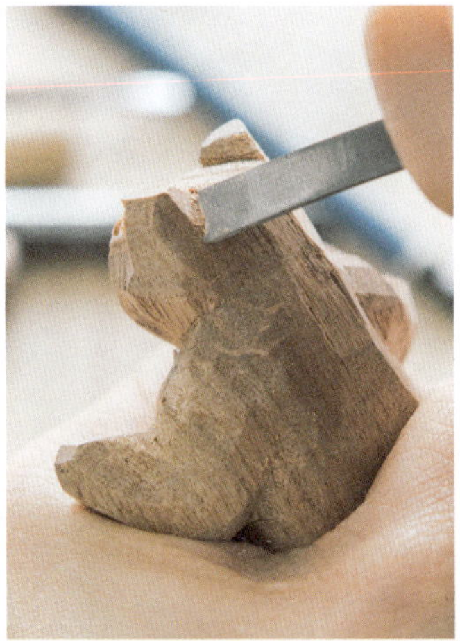

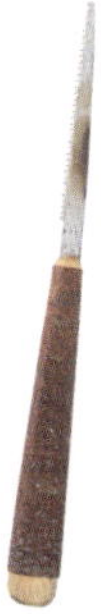

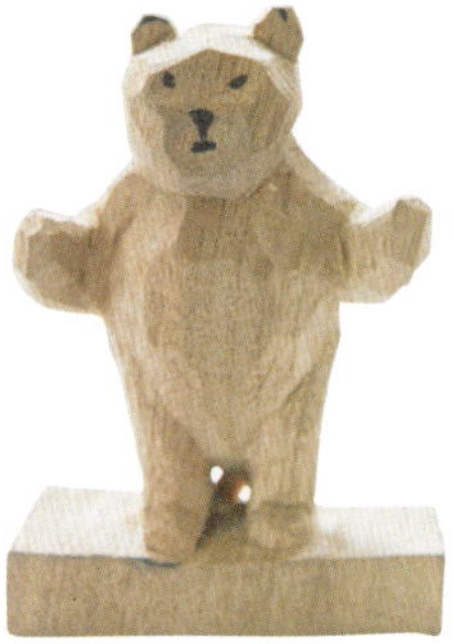

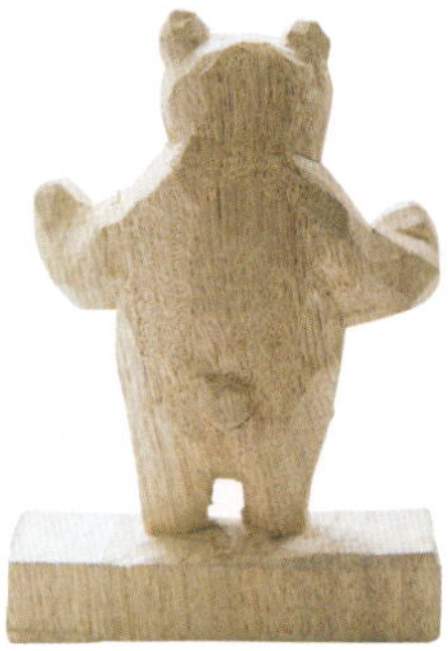

Cut with the saw

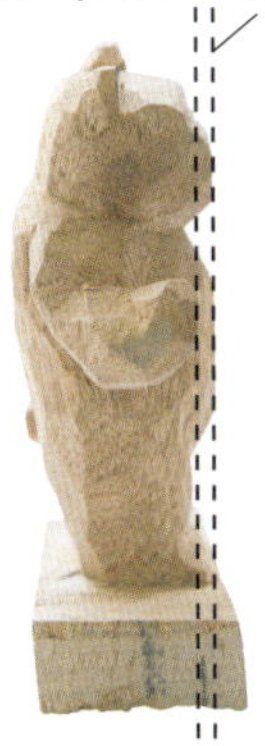

5 Finish

Finish the face

Nose

Erase the preliminary sketch by shaving it off, and then start detailing from the nose. First, carve a significant slope from the nose to the eyes. Carve the cheeks and lower jaw as well.

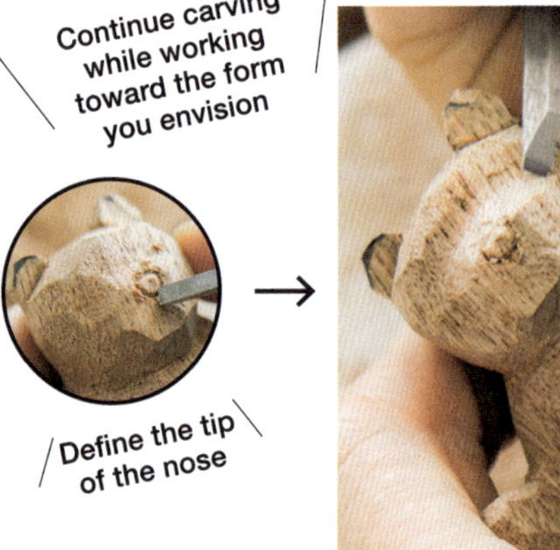

After delineating the nose, carve the nostrils with the corner of the chisel to bring them to life when adding color. Lightly shave the mouth into a slight frown.

Muzzle*

*"Muzzle" refers to the nose and mouth area of an animal

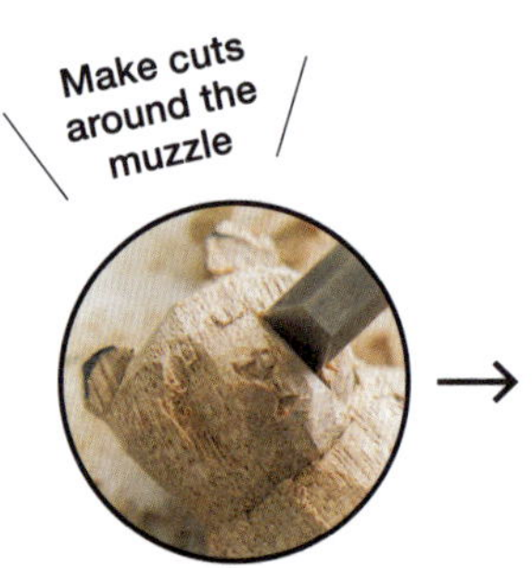

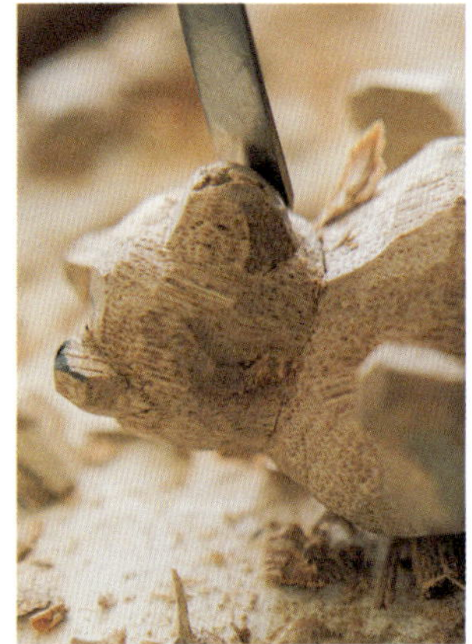

Carve out the muzzle. It is helpful to refer to an animal encyclopedia while carving.

Eyes

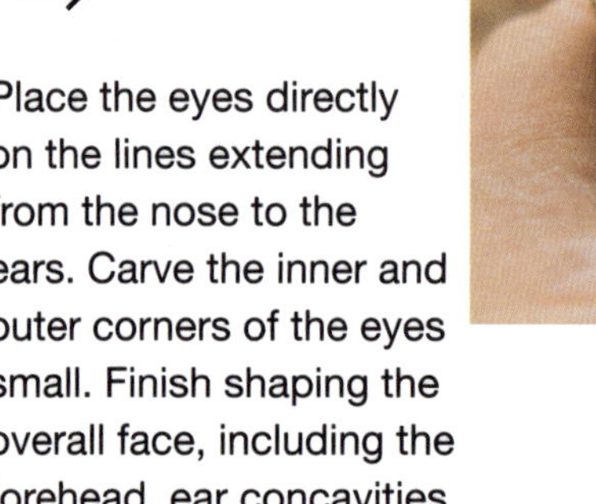

Place the eyes directly on the lines extending from the nose to the ears. Carve the inner and outer corners of the eyes small. Finish shaping the overall face, including the forehead, ear concavities and other indentations.

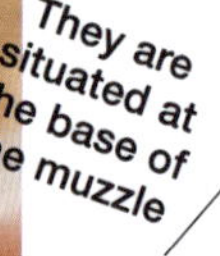

Use a small flat chisel for fine details

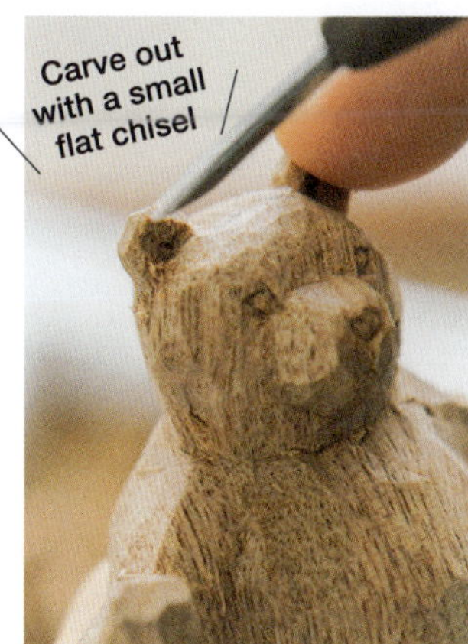

Add detail and texture

Try creating expressions with a gouge!

Don't be confined to a specific order for the details, carve wherever you feel like. There is no correct way to carve, so cherish the shape that you find cute.

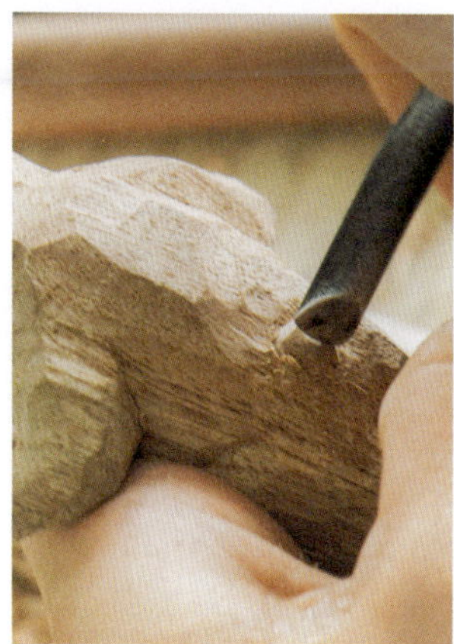

Carve the fore and hind paws, making the forepaws look as if they are holding the cords that you will install later. If desired, make fine cuts with a thin blade to define the toes.

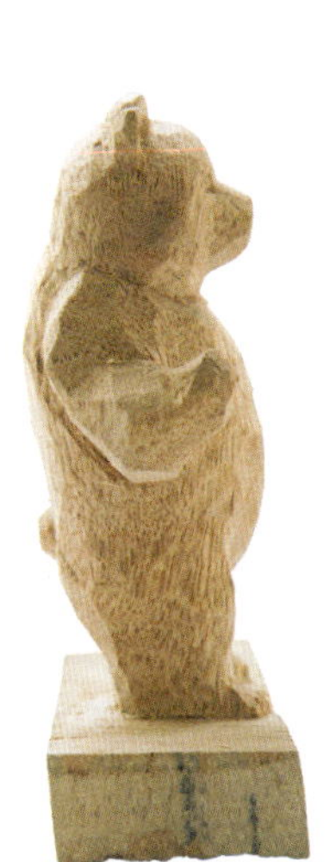

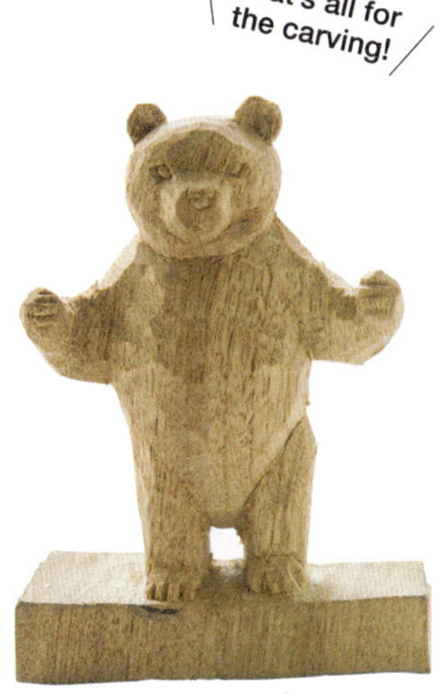

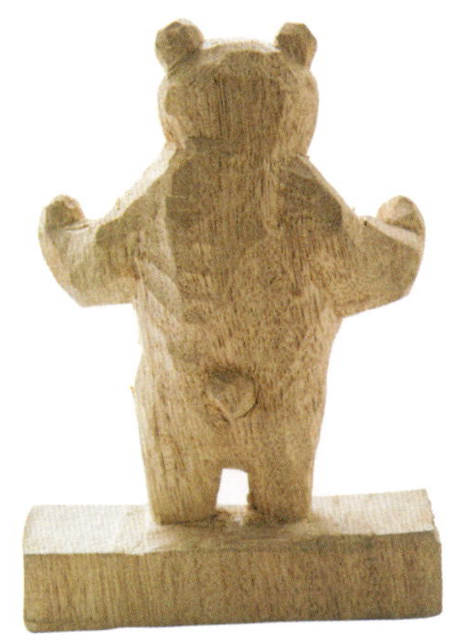

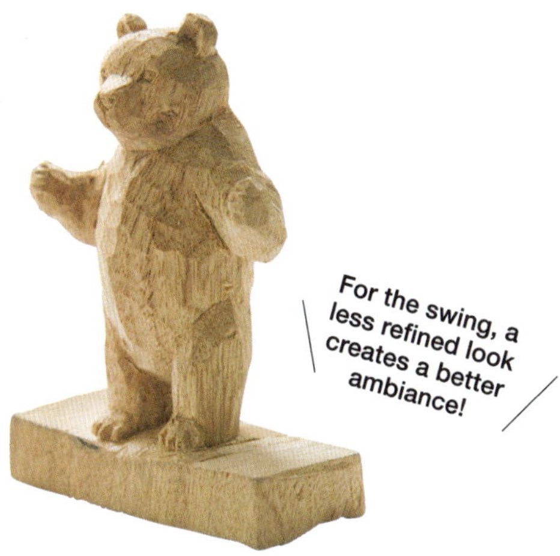

6 Adding color

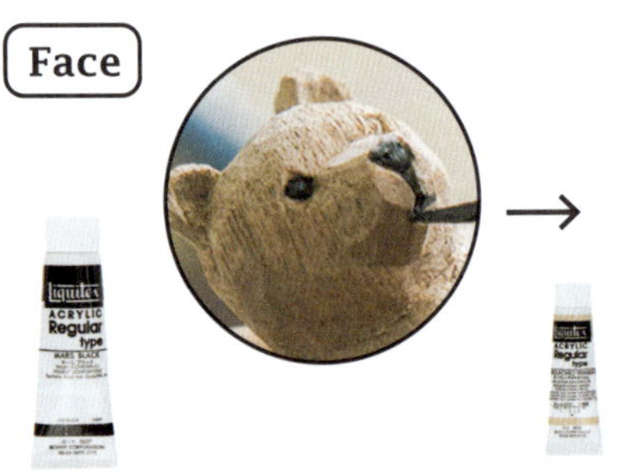

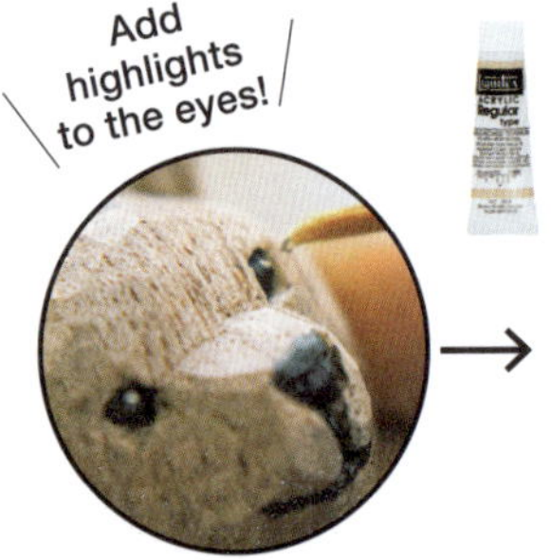

Paint the eyes, nose and mouth black. Finally, add a highlight to the eyes with white.

Use white with a dry brush (refer to page 44) to paint so that the carving marks are visible. Color the swing as you like.

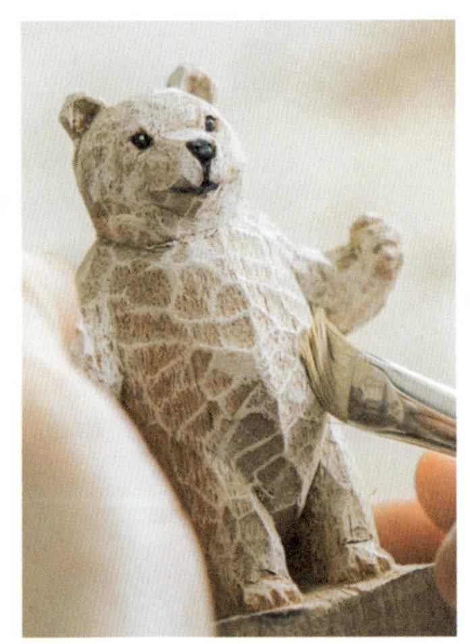

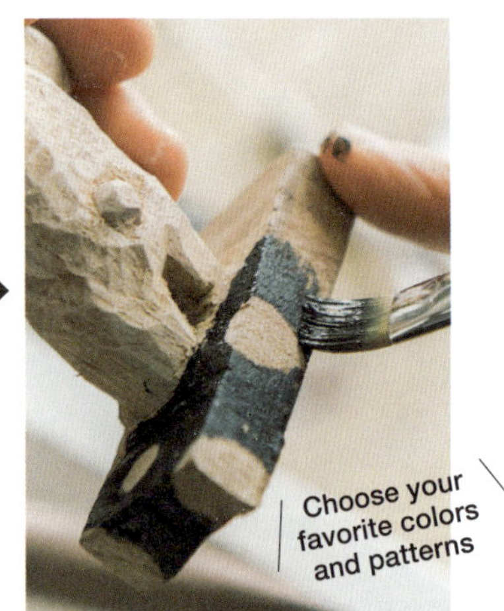

7 Install the cords

Mark the positions for the holes to be drilled vertically into the paws and swing. Carefully drill the holes, and then thread the cords through, tying the ends beneath.

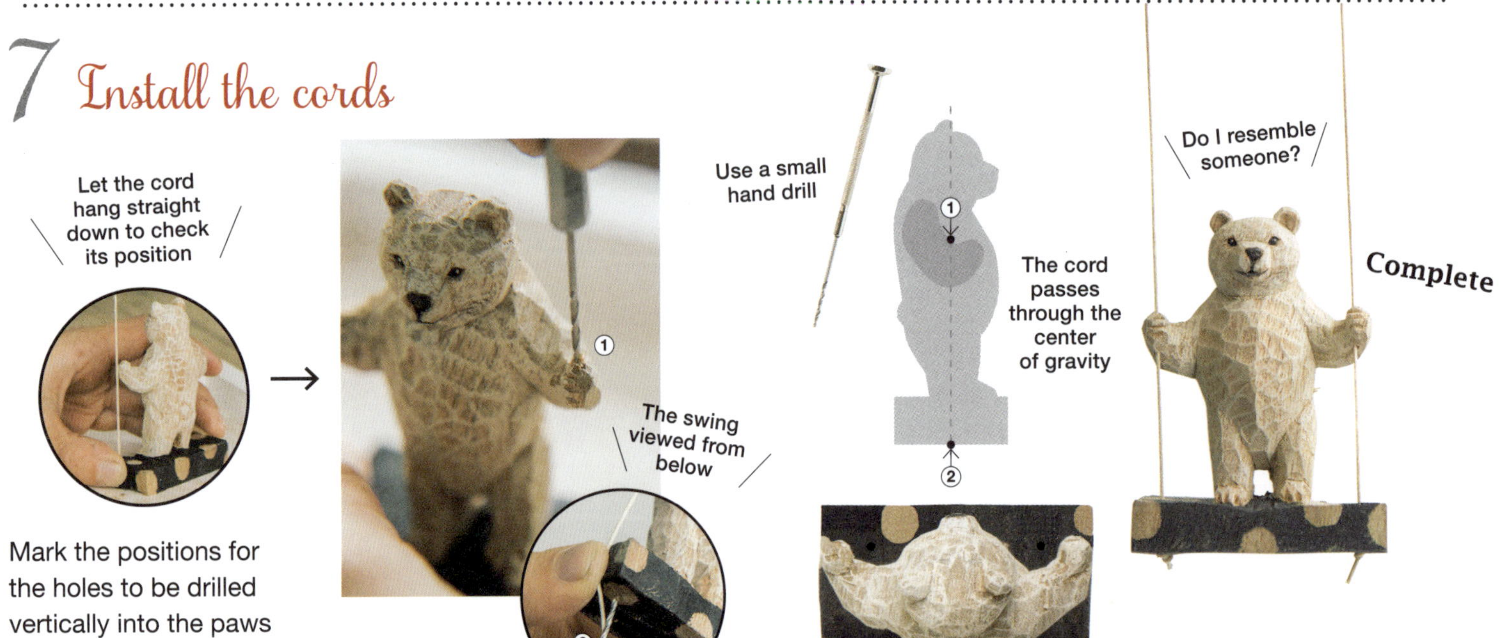

Miniature Donkey

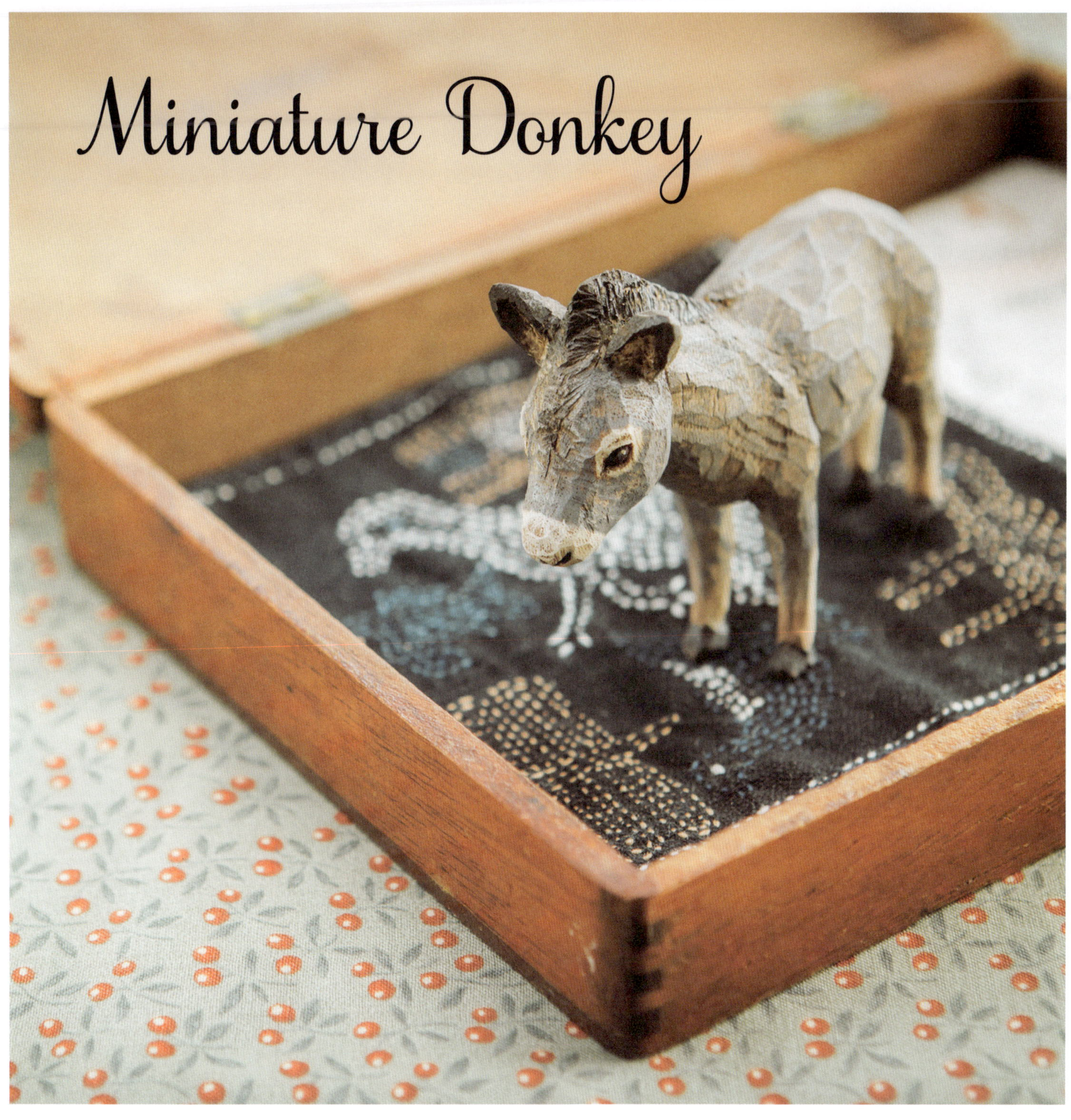

A donkey sculpture with a sturdy quadruped
stance, large ears and gentle eyes ... there
are many features to carve in this figurine.
Use resources like animal encyclopedias, and
consider visiting a zoo for research to observe and
meticulously carve the details.

Miniature Donkey

Materials:

- Wood
- Pen or pencil
- Saw
- Flat chisel
- Gouge
- Acrylic paint

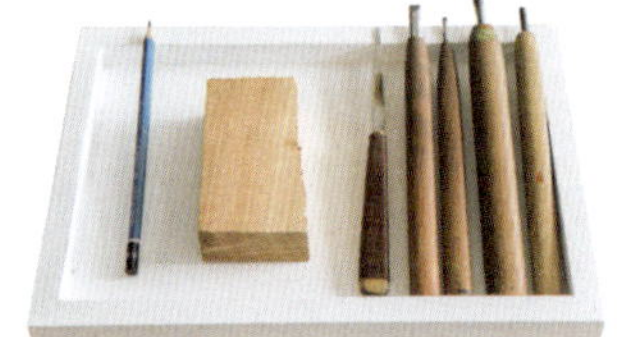

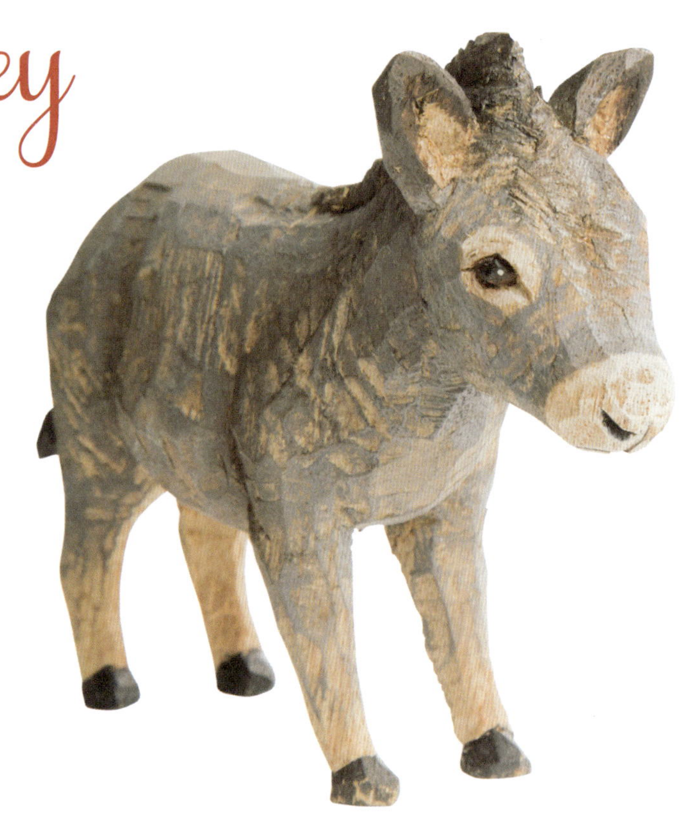

1 Sketch

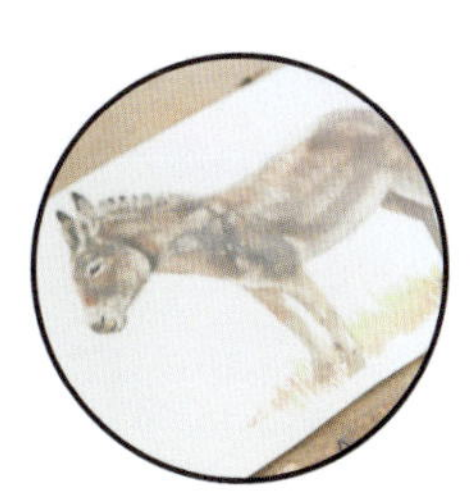

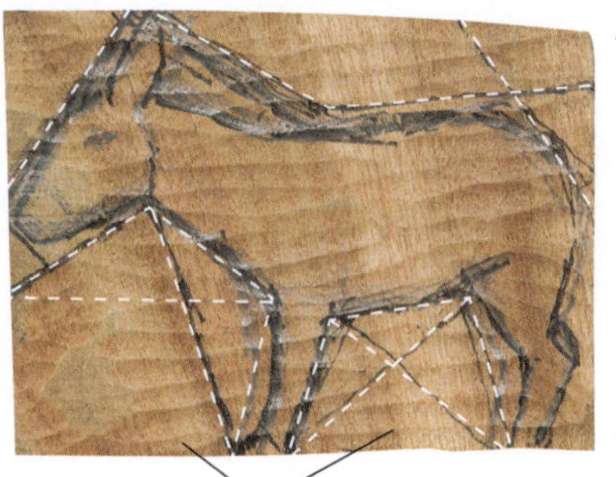

Make the preliminary sketch while referring to illustrations, photos or animal encyclopedias.

Make U-shaped cuts (refer to page 69)

2 Saw

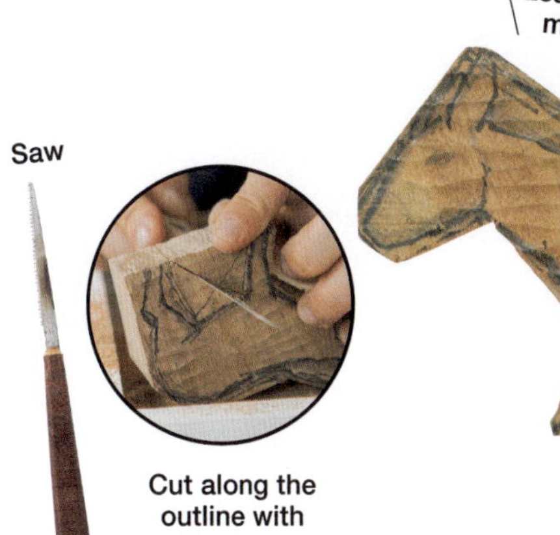

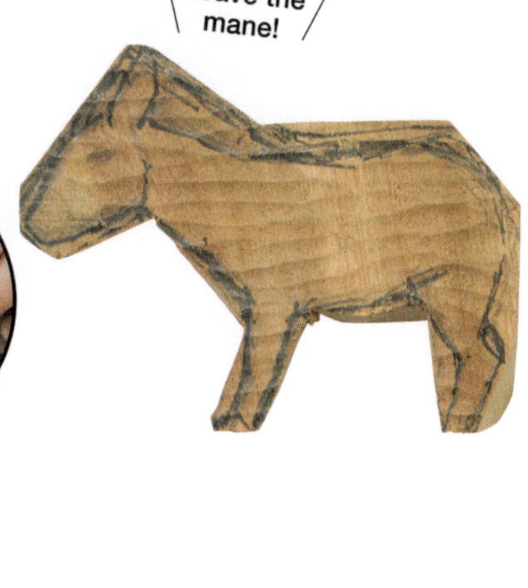

Cut along the outline with the saw

3 Rough out

[Legs]

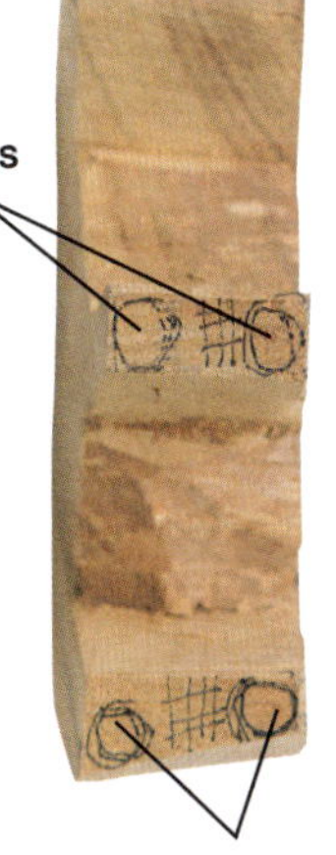

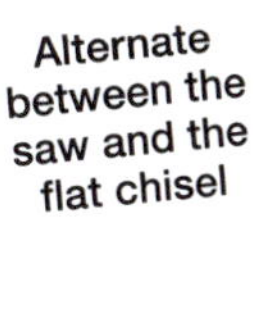

Mark the soles of the feet to determine the spaces between the forelegs and hind legs. Work the saw into the bases between both sets of legs and shave with a chisel from above to open up the spaces.

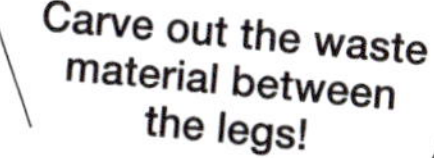

Alternate between the saw and the flat chisel

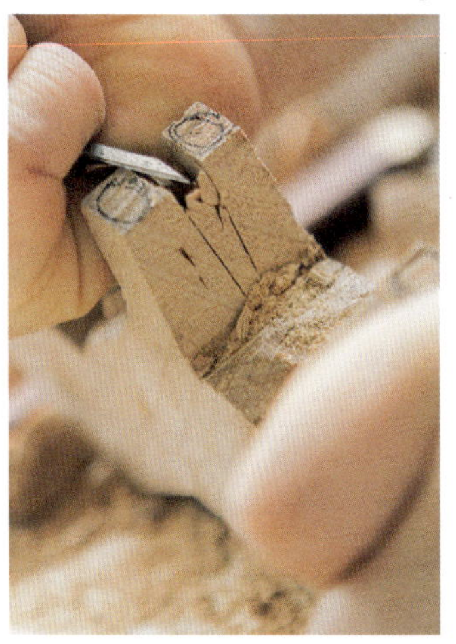

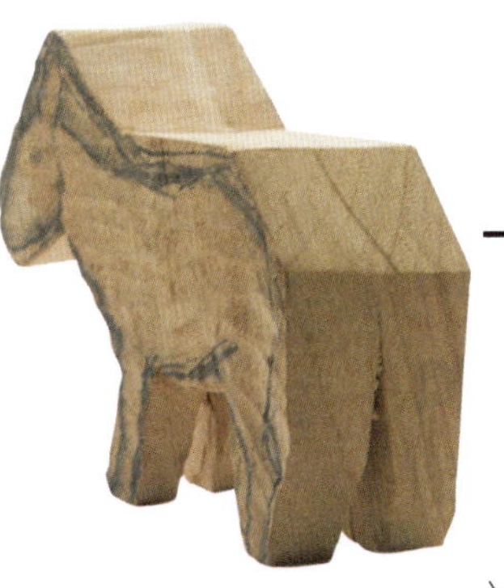

The space between the hind legs should be cut into a triangular notch

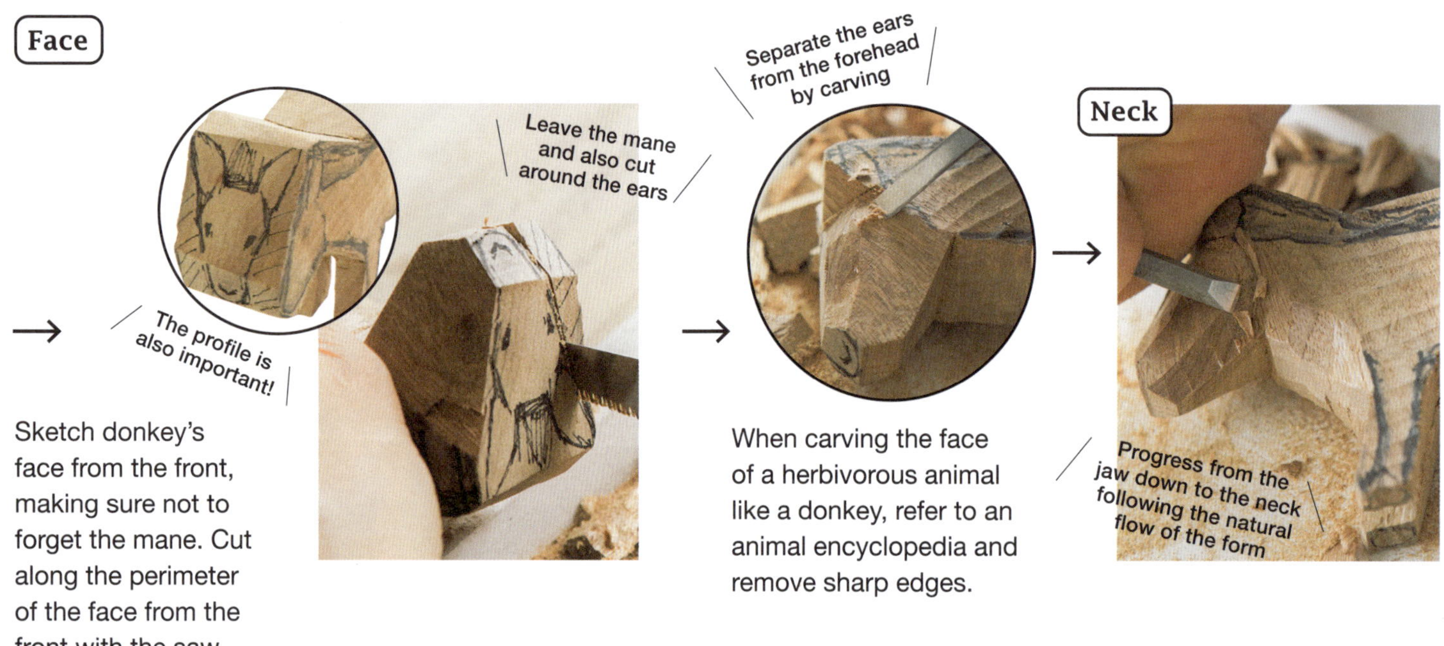

→ Sketch donkey's face from the front, making sure not to forget the mane. Cut along the perimeter of the face from the front with the saw.

→ When carving the face of a herbivorous animal like a donkey, refer to an animal encyclopedia and remove sharp edges.

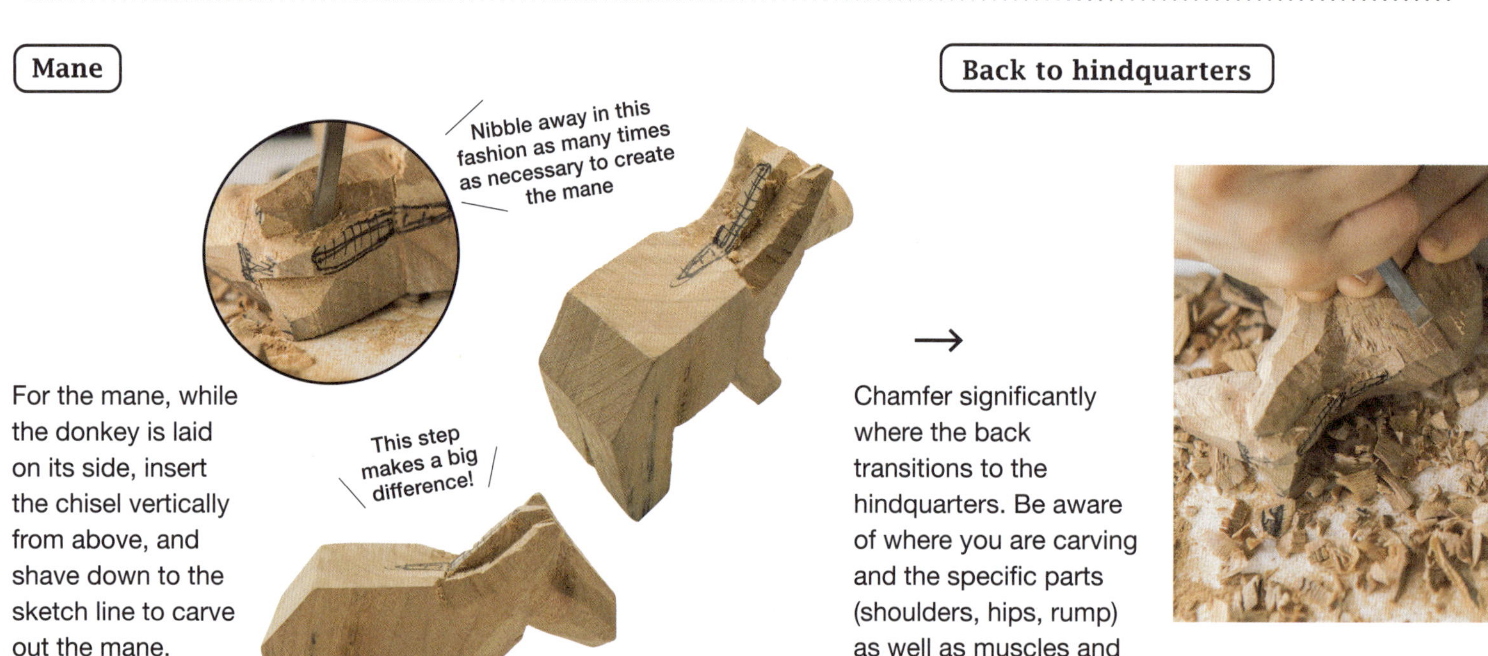

For the mane, while the donkey is laid on its side, insert the chisel vertically from above, and shave down to the sketch line to carve out the mane.

→ Chamfer significantly where the back transitions to the hindquarters. Be aware of where you are carving and the specific parts (shoulders, hips, rump) as well as muscles and the skeletal structure.

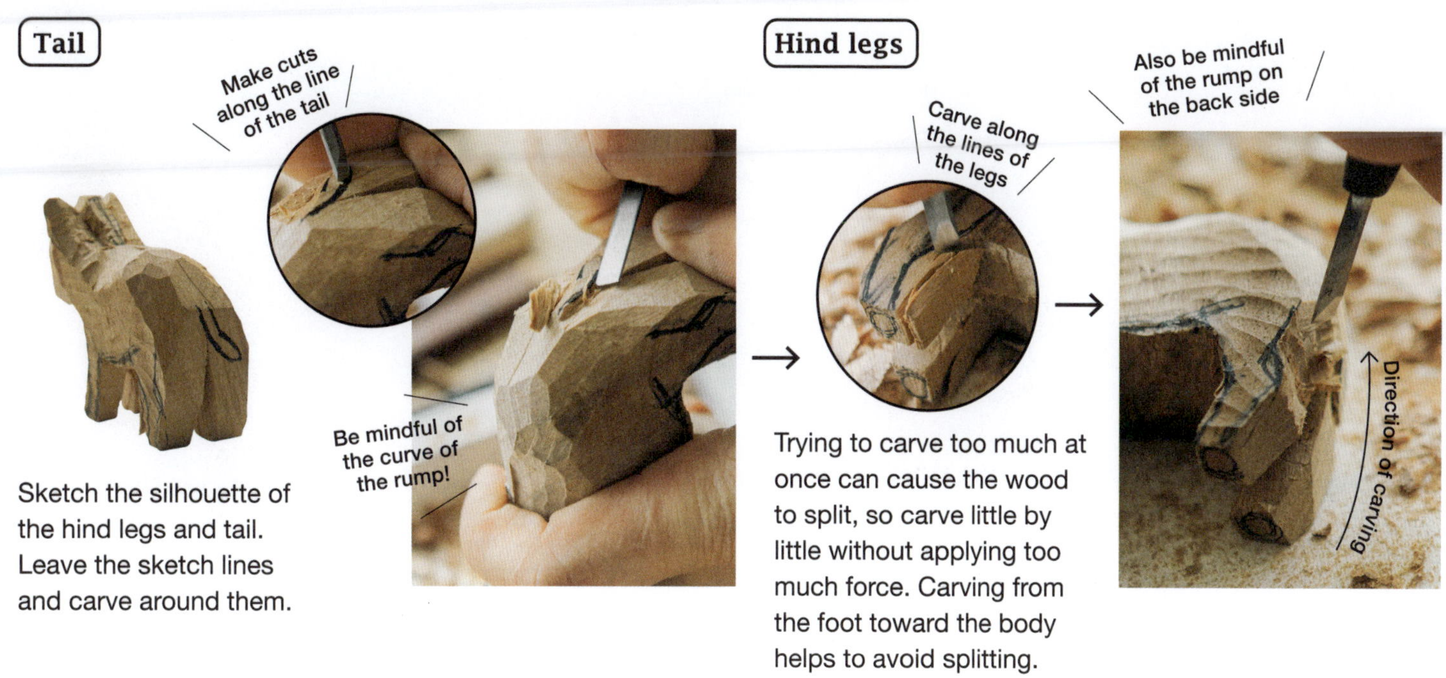

Sketch the silhouette of the hind legs and tail. Leave the sketch lines and carve around them.

Trying to carve too much at once can cause the wood to split, so carve little by little without applying too much force. Carving from the foot toward the body helps to avoid splitting.

4 Refine

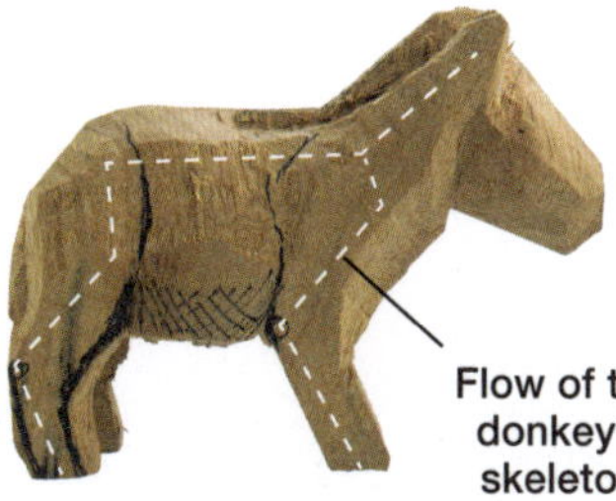

The bones of a donkey's legs, shoulders and hips connect in series to the spine. Sketch the lines of the legs, hips and shoulders, and then carve down the belly area.

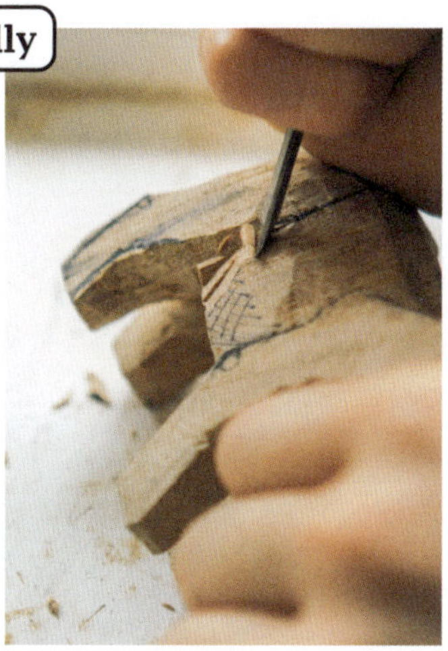

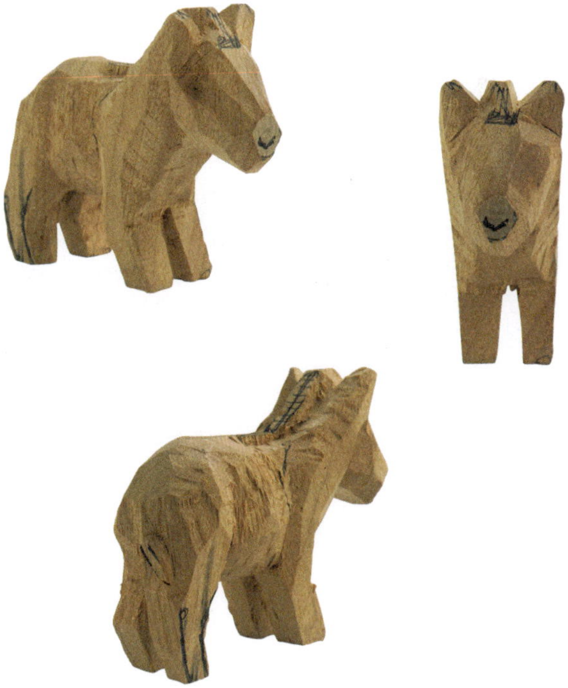

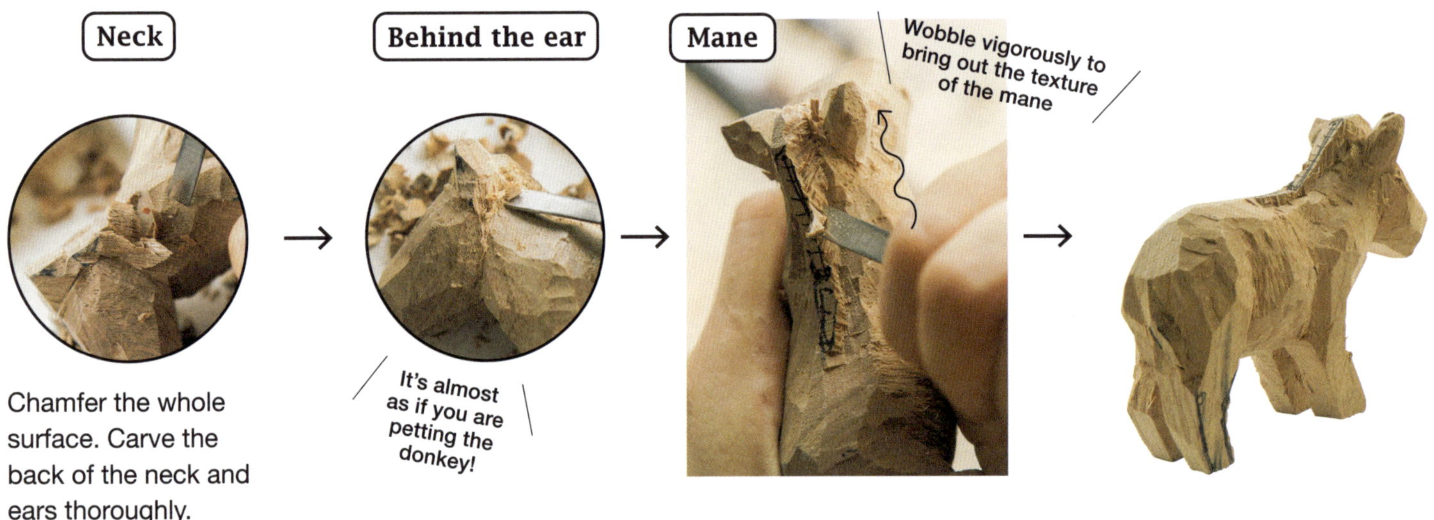

Chamfer the whole surface. Carve the back of the neck and ears thoroughly.

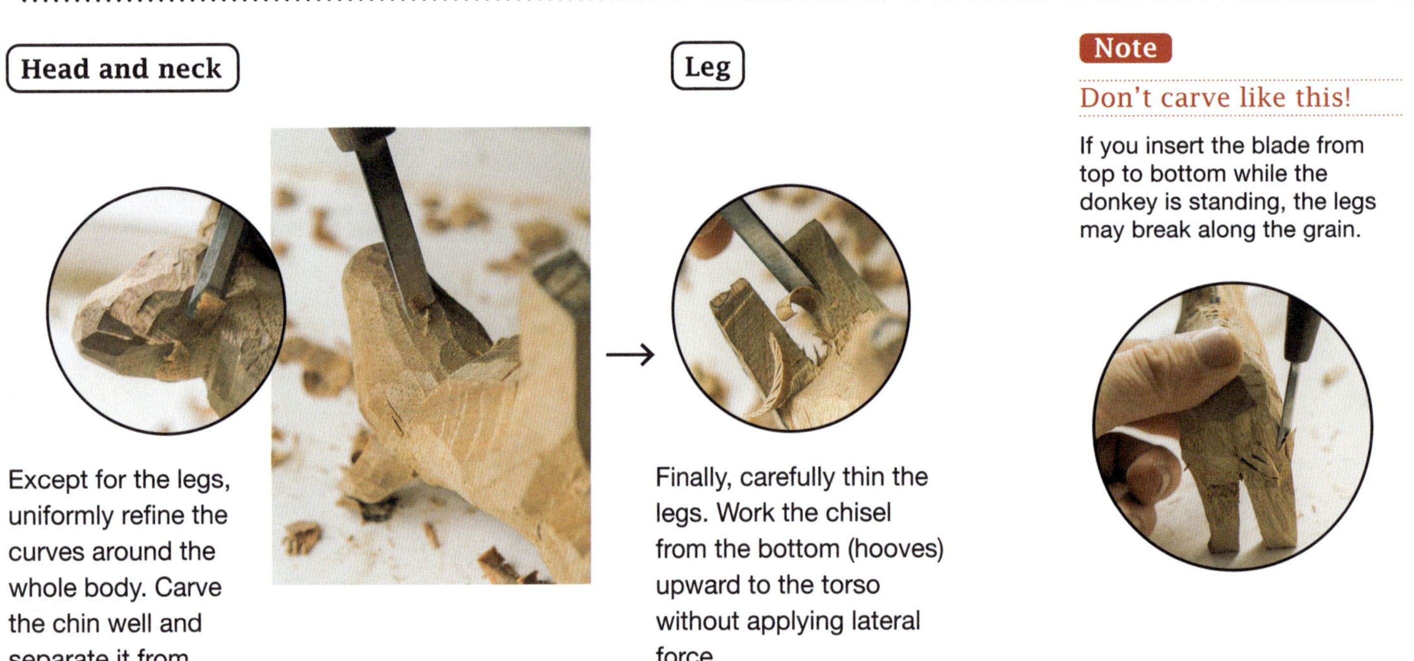

Except for the legs, uniformly refine the curves around the whole body. Carve the chin well and separate it from the neck.

Finally, carefully thin the legs. Work the chisel from the bottom (hooves) upward to the torso without applying lateral force.

Don't carve like this!

If you insert the blade from top to bottom while the donkey is standing, the legs may break along the grain.

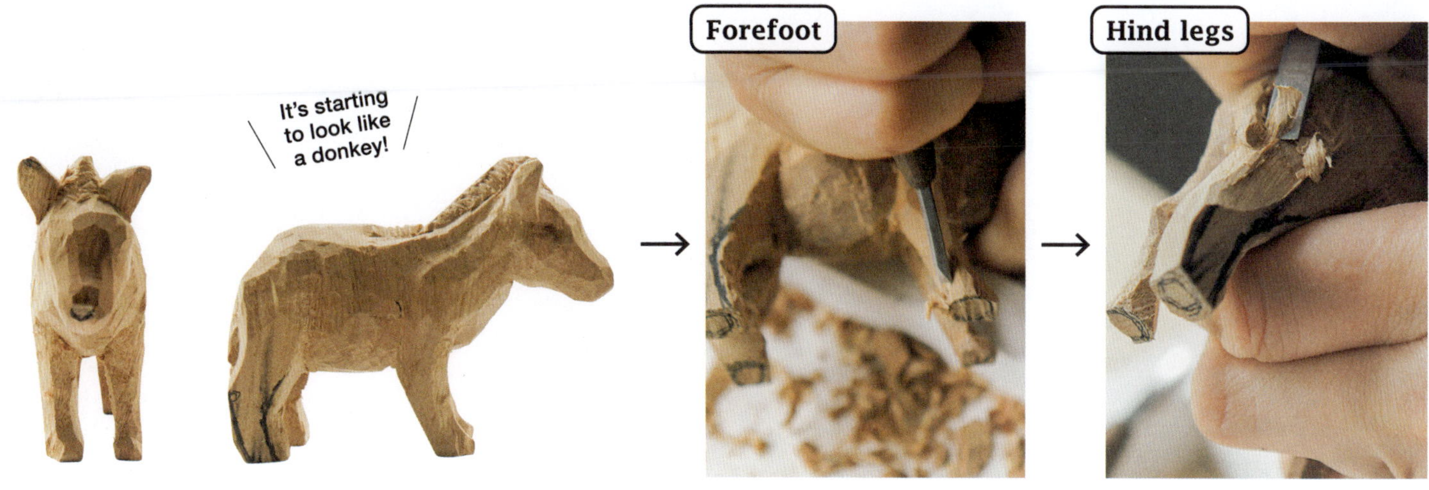

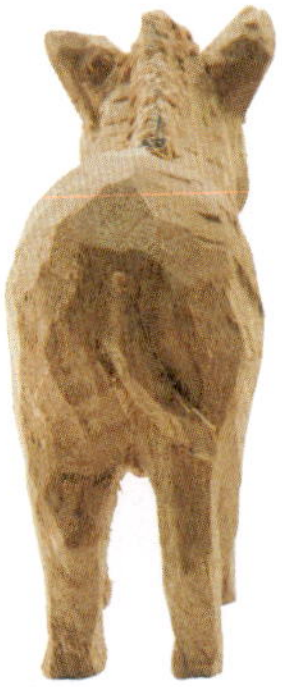

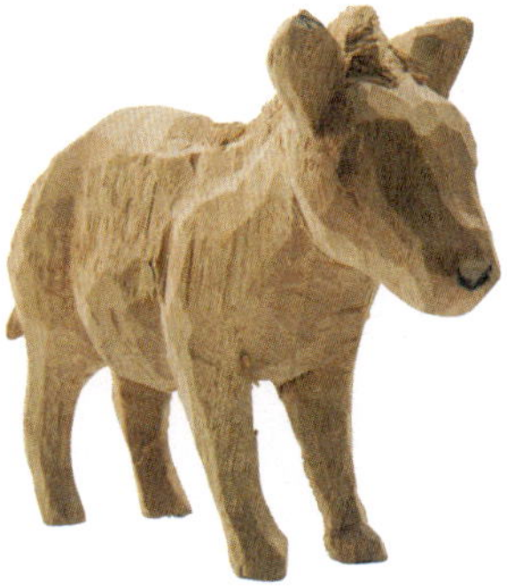

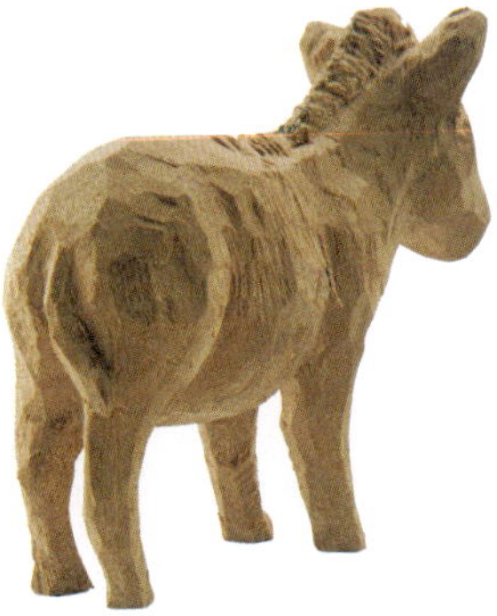

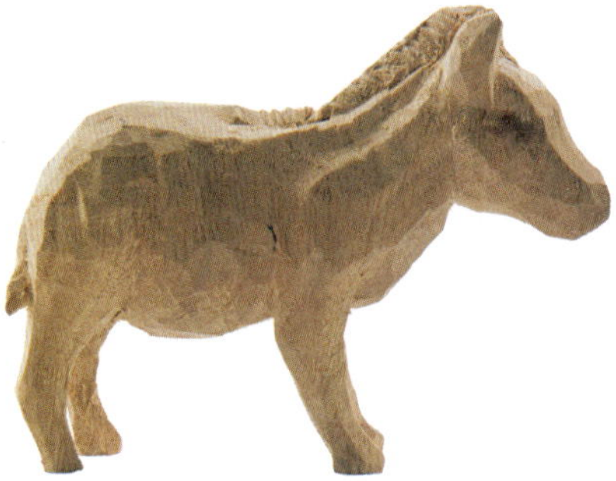

Note

If a leg breaks...

Use super glue for temporary fixes. For a strong bond, use wood glue, secure the repair with rubber bands, and leave to cure overnight.

5 Finishing touches

Adding details

Hooves

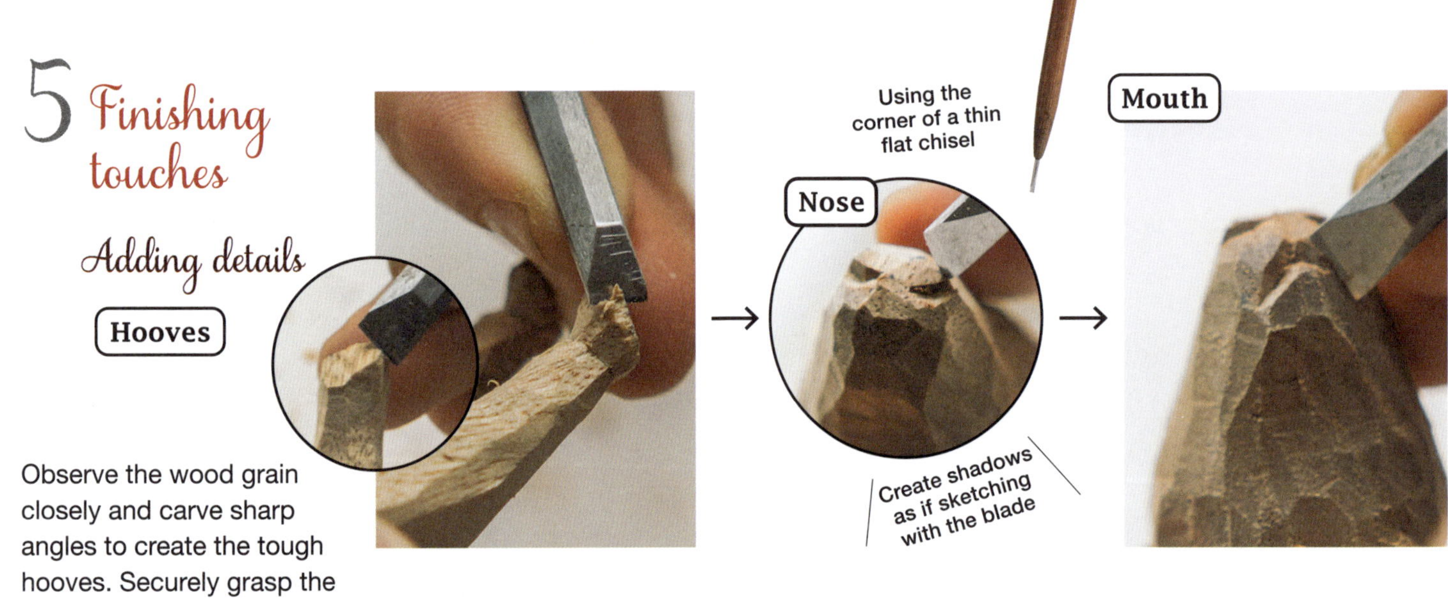

Observe the wood grain closely and carve sharp angles to create the tough hooves. Securely grasp the sculpture and meticulously carve the final shape.

Eyes

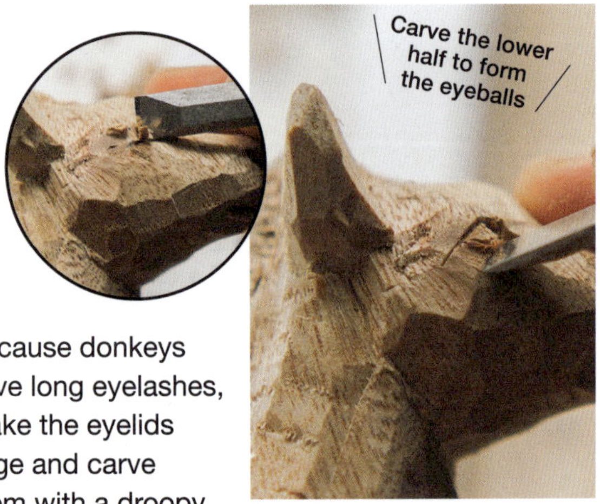

Because donkeys have long eyelashes, make the eyelids large and carve them with a droopy look. Adding a deep crease to the lids makes it more characteristic of a donkey.

Mane

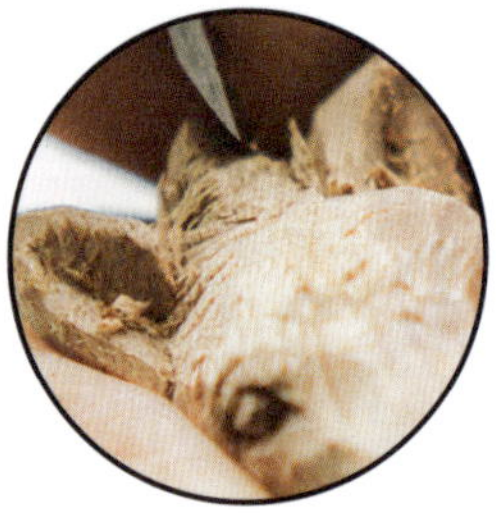

Cheeks

Carve the ear concavity, mane and cheeks in detail. Work toward achieving a realistic donkey figurine by evaluating the whole carving and adjusting as needed while wrapping up.

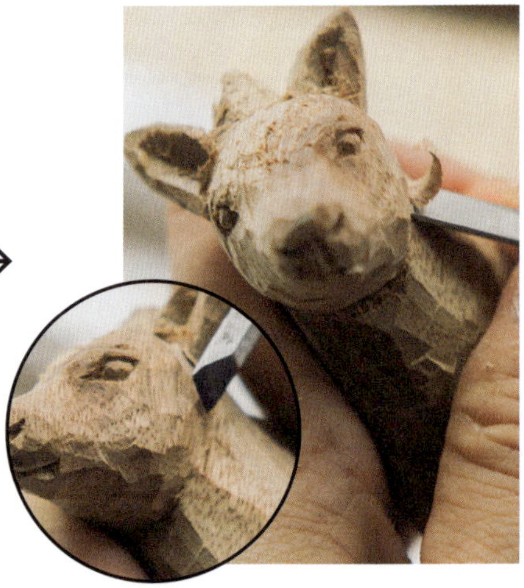

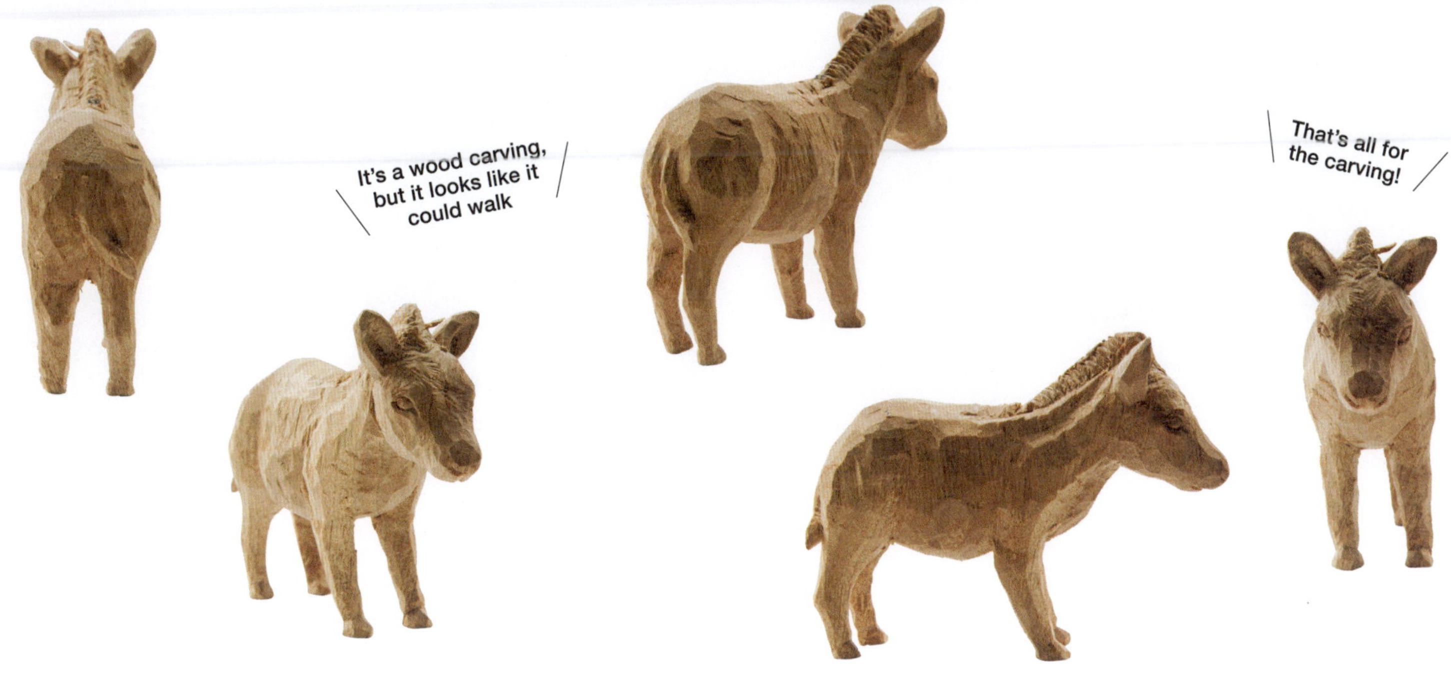

6 Adding color

Black

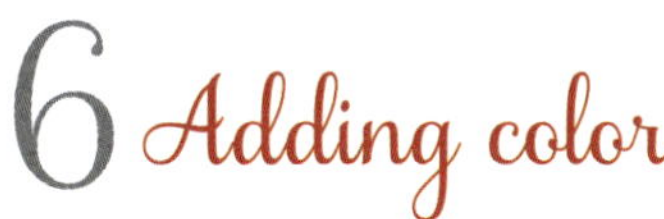

Eyes, nose and mouth

Paint the eyes first as in the other projects. Add brown, black, and finally white (for the highlights).

Gray

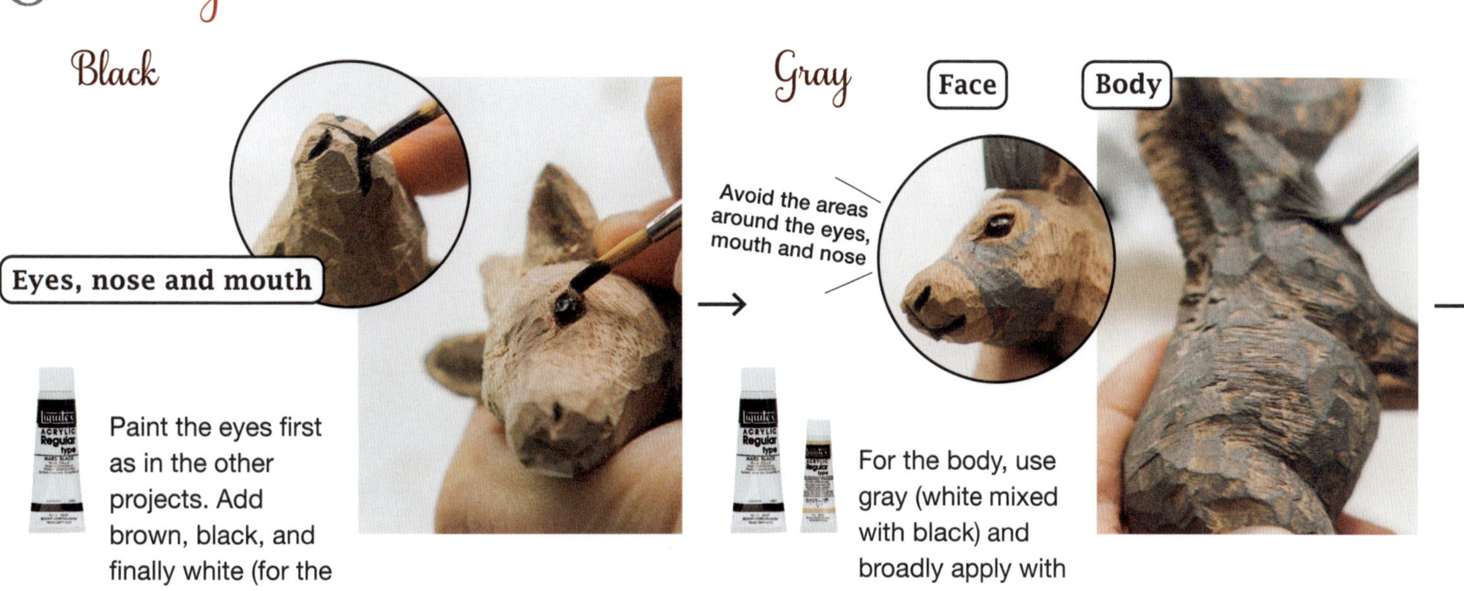

For the body, use gray (white mixed with black) and broadly apply with a dry brush (refer to page 44).

Black

Tail / Hooves

Apply black to the hooves, the tip of the tail and the edges of the ears. Also, paint the mane.

White

Ears and mane / Around the eyes and tip of the nose

Finish by applying white to the tip of the nose and around the eyes, adding an overall fleecy and glossy appearance.

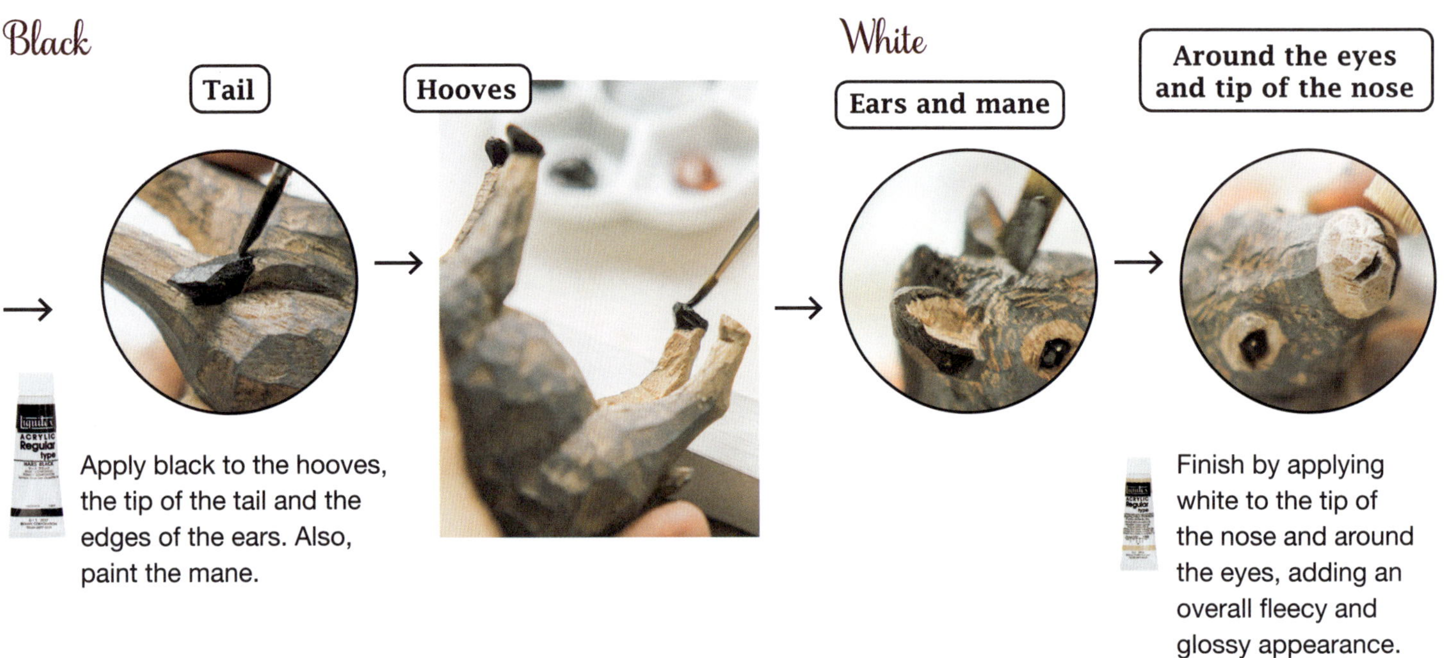

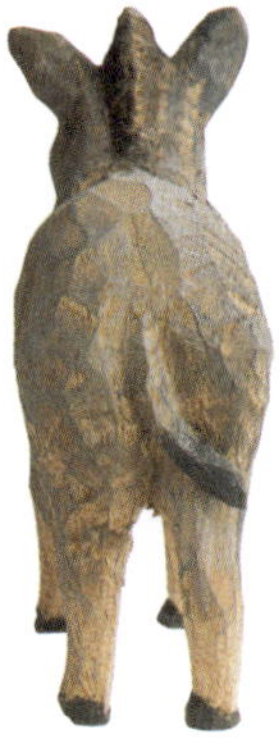

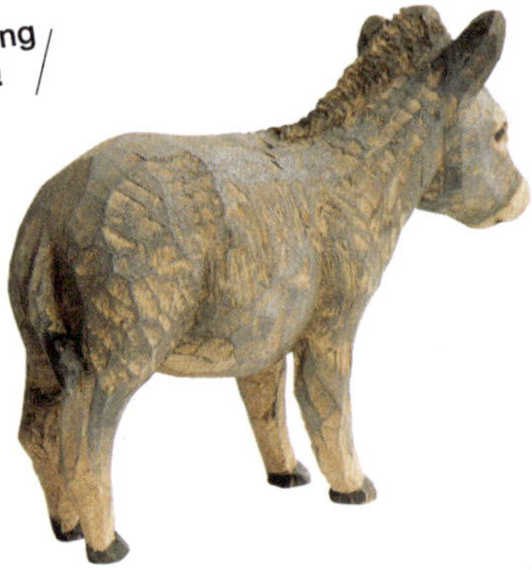

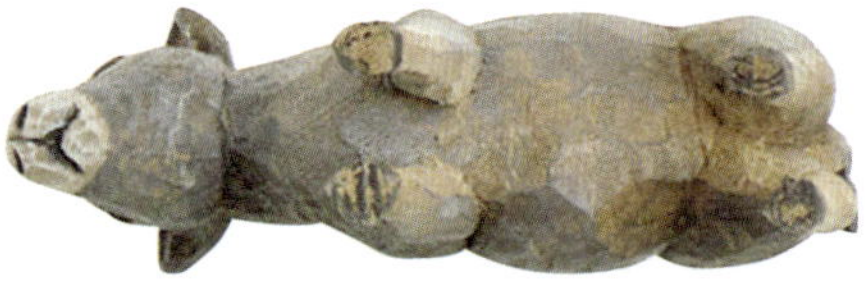

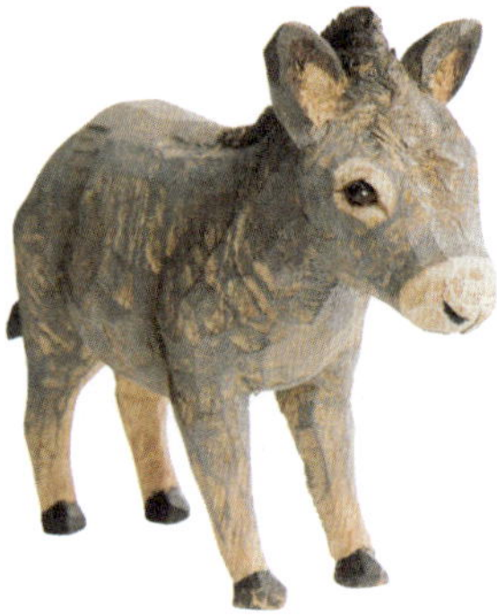

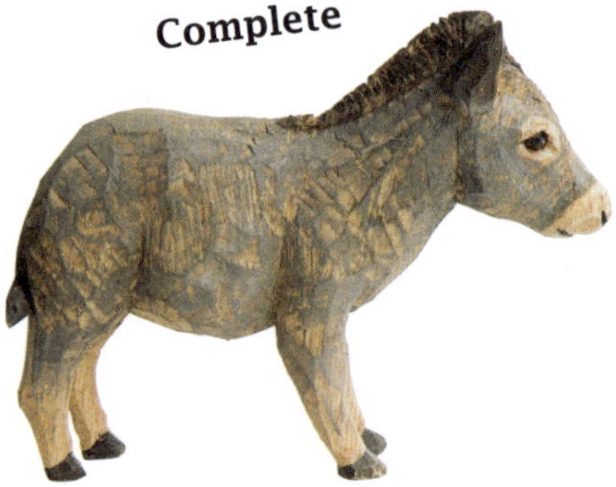

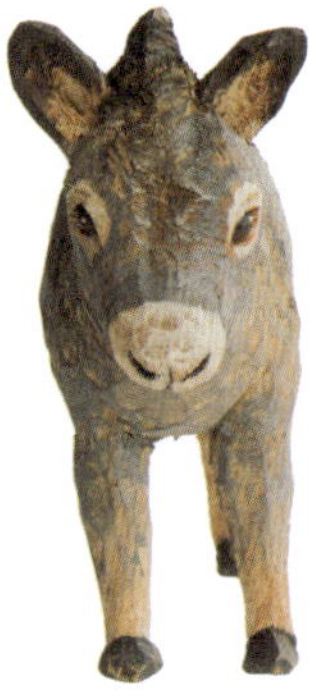

More of My Friends

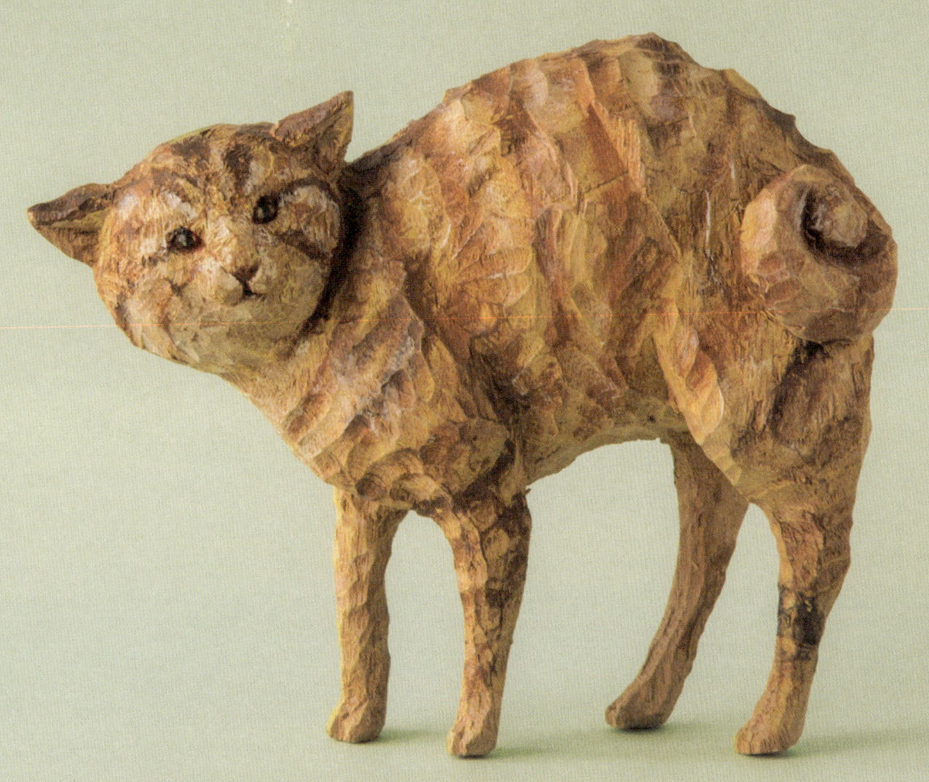

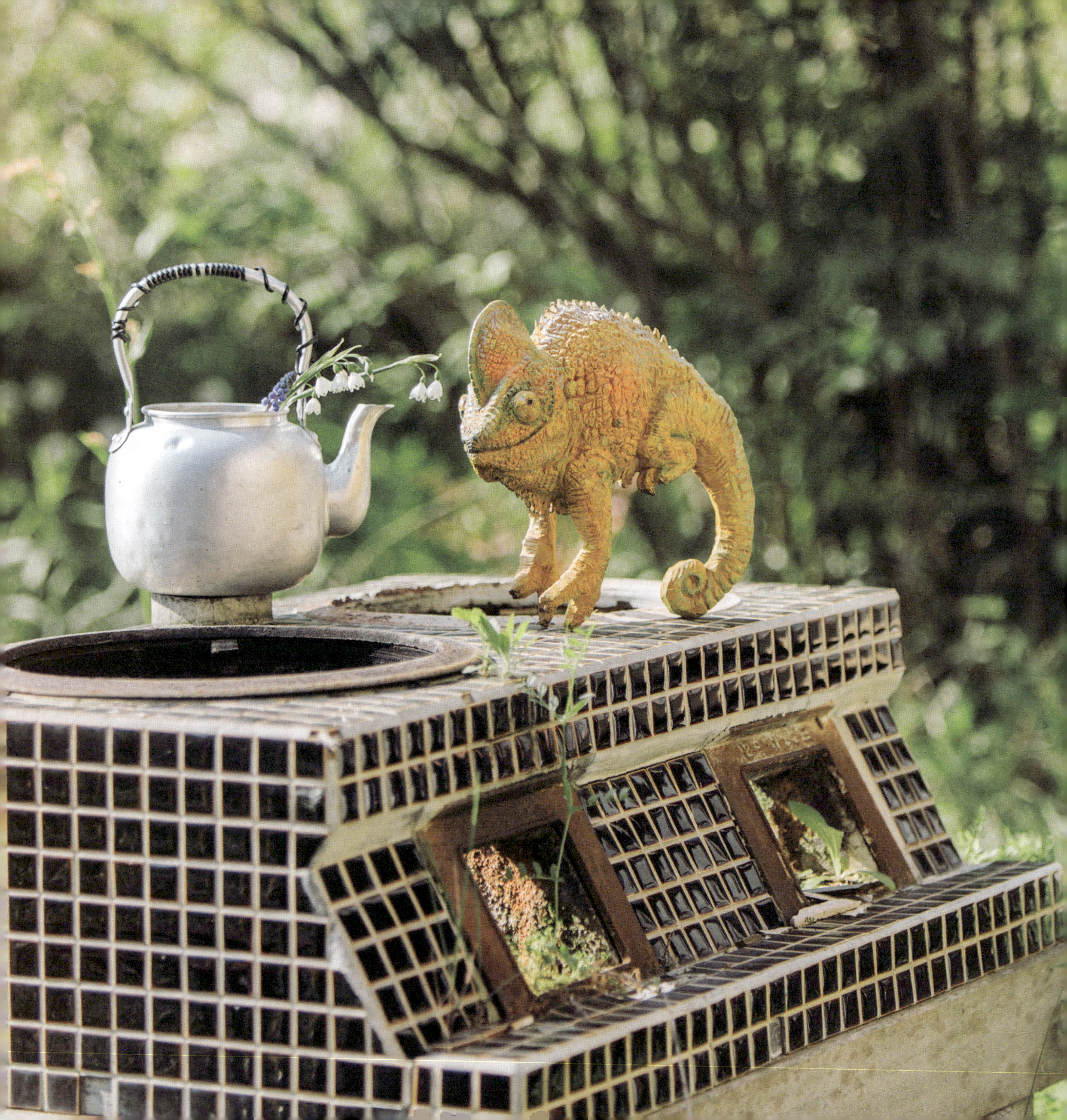

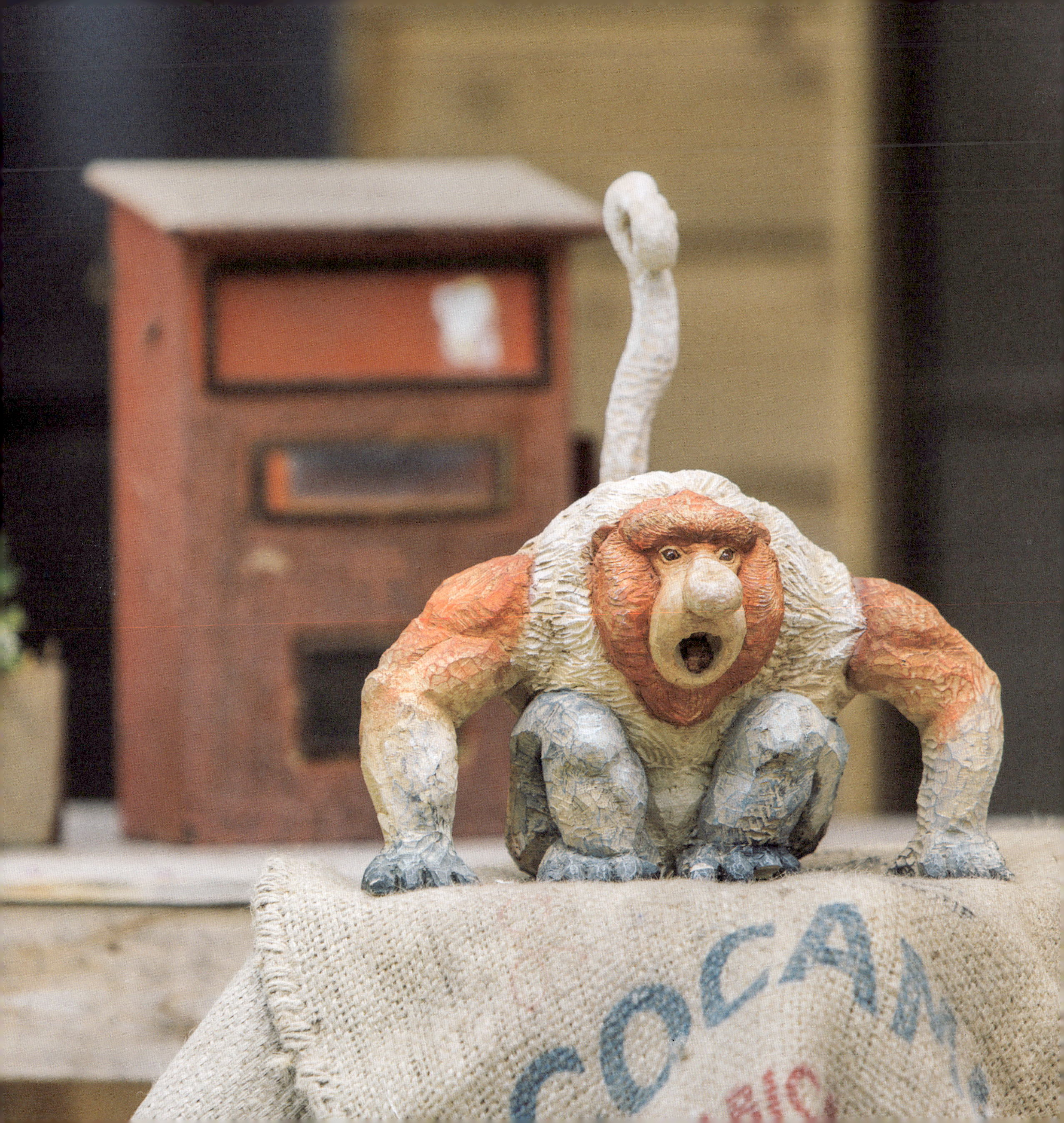
COCAN

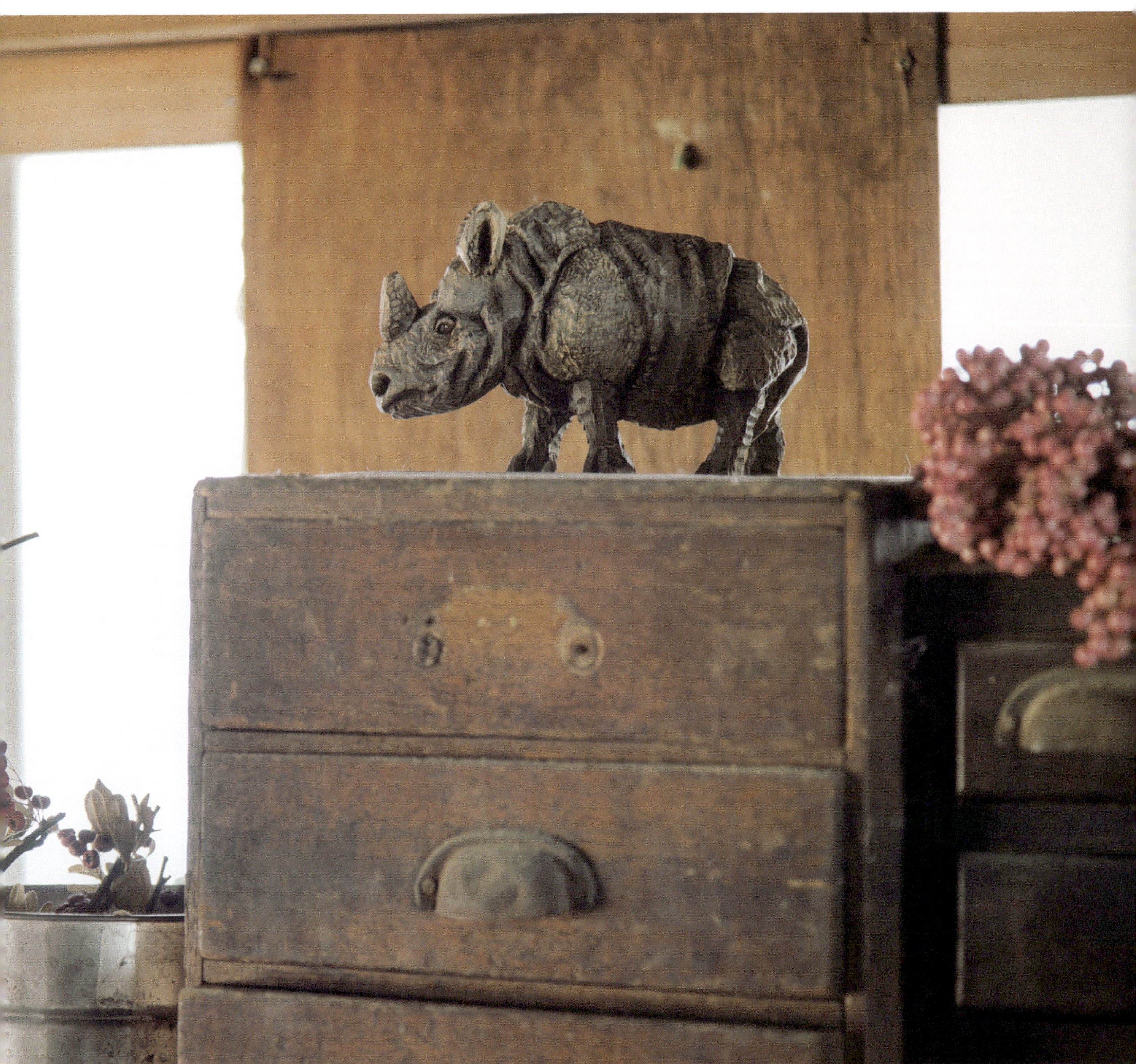

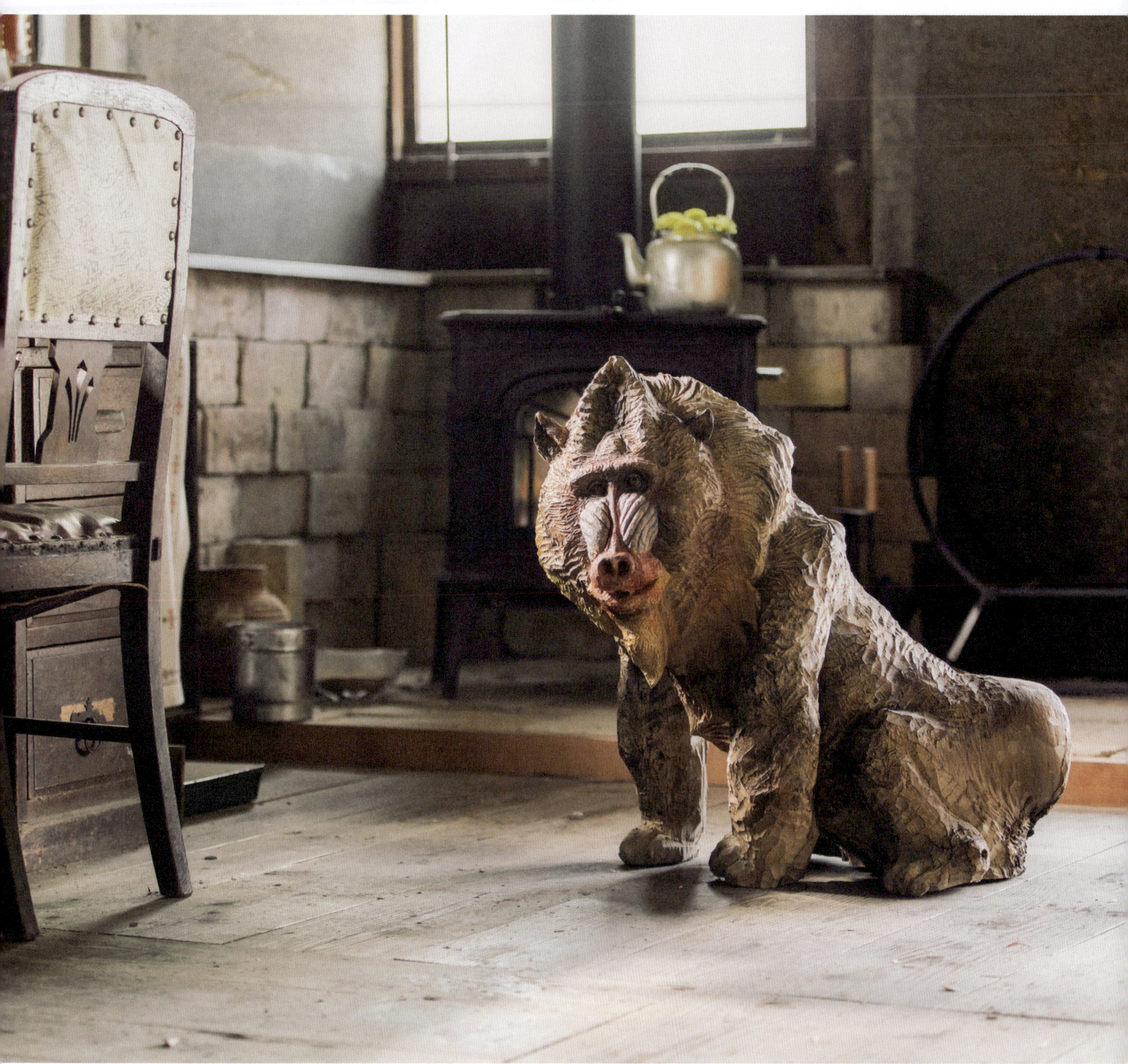

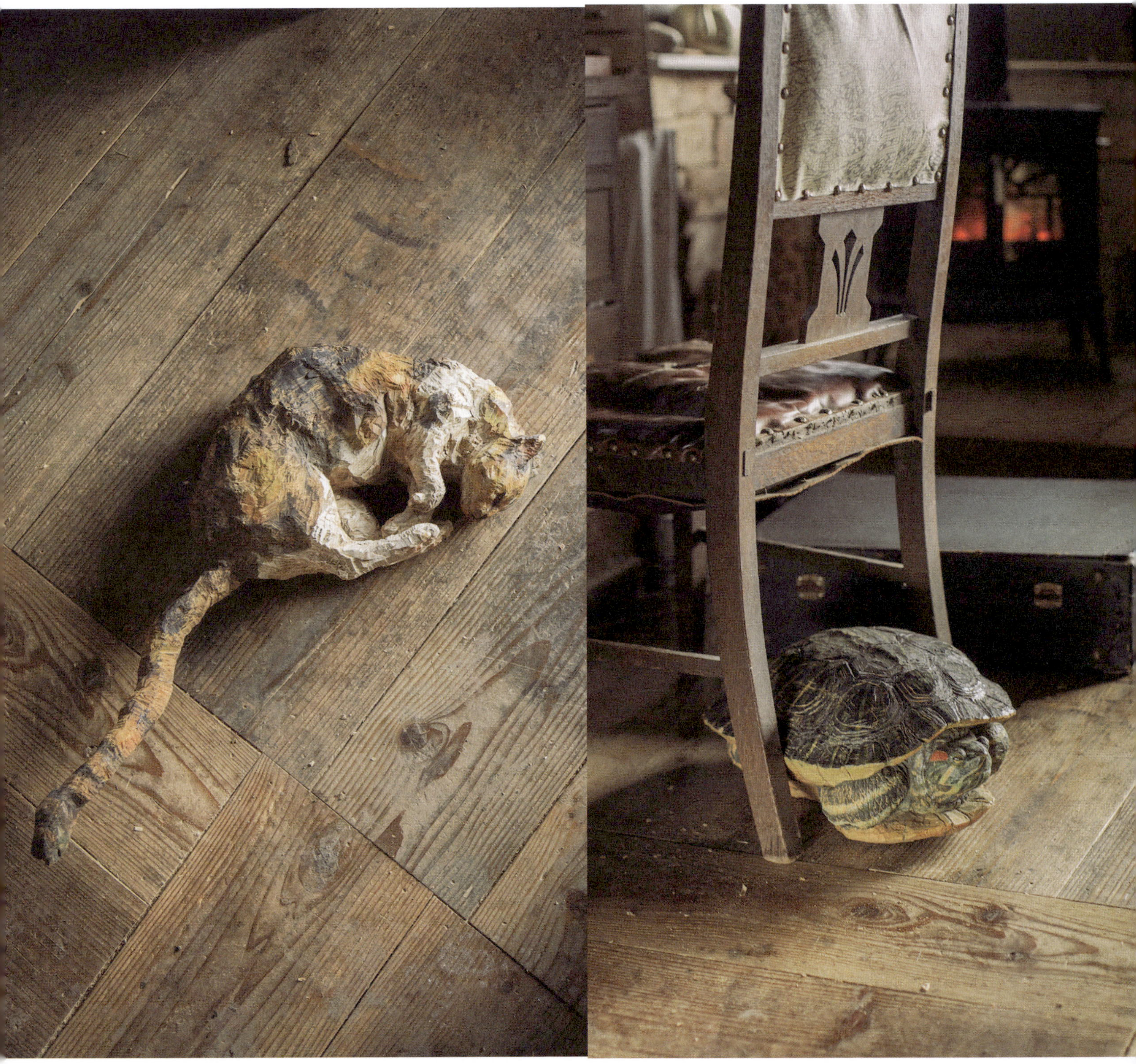

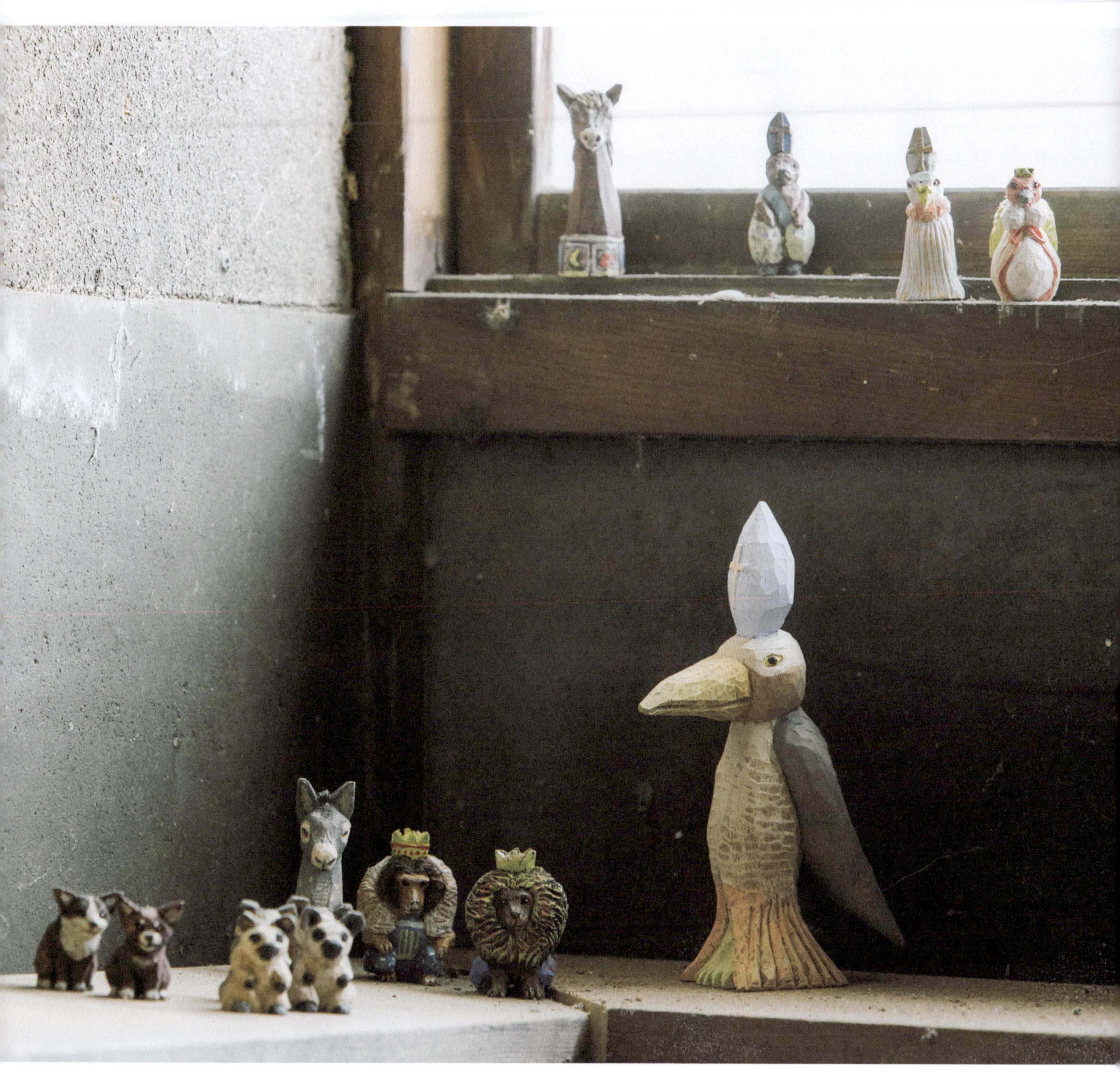

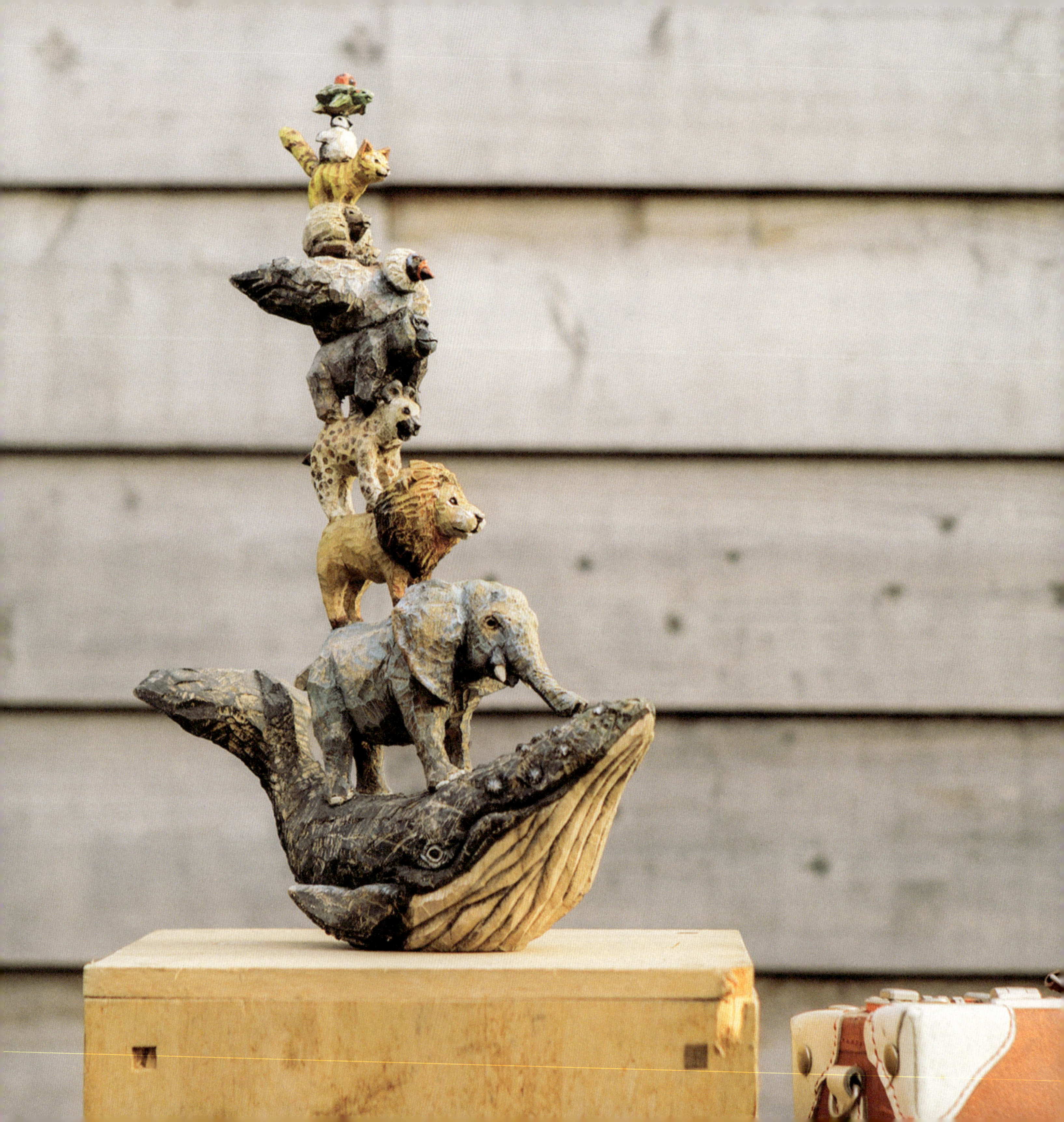

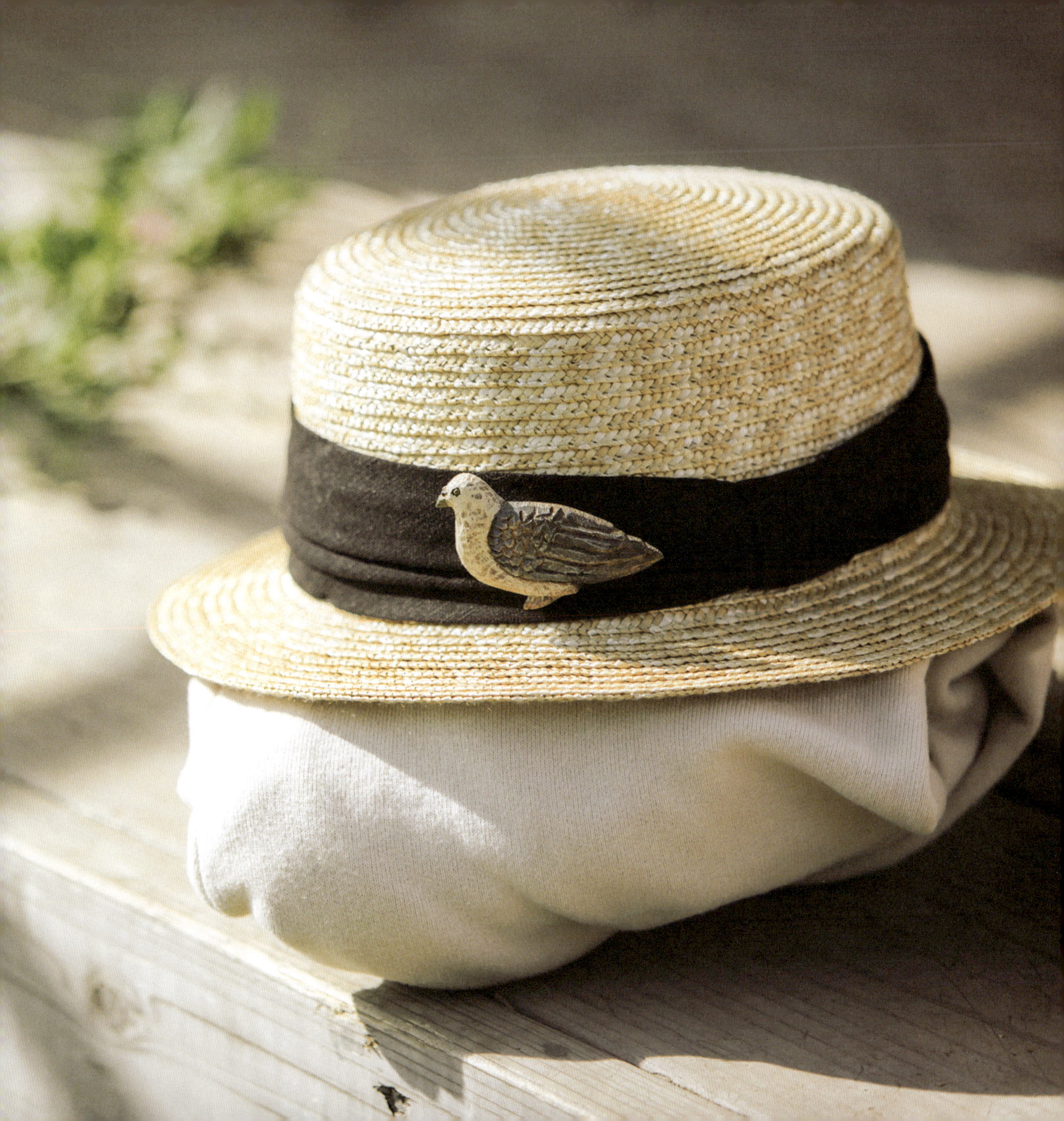

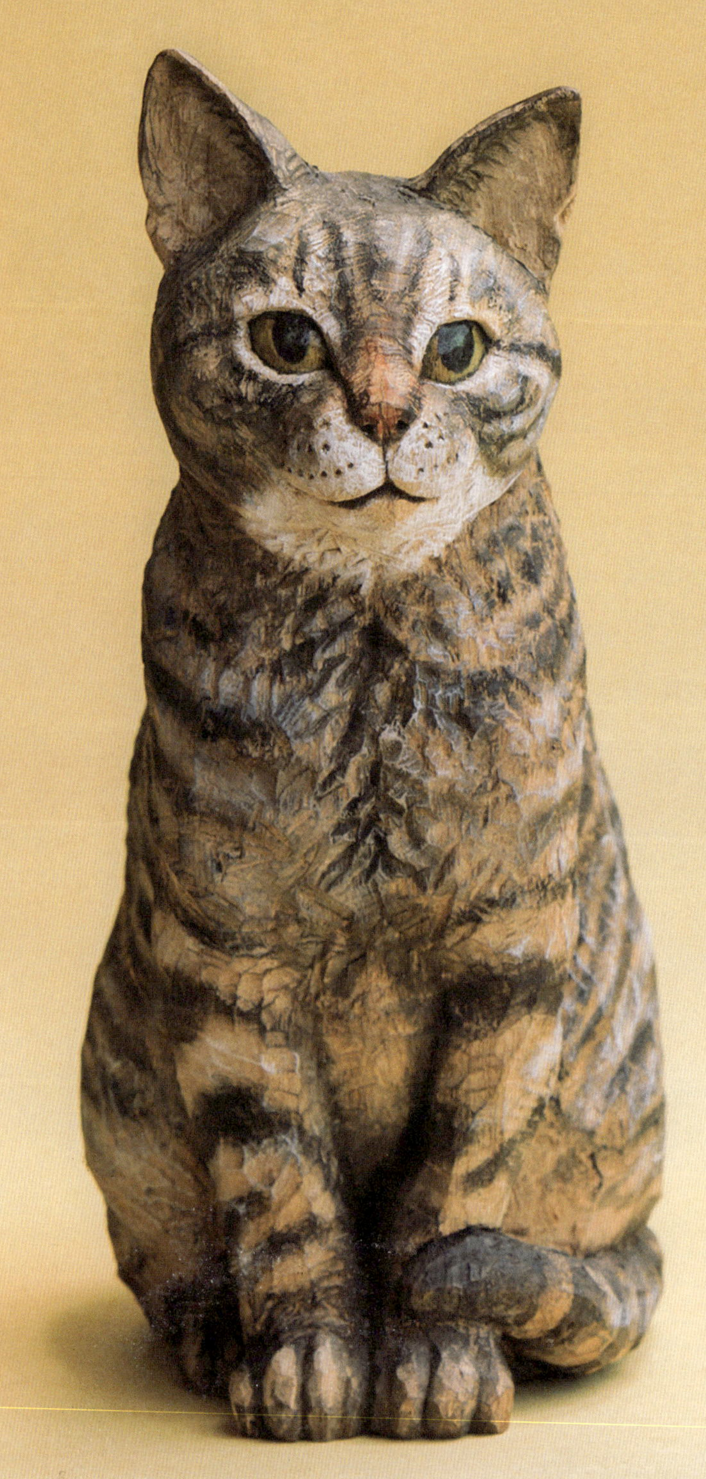

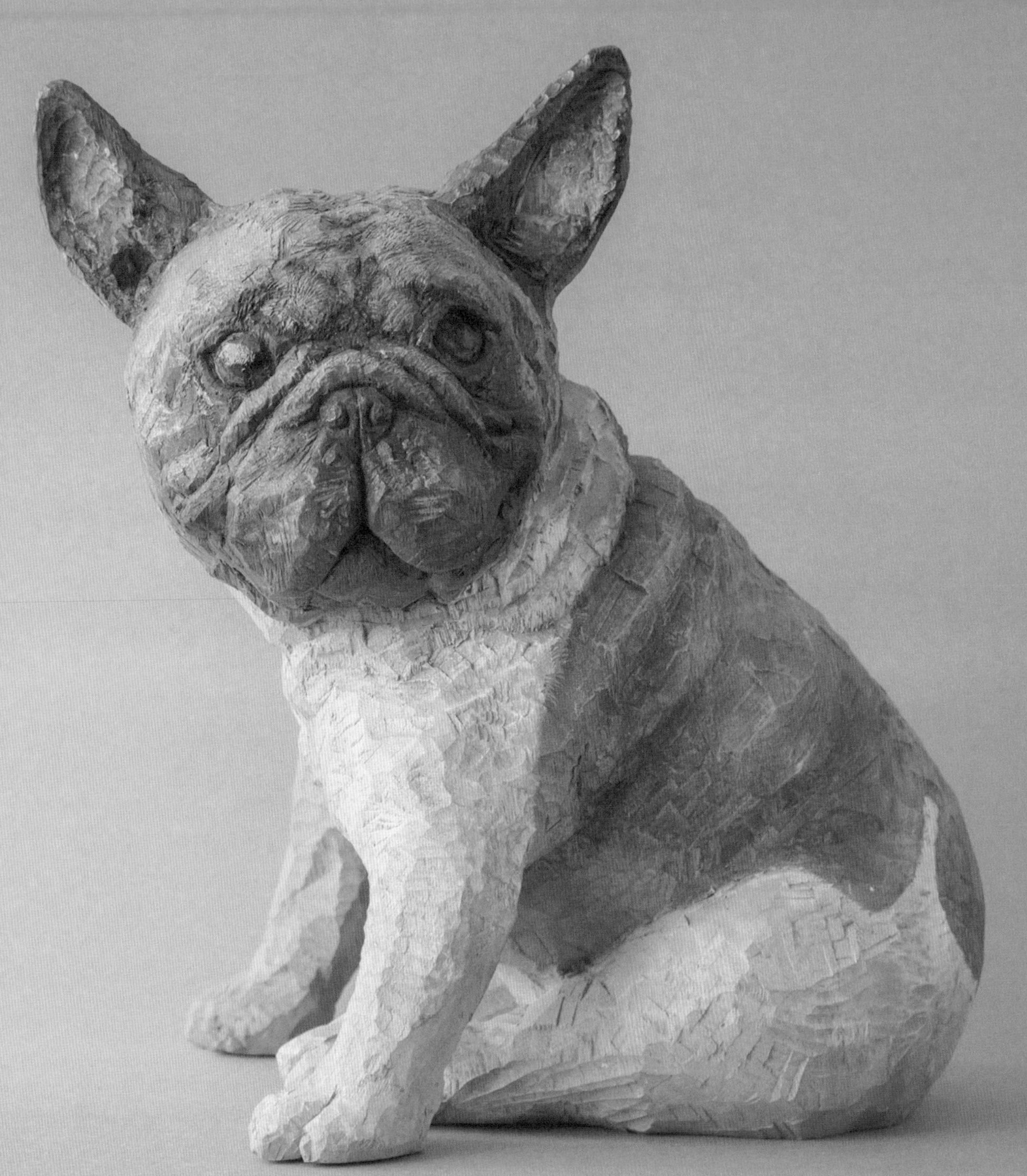

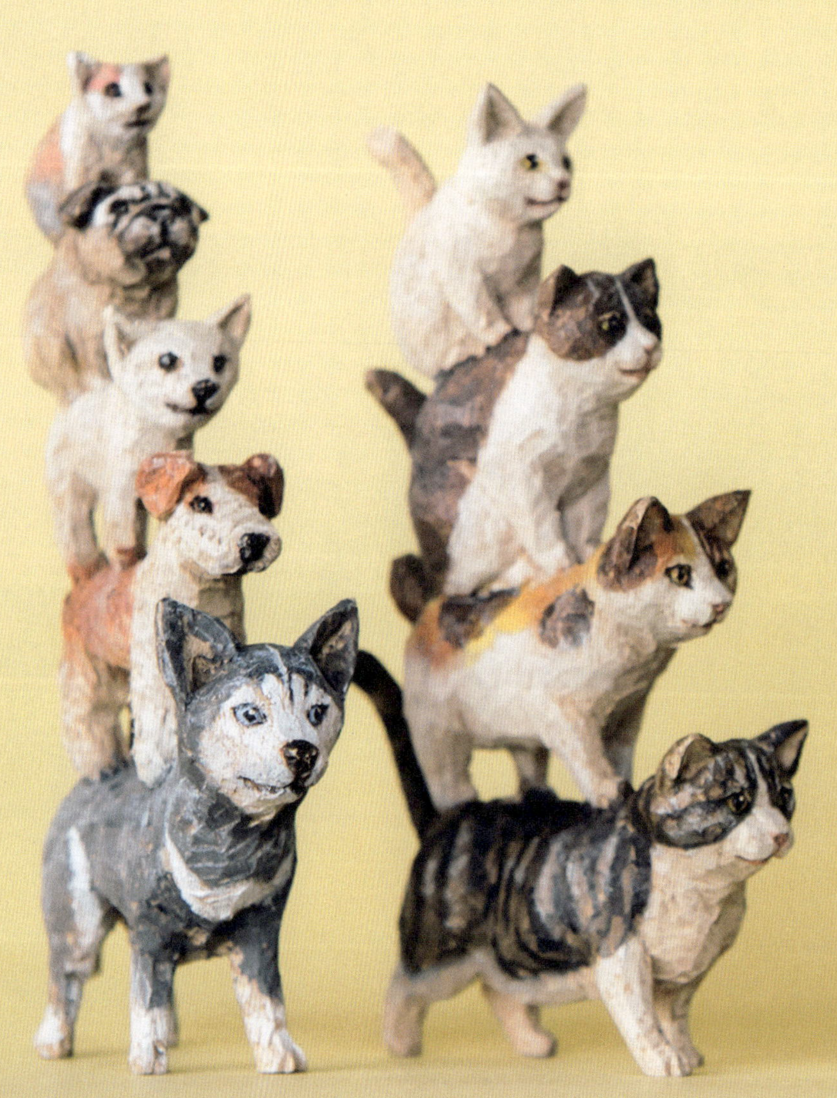

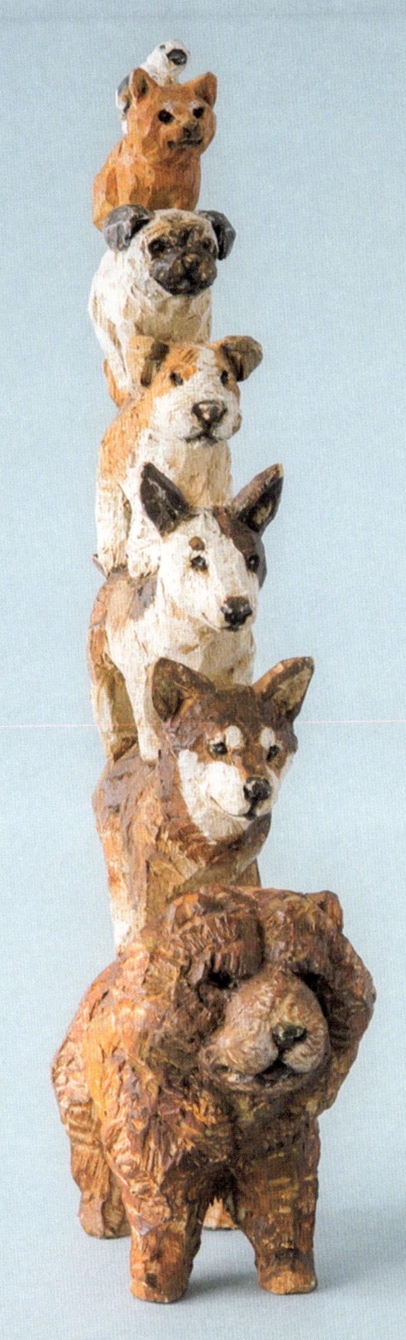

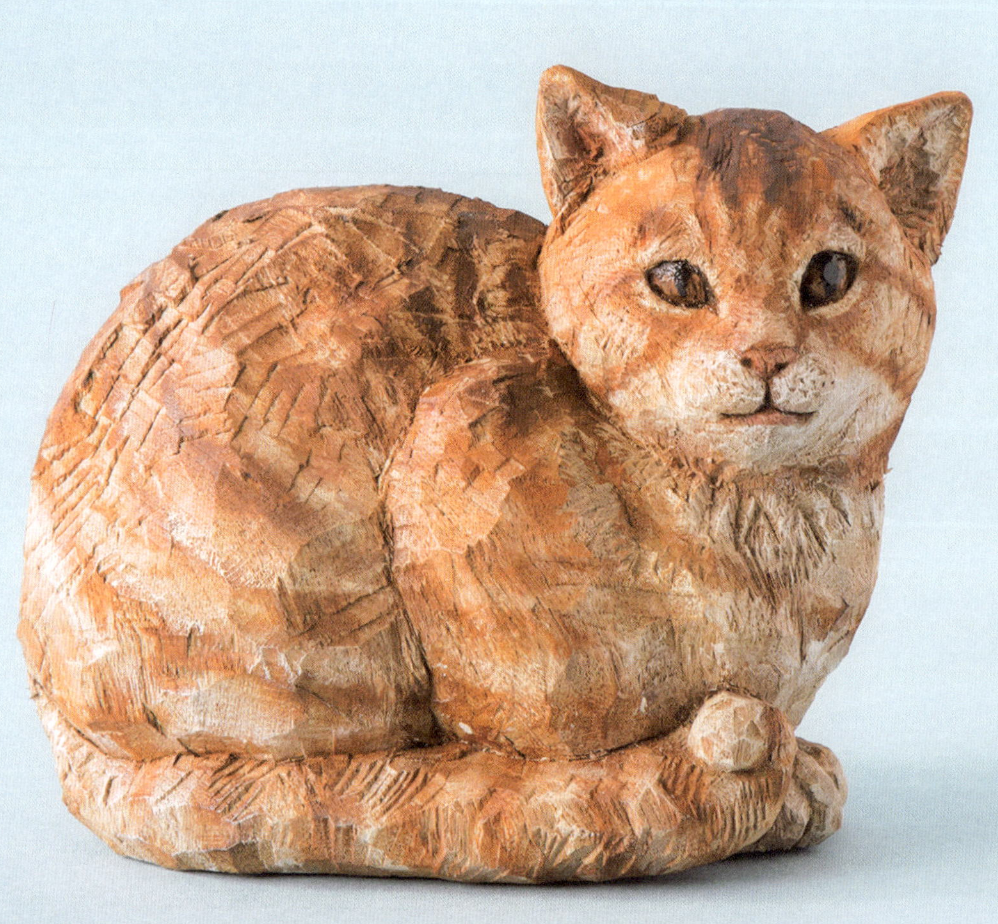

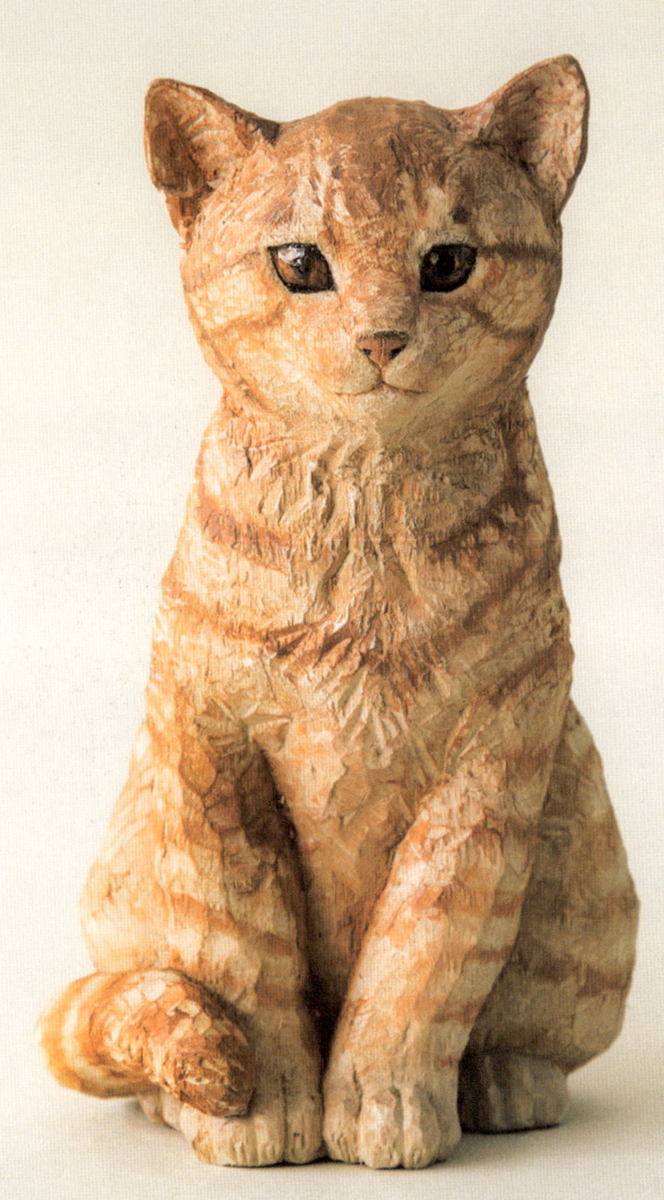

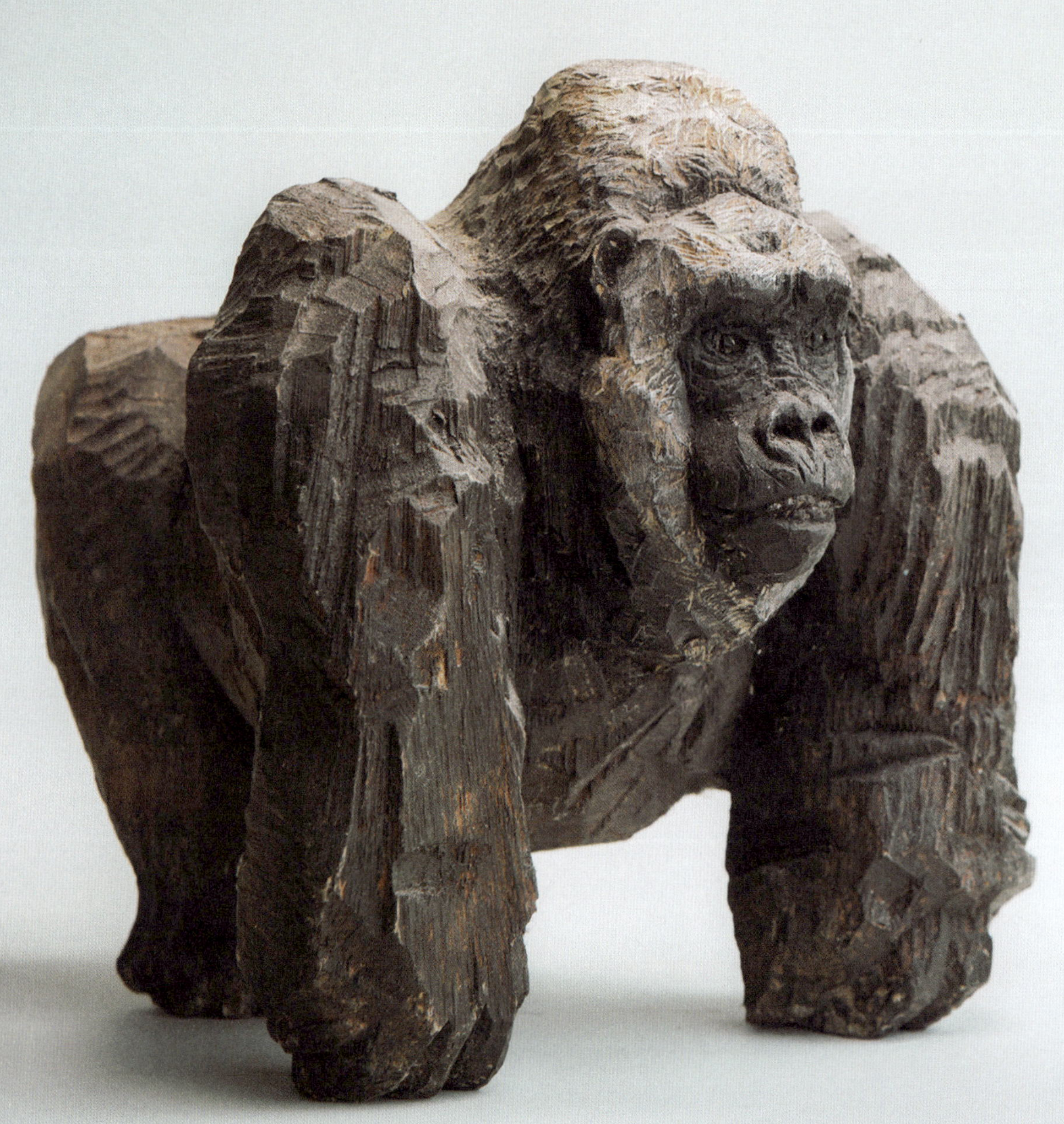

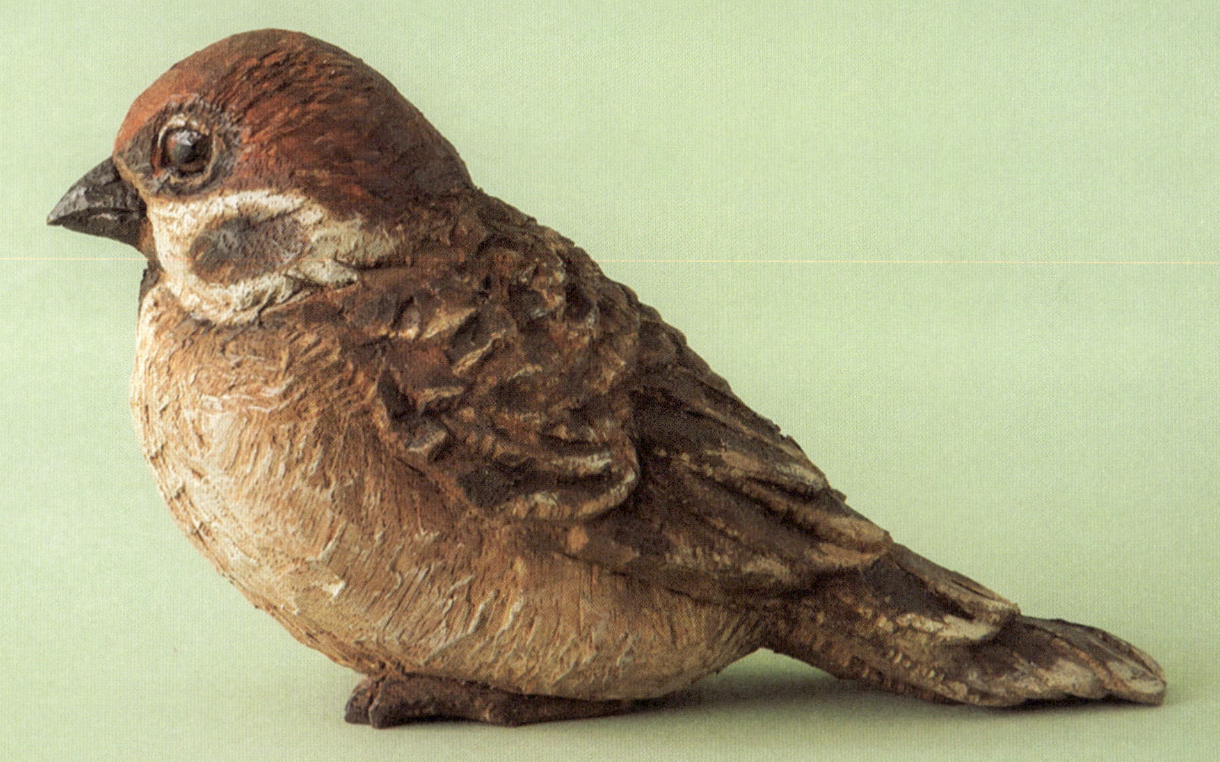

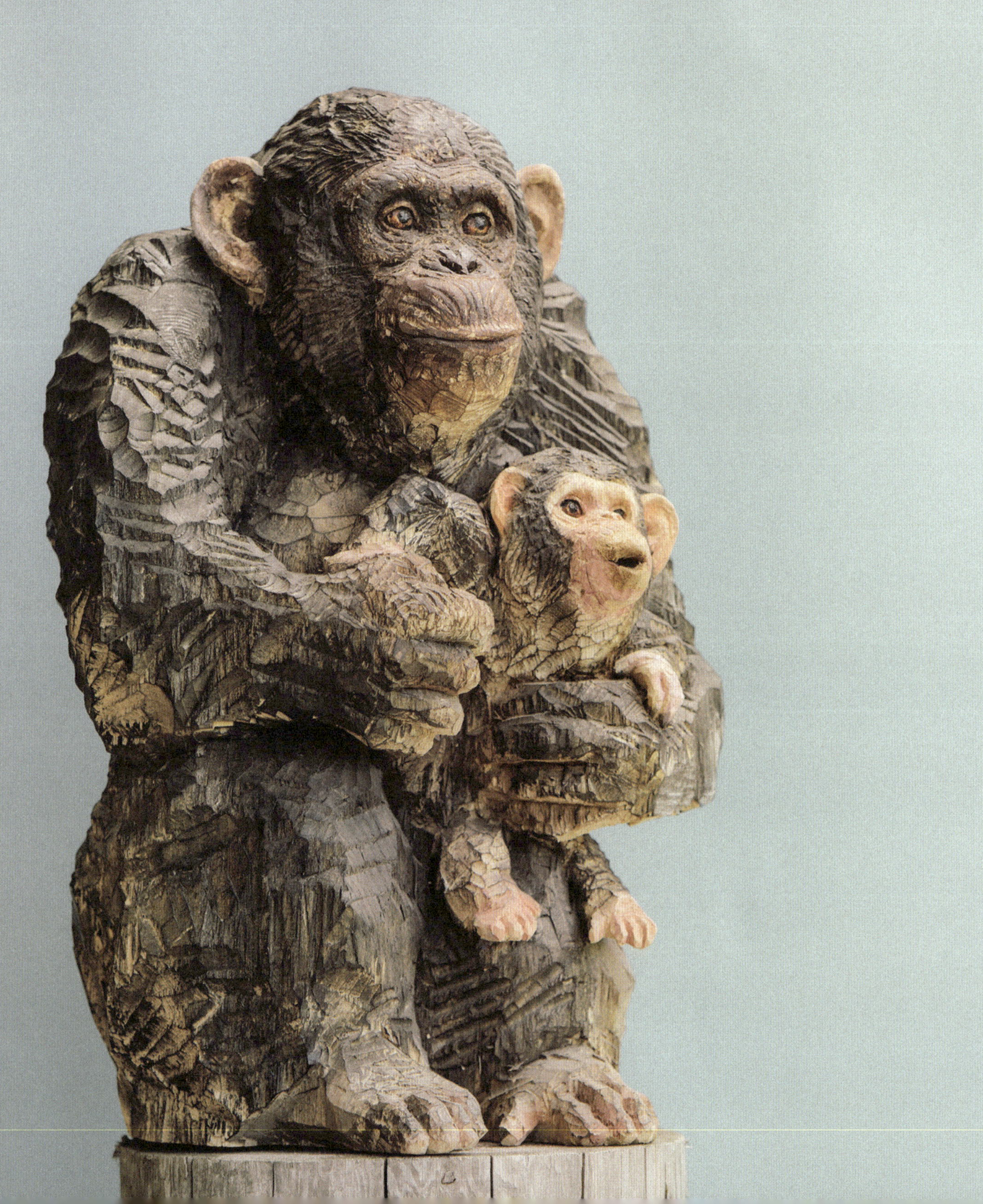

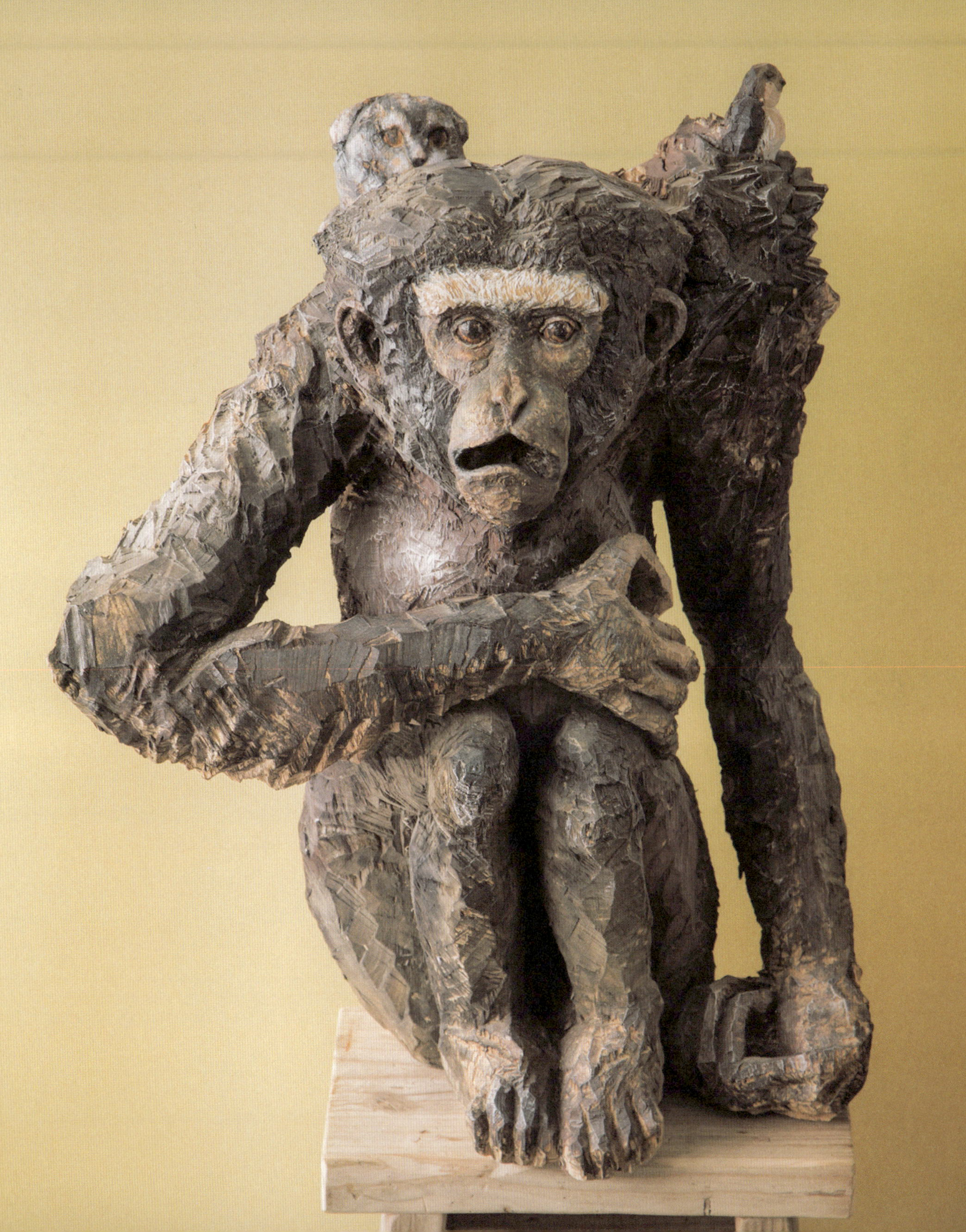

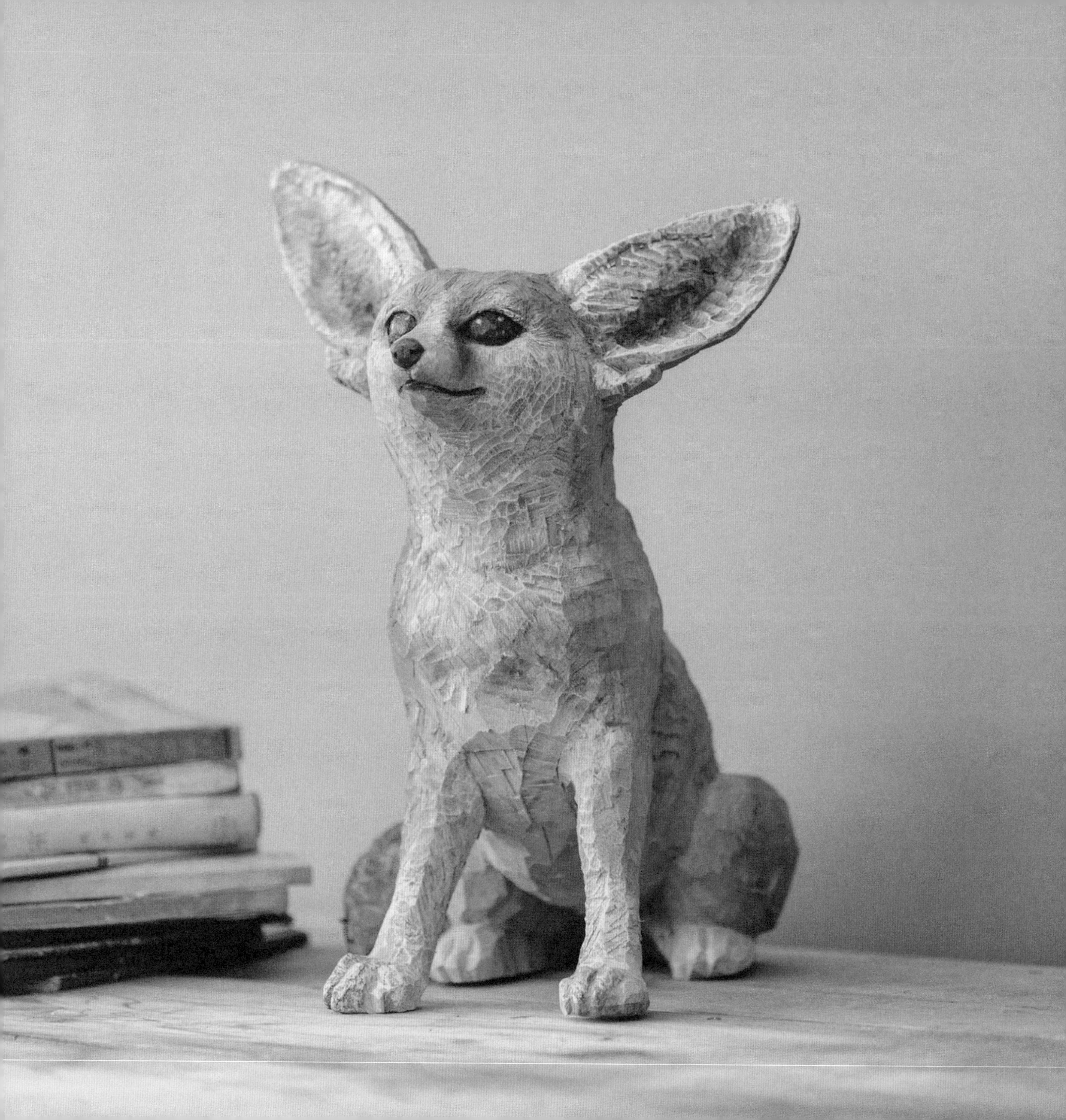

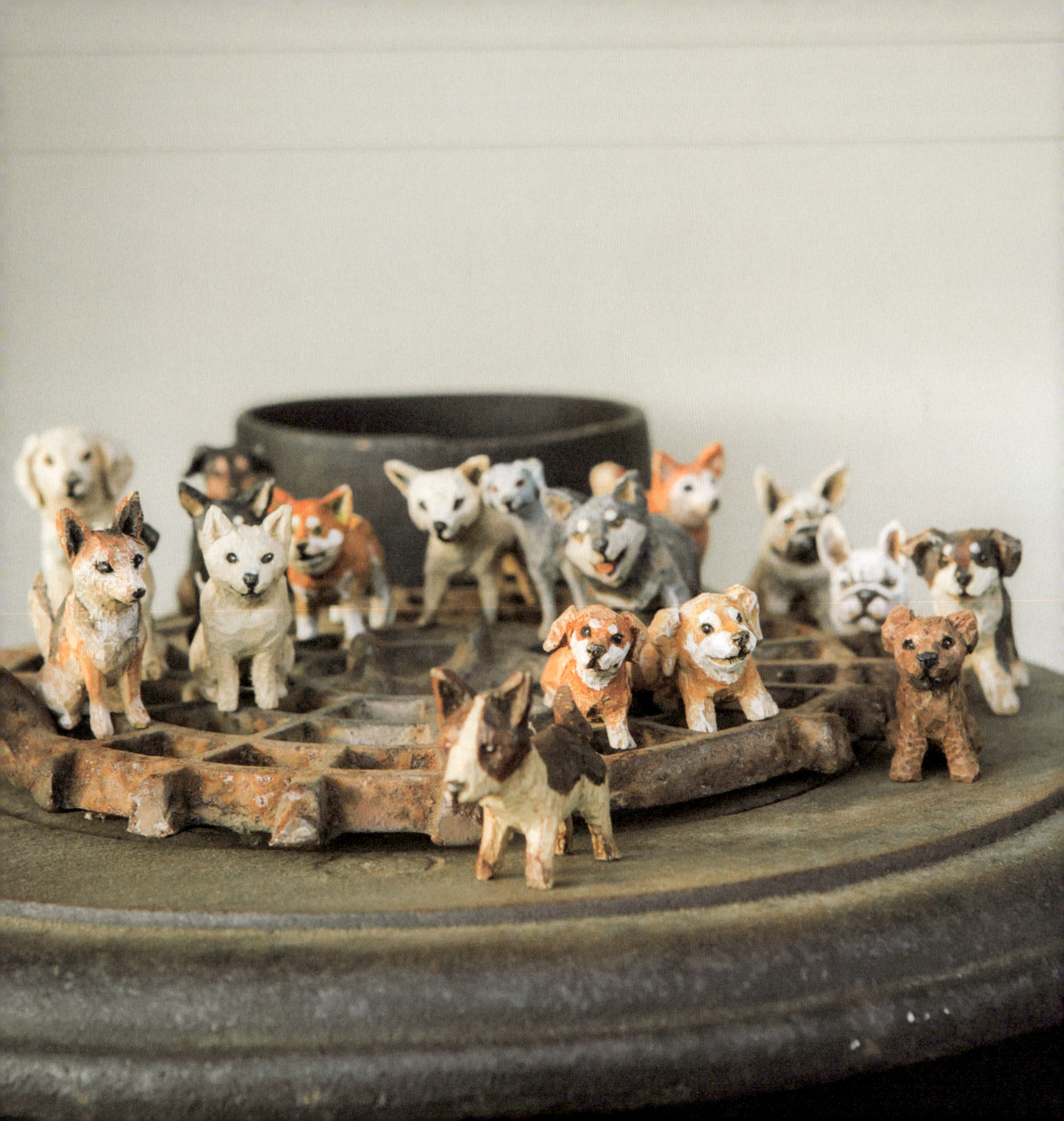

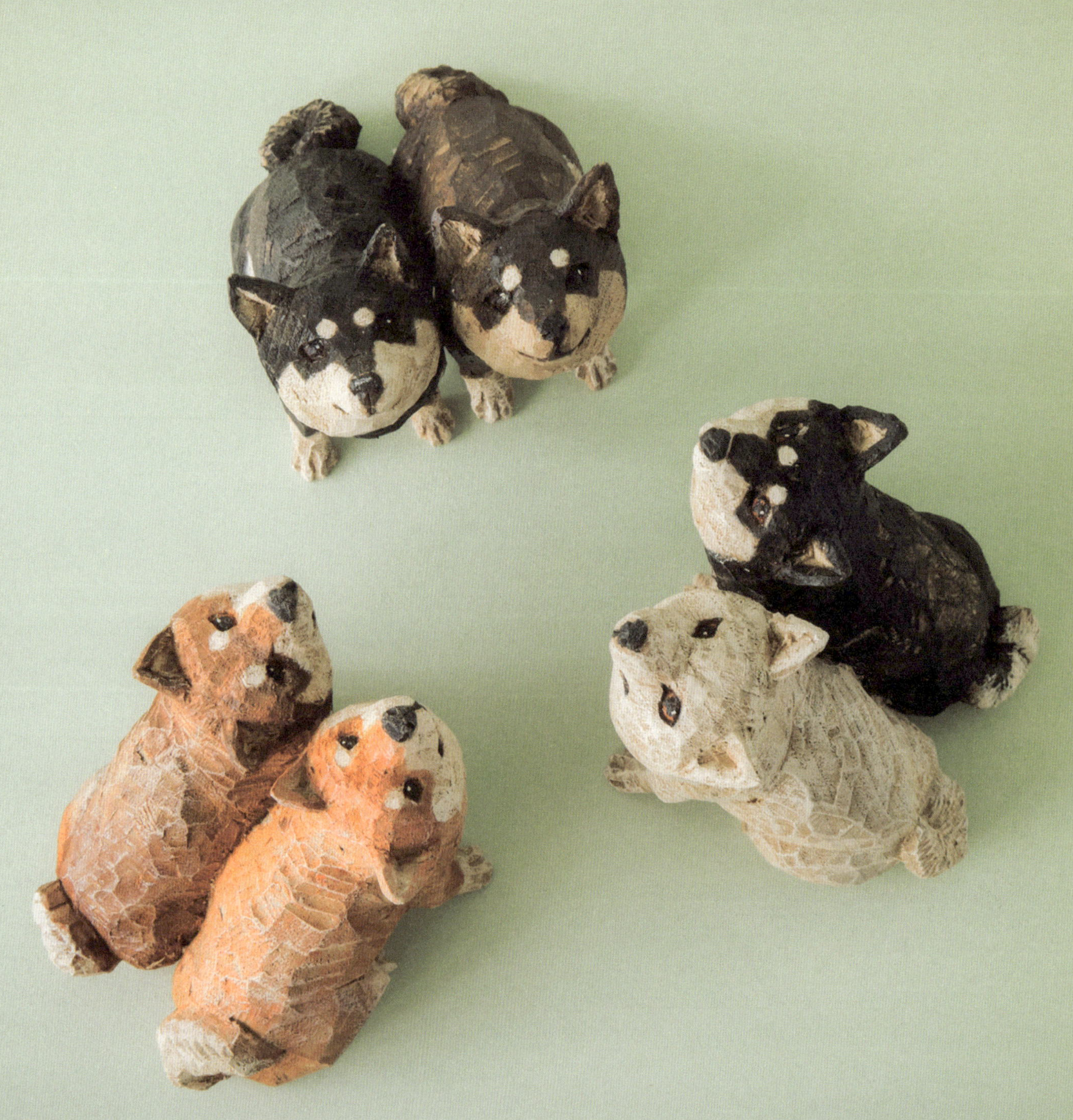

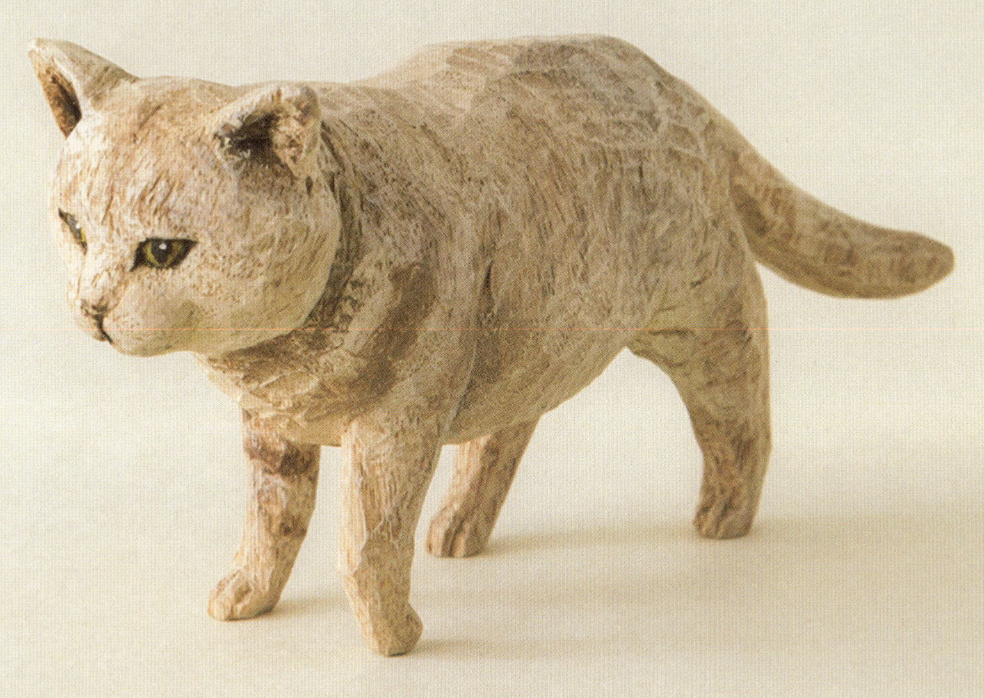

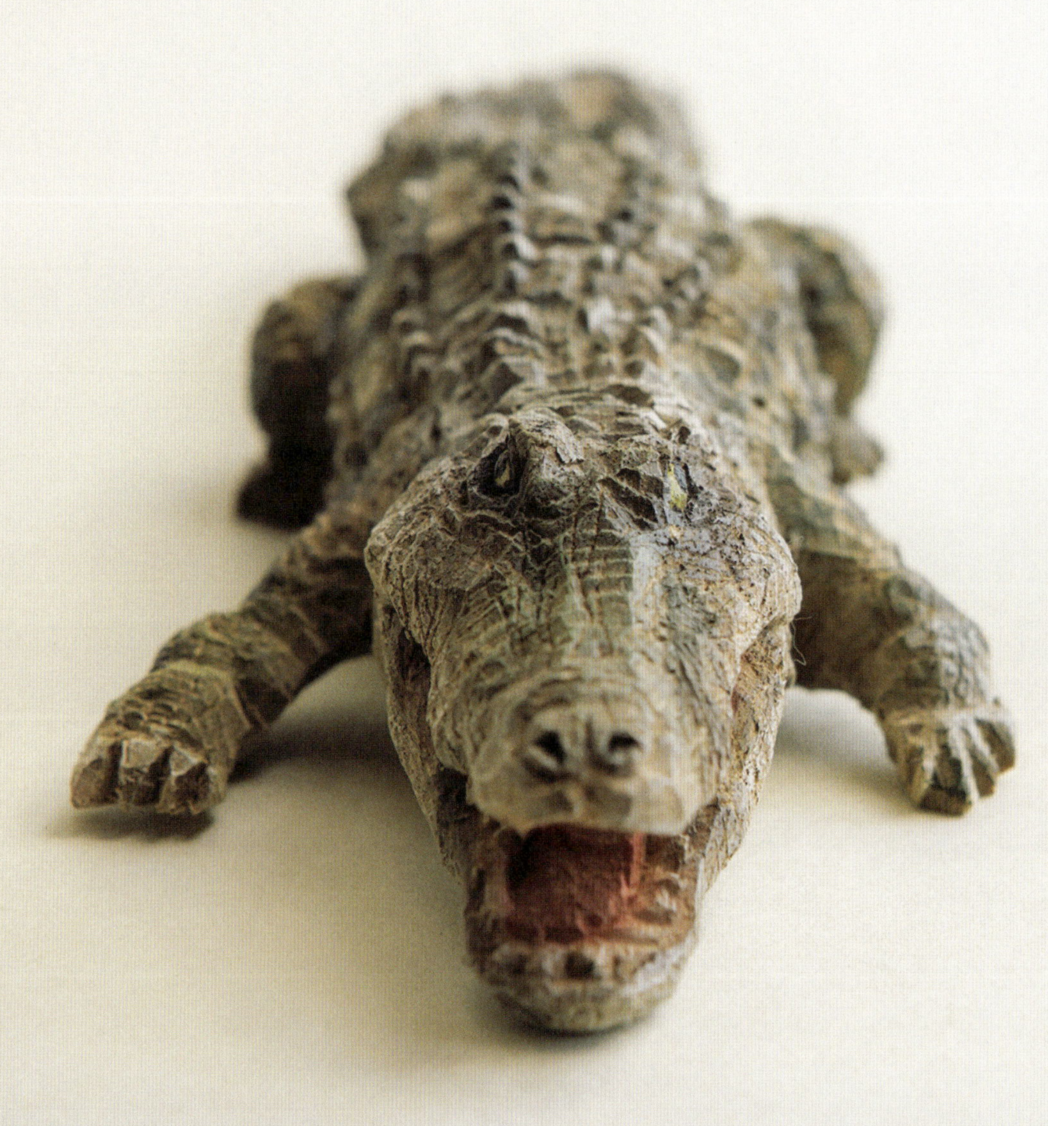

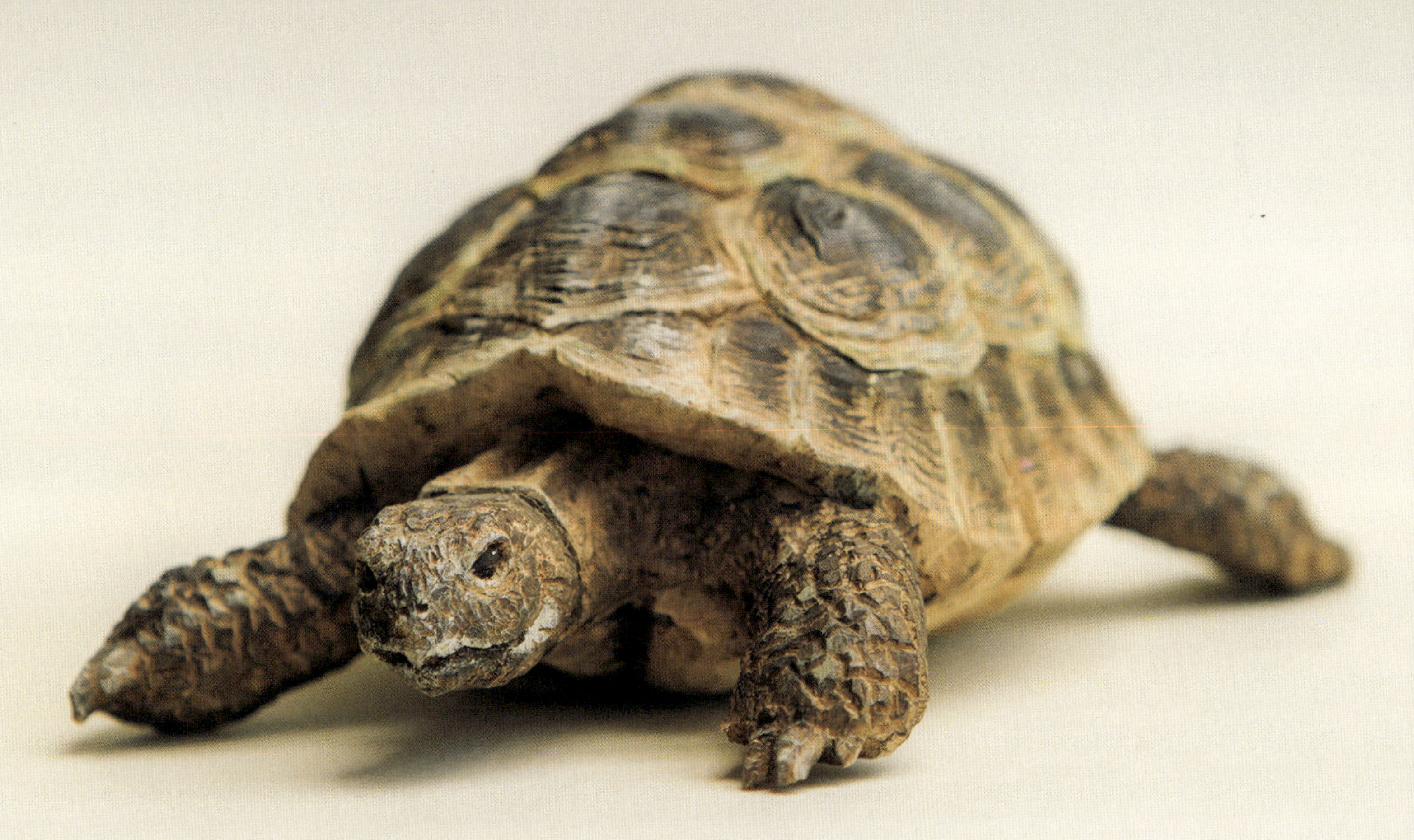

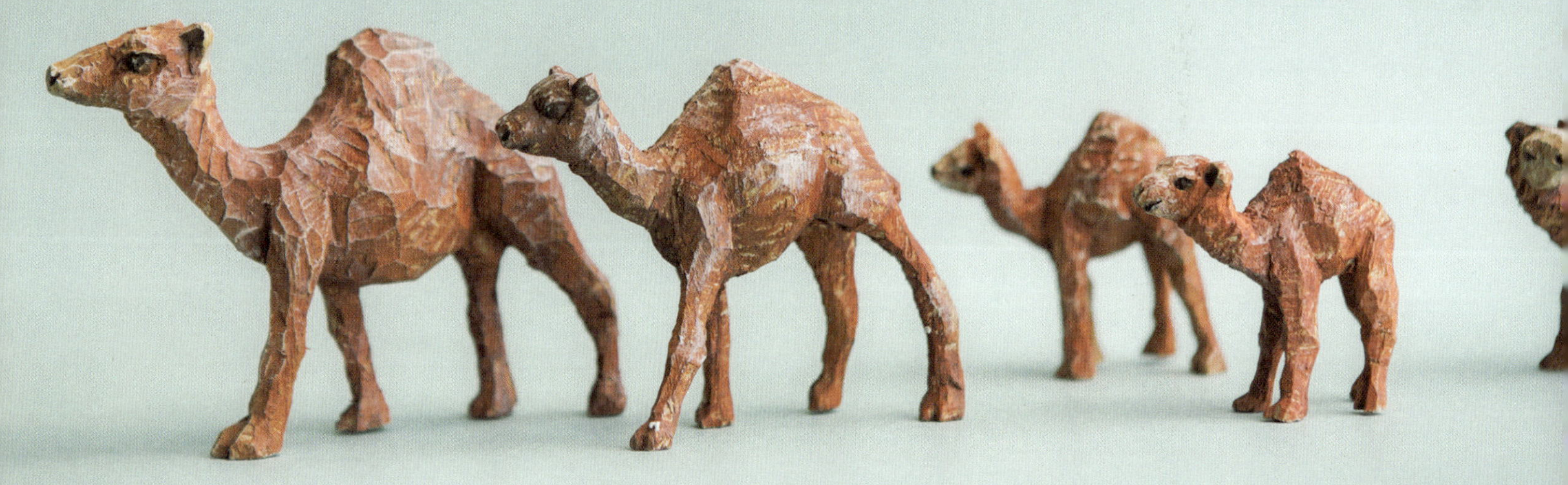

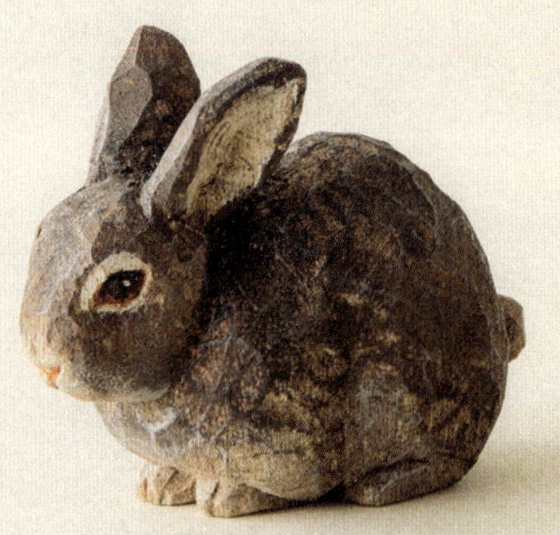
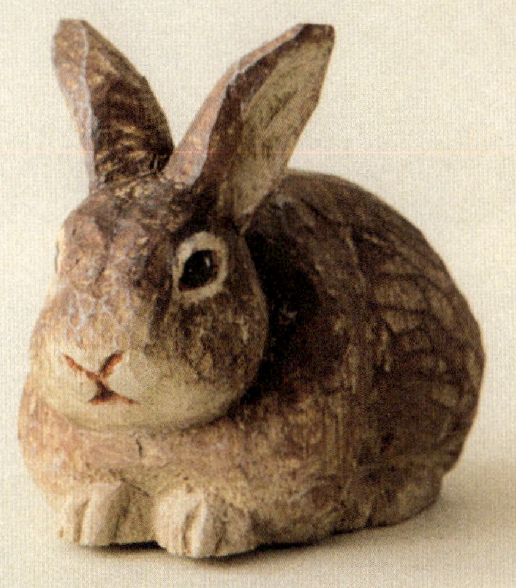

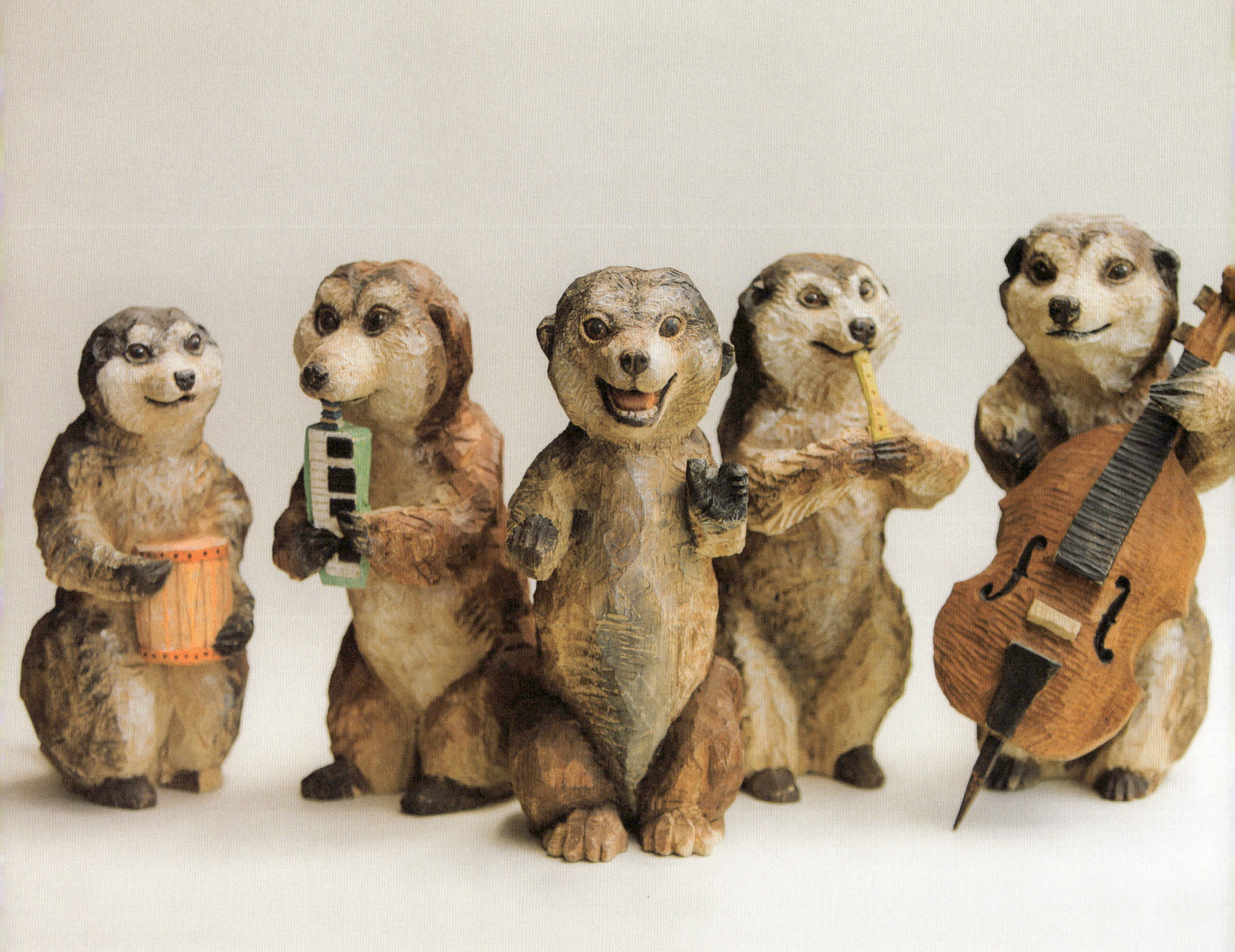

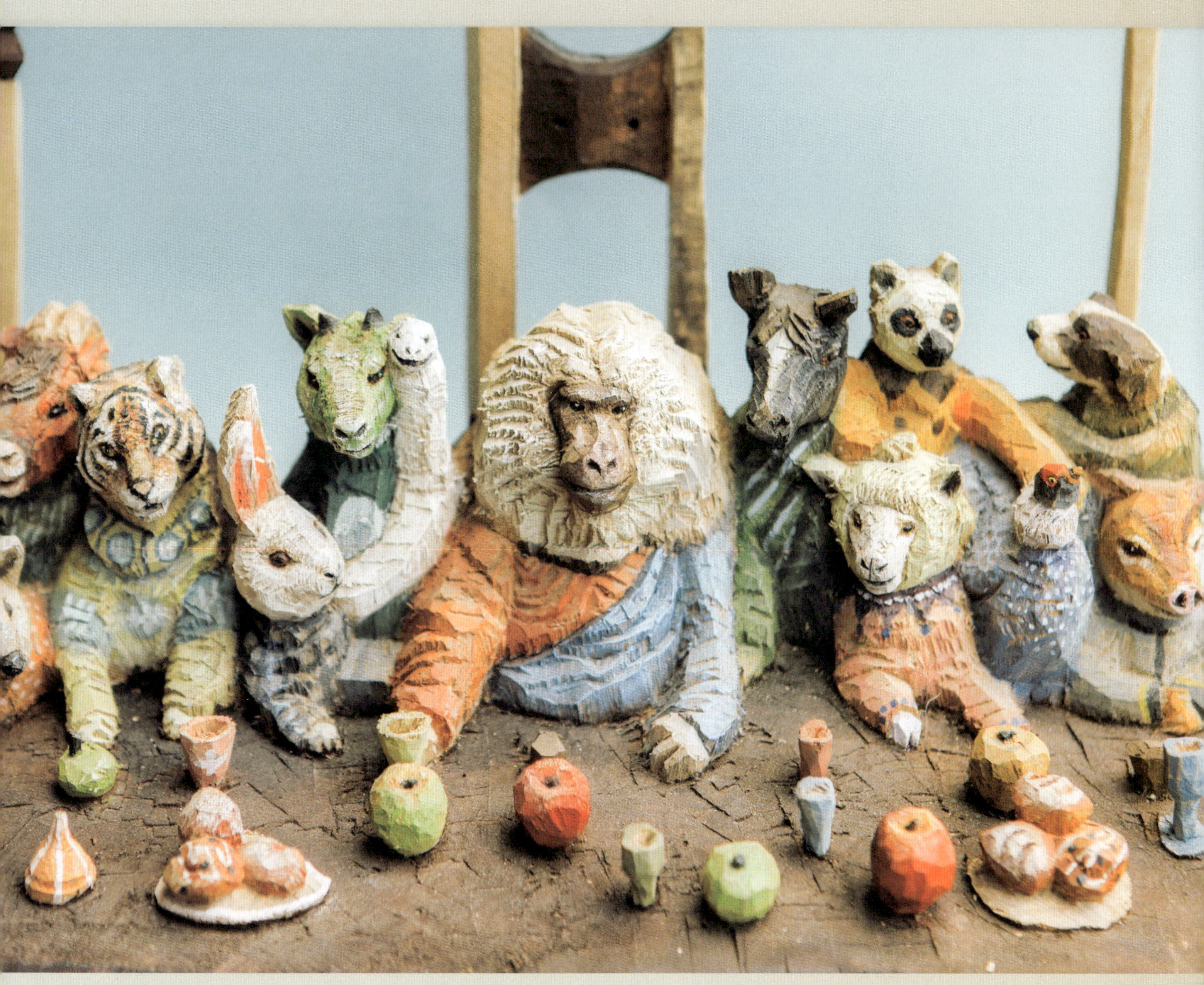

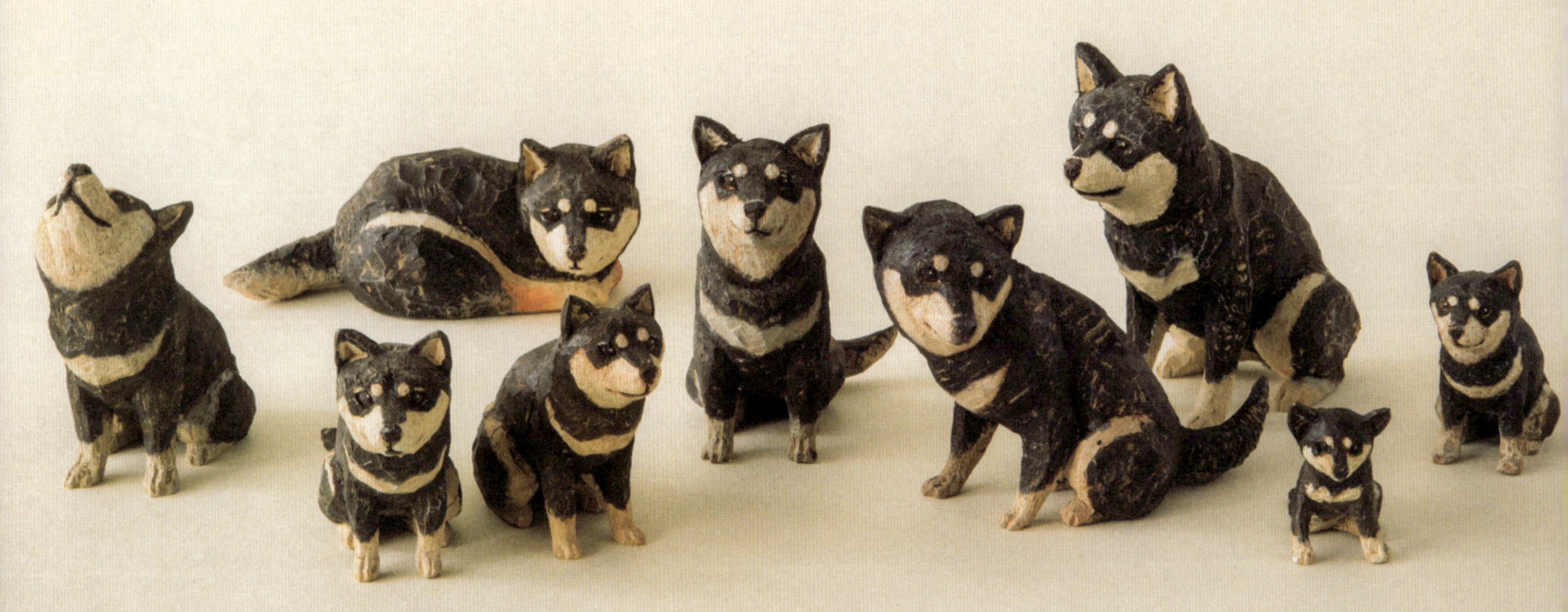

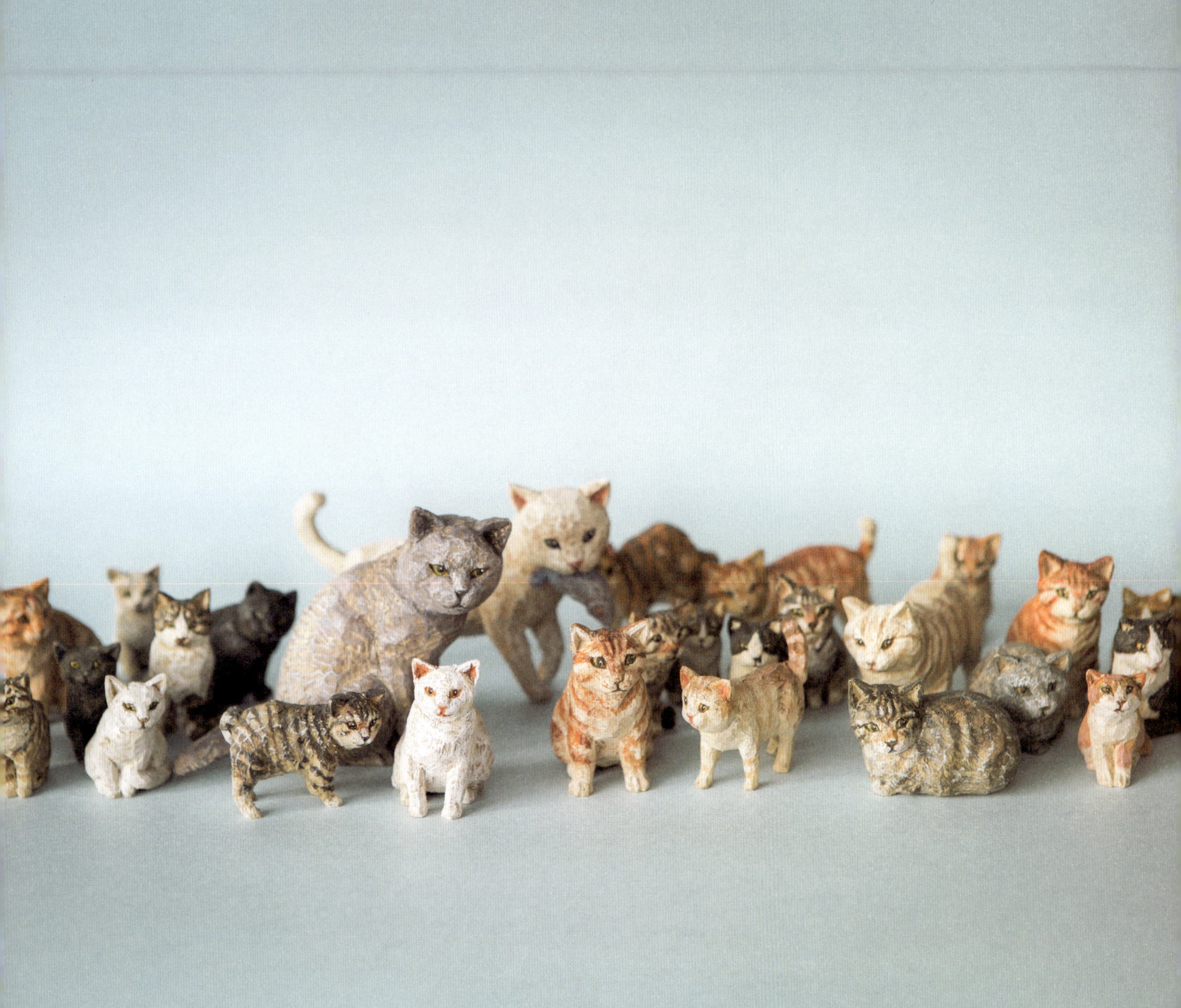

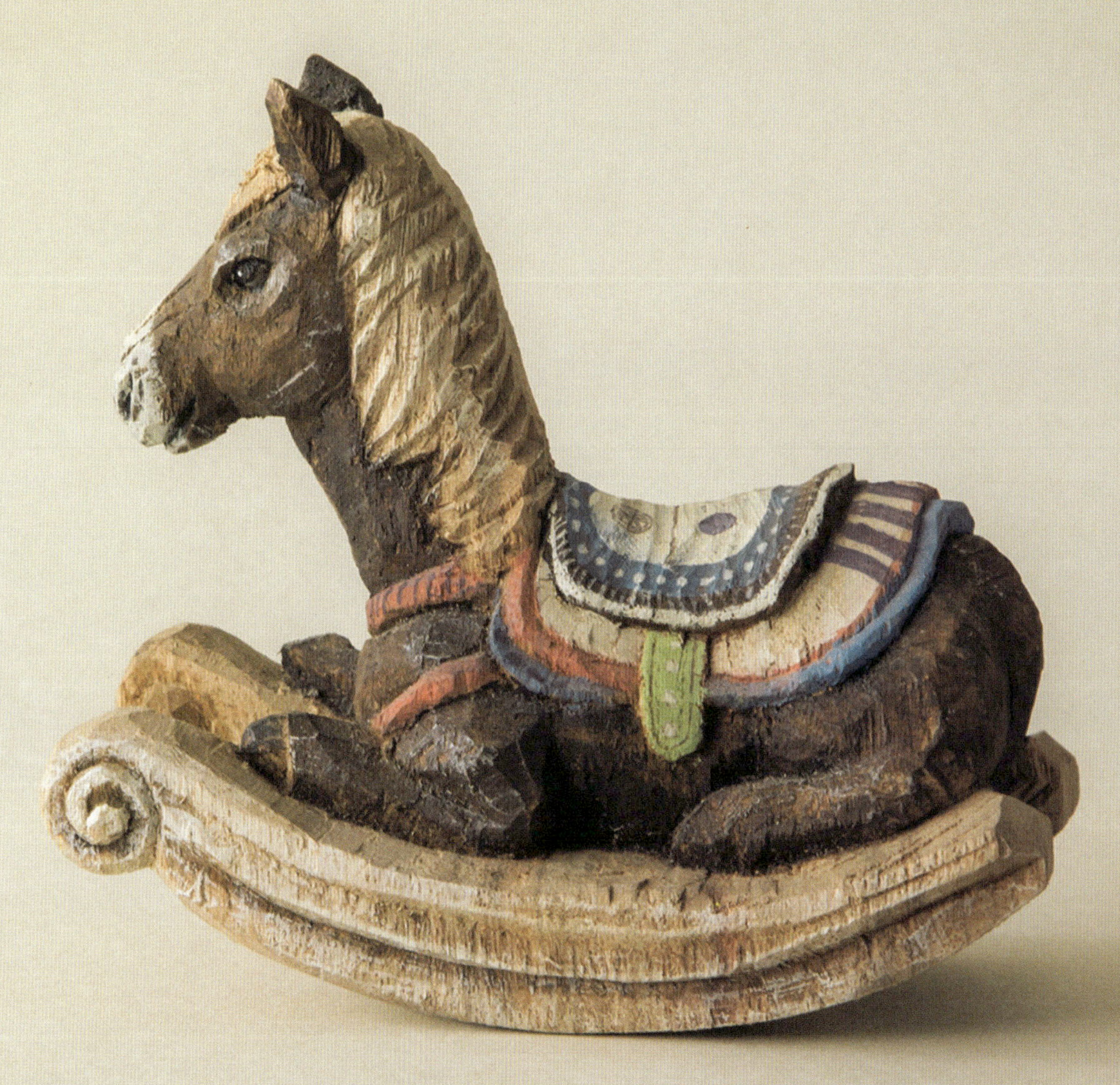

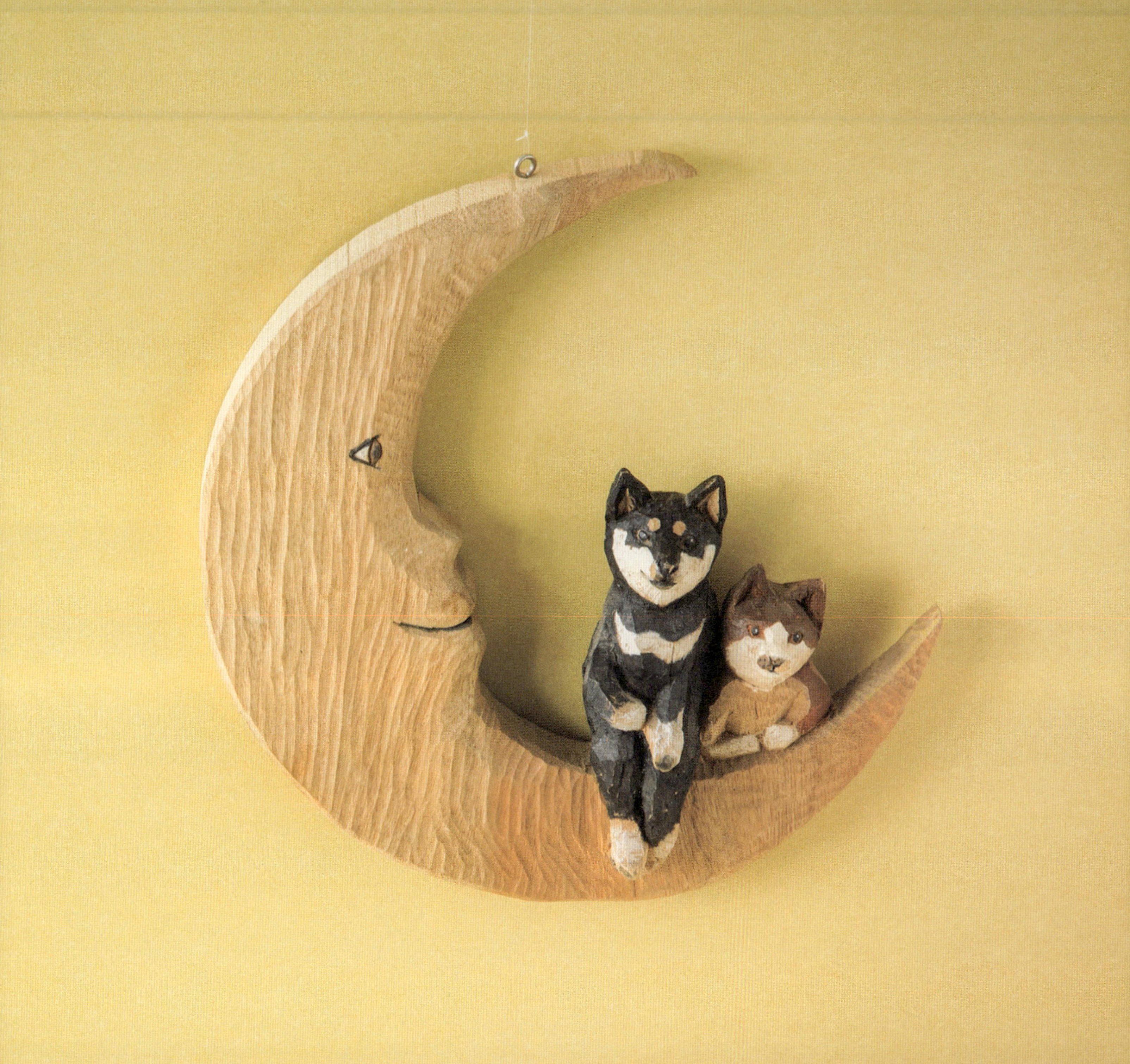

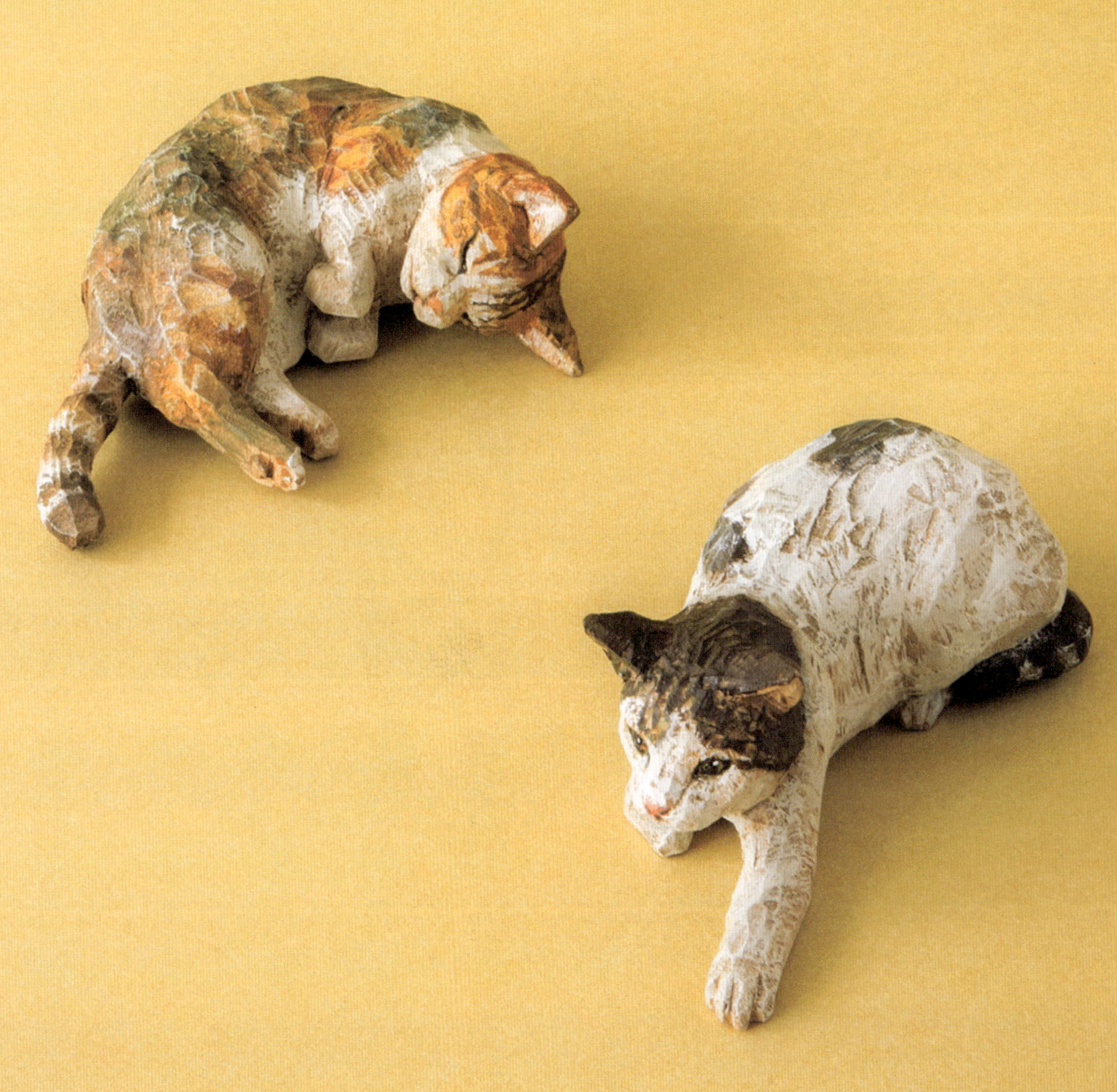

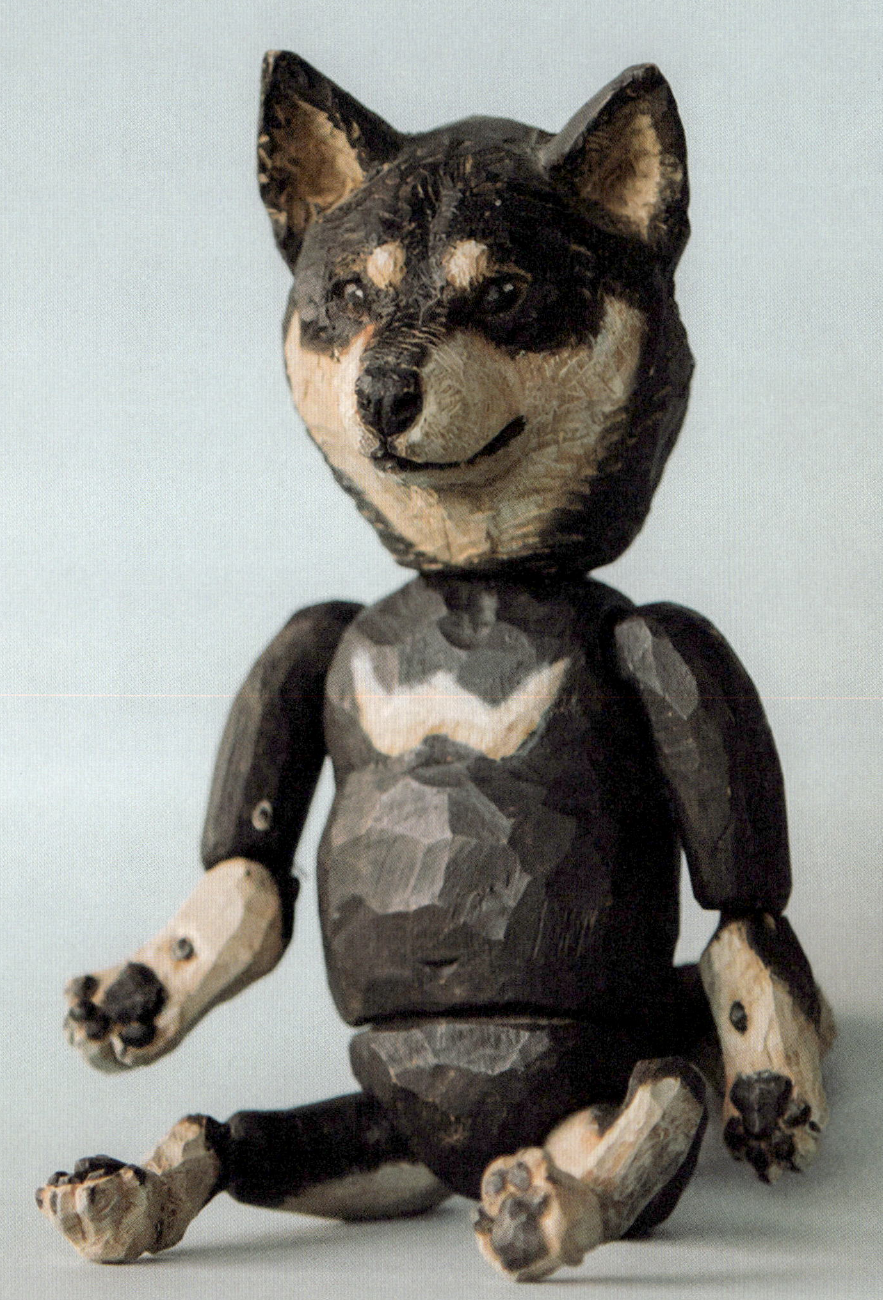

Photo Reference

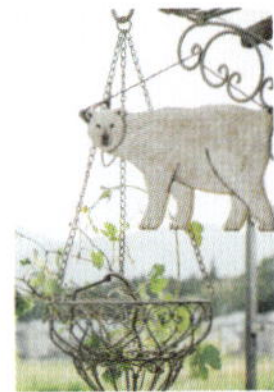

Shirokuma-kun [polar bear / Atelier signboard]

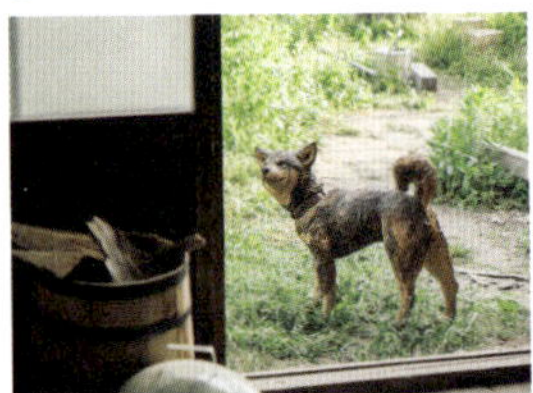

Tsuki [black Shiba Inu / Mie Prefecture]

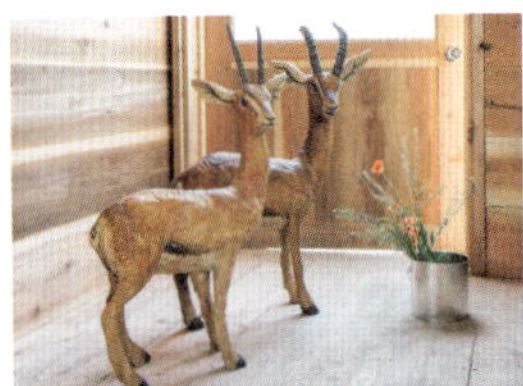

Sarmel and *Damani* [gazelles / UAE]

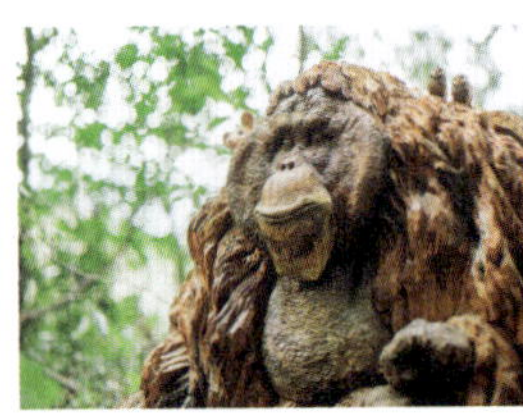

Q [orangutan / Tama Zoological Park]

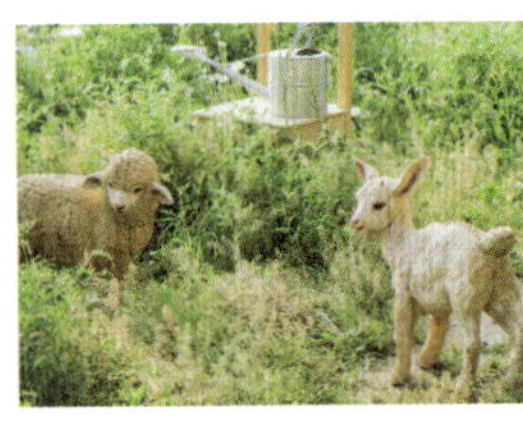

Sova [sheep] and *Choco* [goat]

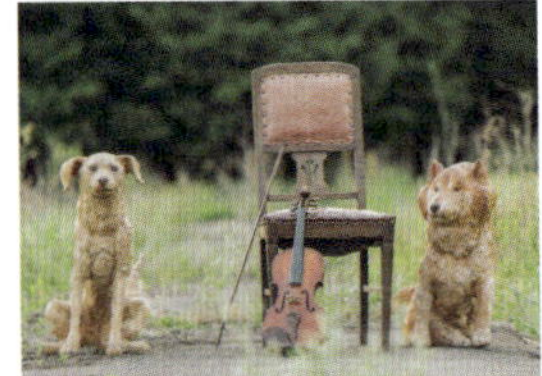

Left: *Vel* [mixed breed Shiba Inu]; Right: *Don* [Aichi]

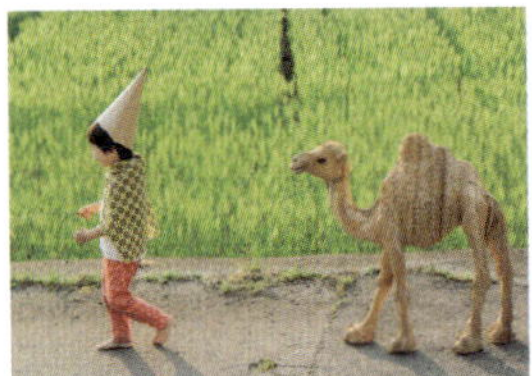

Camel [UAE]

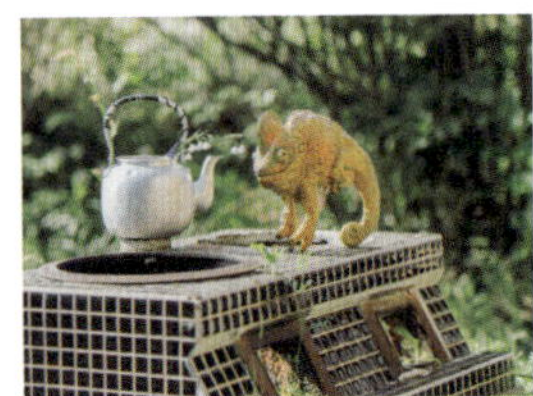

Leon [chameleon]

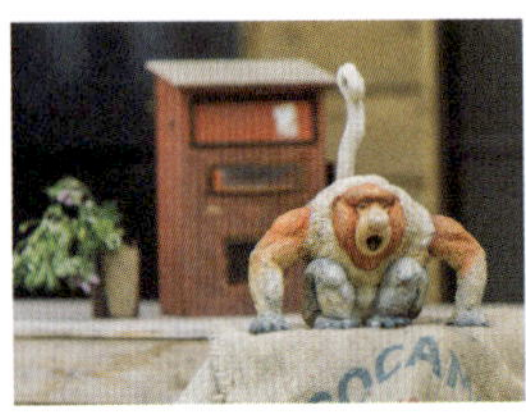

Tengu Monkey [Borneo]

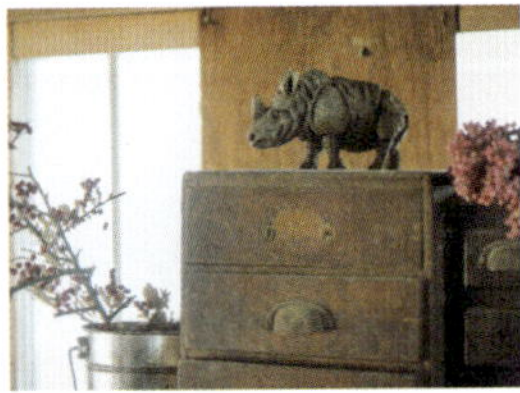

Rhinoceros [Higashiyama Zoo]

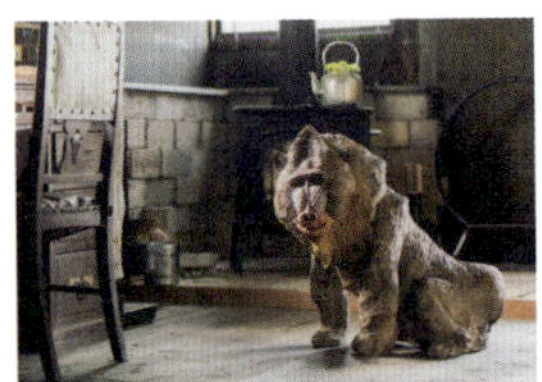

Manjuuro [mandrill / Higashiyama Zoo]

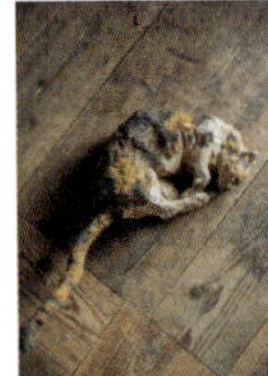

Chibi [calico cat / Tokyo University of the Arts]

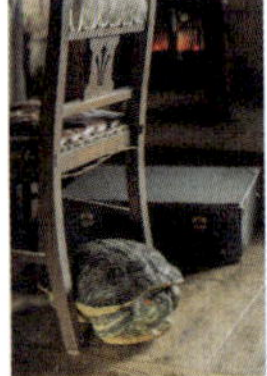

Koma [green turtle / Mie Prefecture]

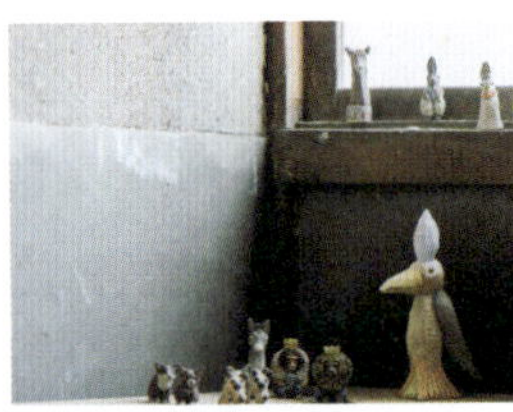

Various chess pieces

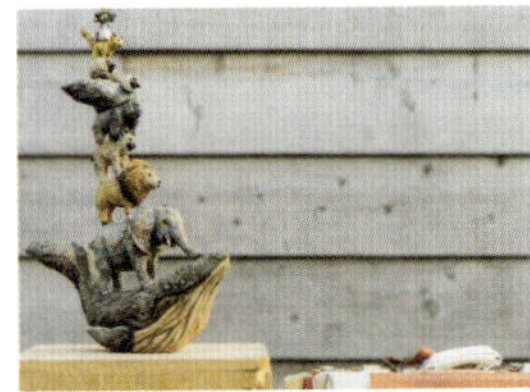

Elephant-whale "Bremen arrangement"

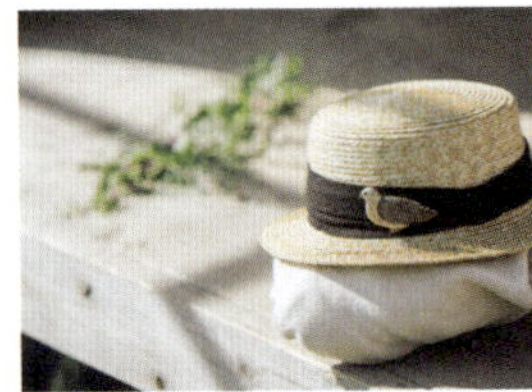

Kubuz [pigeon / UAE]

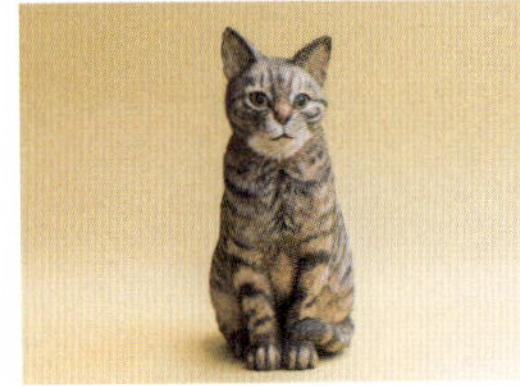

Tara [Tabby Cat / Tokyo]

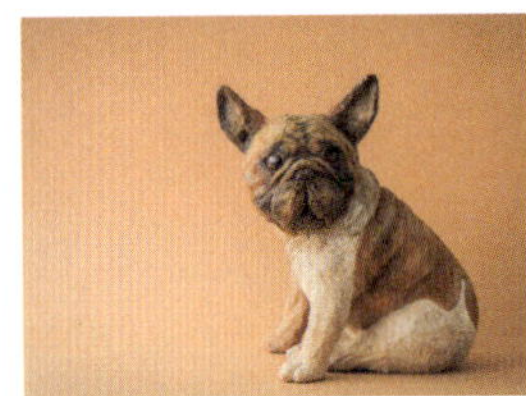

Diego [Bulldog / Tokyo]

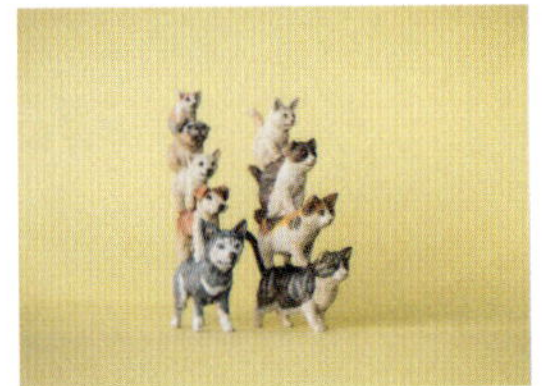

Left: dog "Bremen arrangement"; Right: cat "Bremen arrangement"

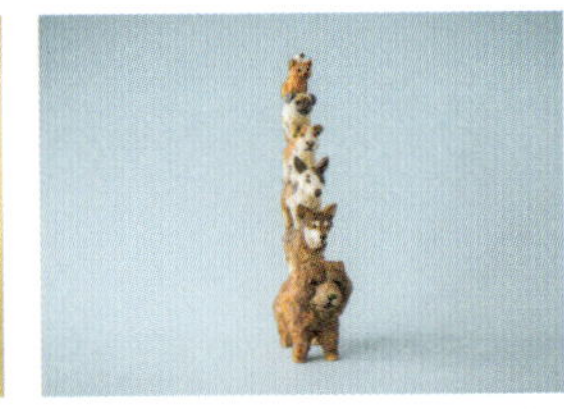

Dog "Bremen arrangement"

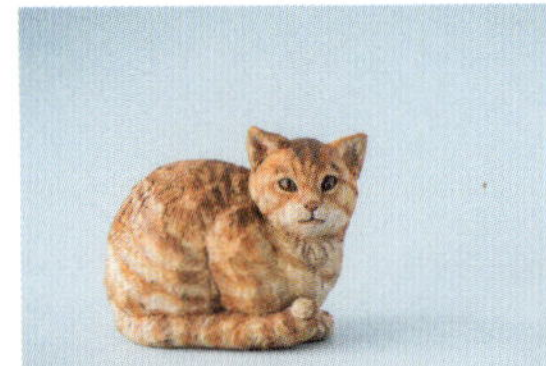

Nyurya [brown Tabby Cat / Fukuoka]

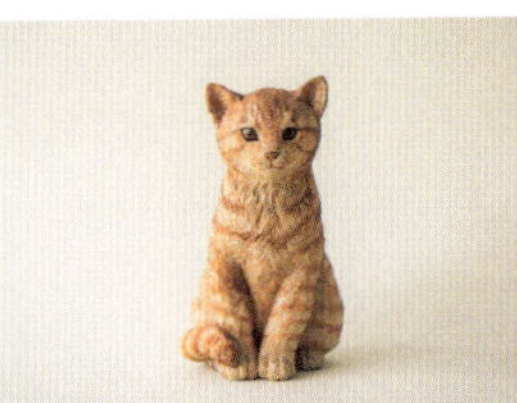

Nyuri [brown Tabby Cat / Fukuoka]

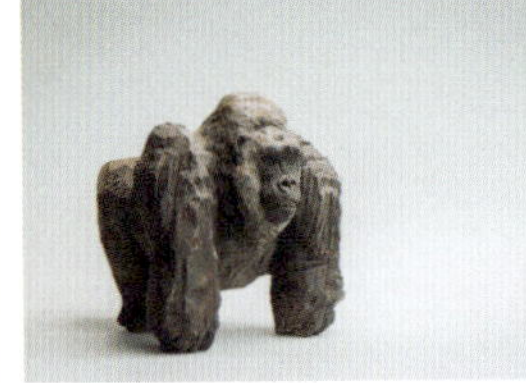

Musashi [gorilla / Ueno Zoological Gardens]

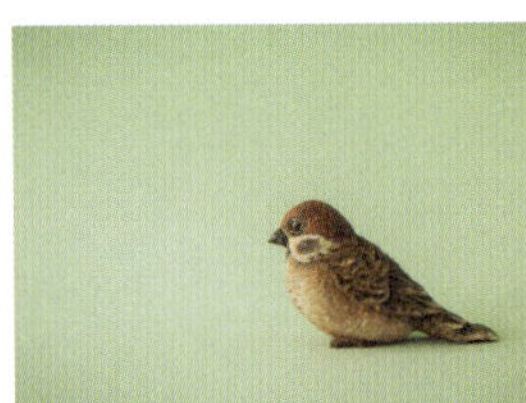

Chiyoko [sparrow / Mie Prefecture]

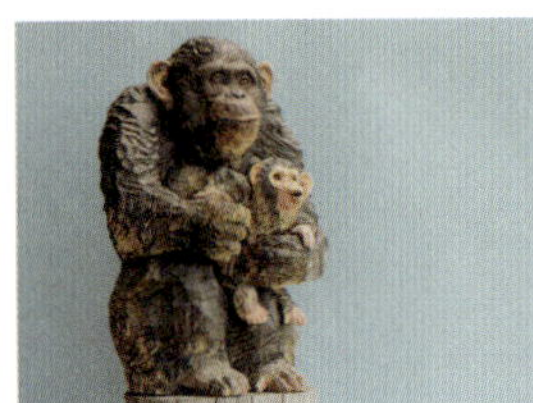

Chimpanzee Family [Tama Zoological Park]

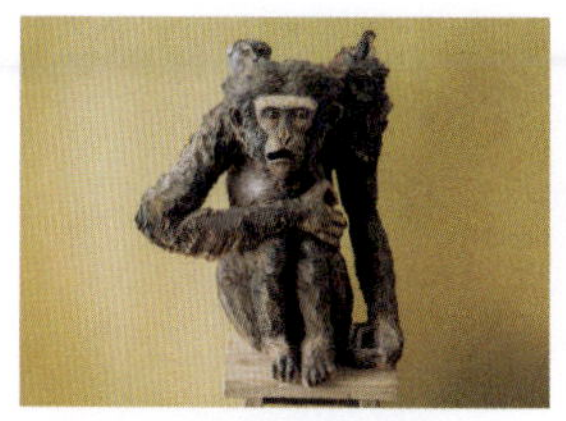

Beegee [white-browed gibbon / Aichi Prefecture]

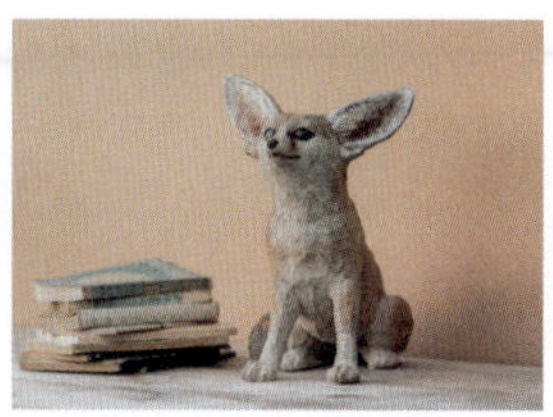

Api [fennec fox / Tokyo]

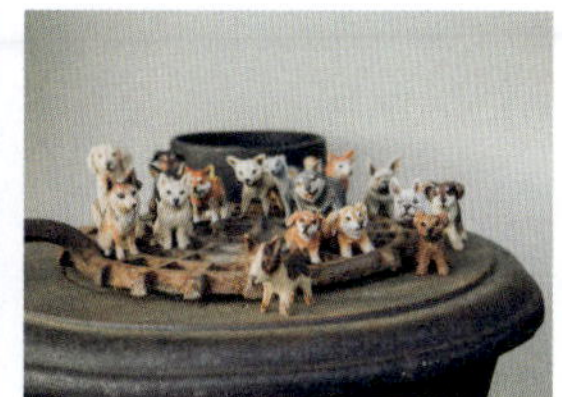

Various dog figurines

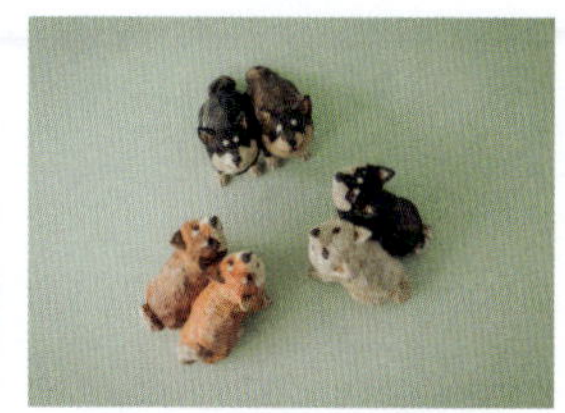

Various paired dog figurines in a ring arrangement

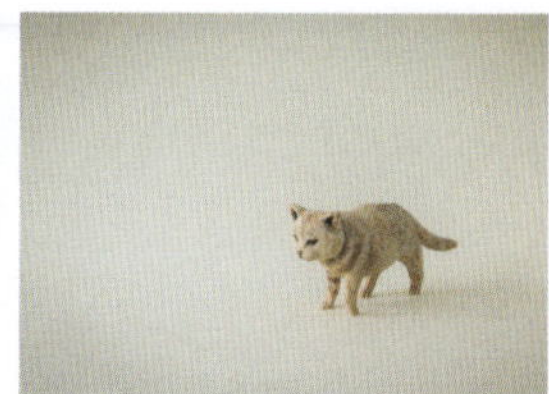

Cinnamon [white tiger cat / Fukuoka]

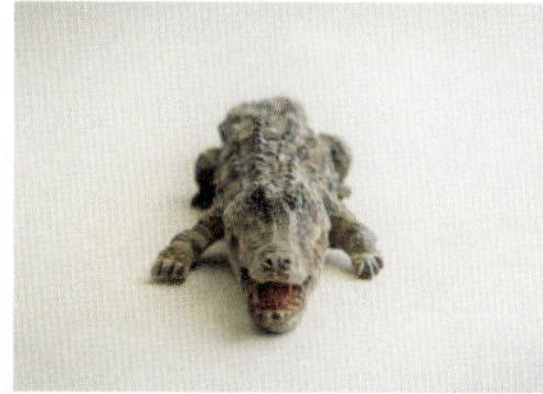

Crocodile [Banana Crocodile Park]

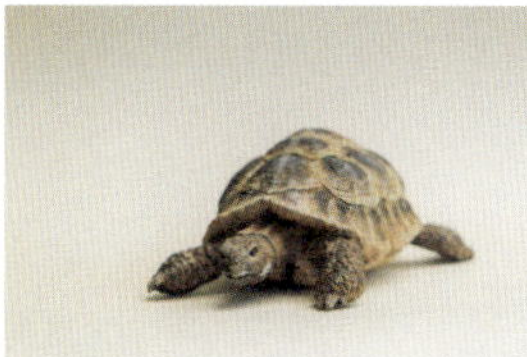

Kamekichi [Russian tortoise / Okinawa]

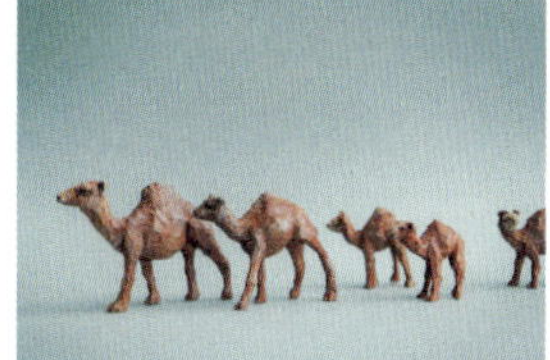

Camel Caravan [UAE]

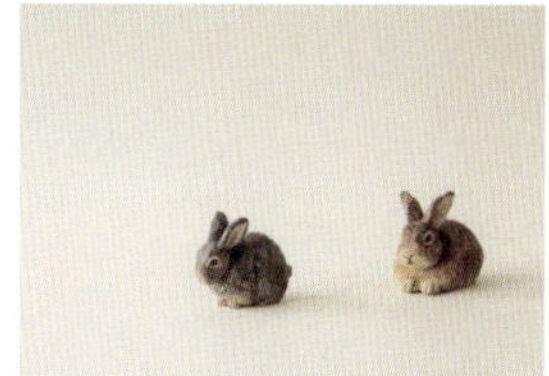

Left: *Mickey*; Right: untitled [Netherland Dwarf rabbits / Fukuoka]

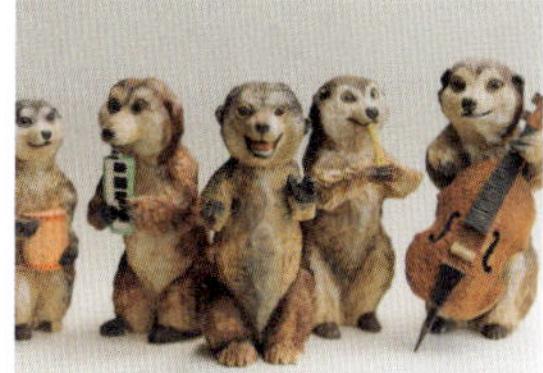

Meerkat Band [East Park Zoo]

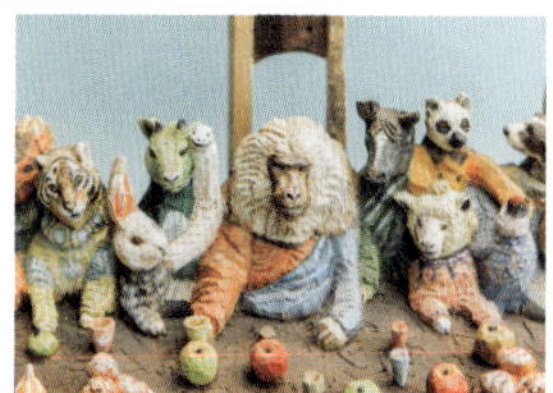

The Last Supper of the Animals

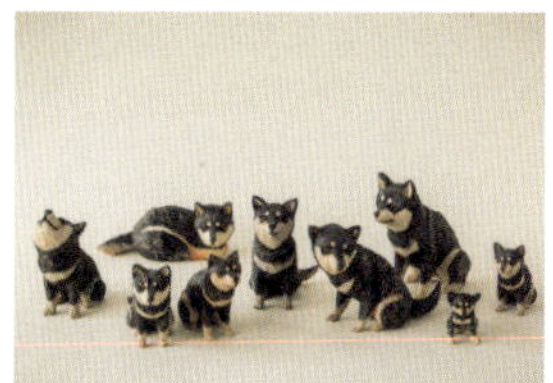

Various *Tsuki* figurines [black Shiba Inu / Mie Prefecture]

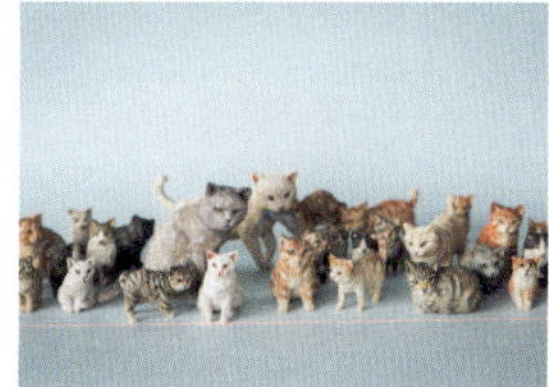

Various cat figurines [Fukuoka]

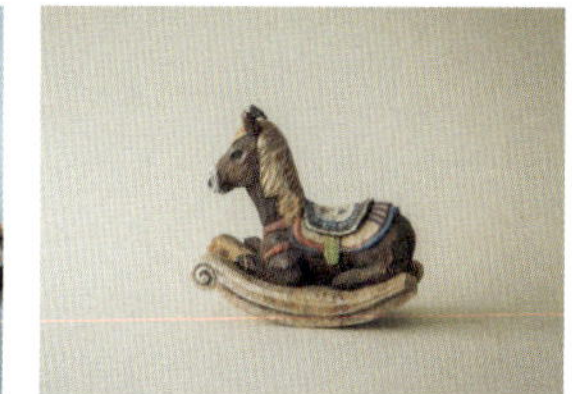

Wooden Horse

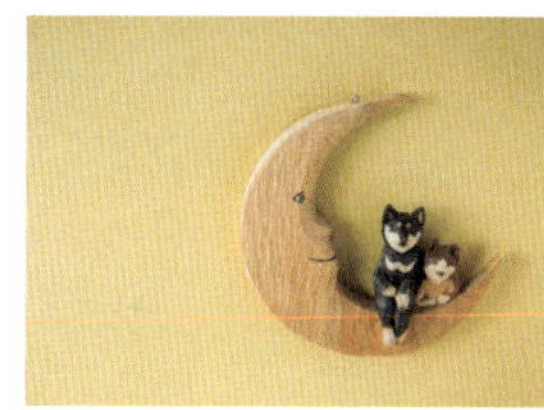

Moon with Moon and Cat

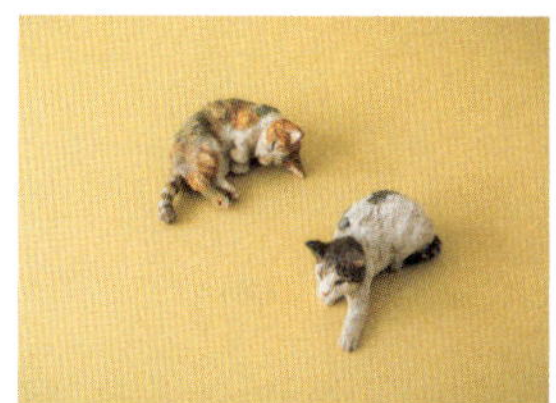

Left: *Ikura* [calico cat]; Right: *Nico* [Tabby Cat] [Tokyo]

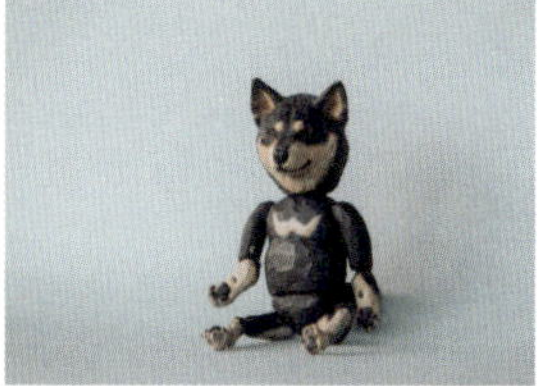

Moon's Marionette [black Shiba Inu / Mie Prefecture]

Carving Block Dimension Reference

These are examples of the five animal carvings described in this book. The size of the wood is just a guideline, so precise measurement is not necessary. As you become accustomed to wood carving, you'll become comfortable adjusting the size and shape of the figures you carve without lots of planning.

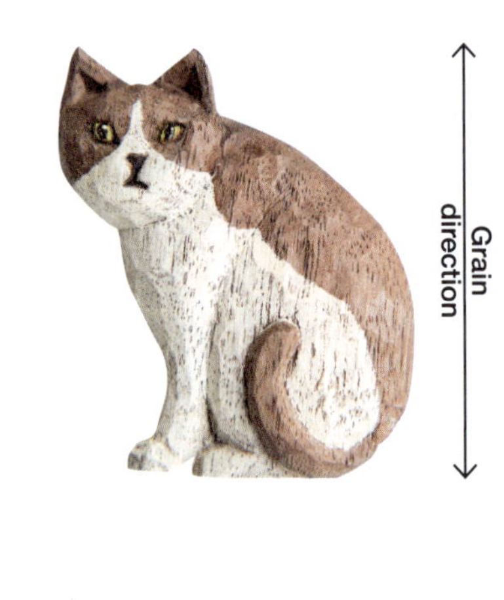

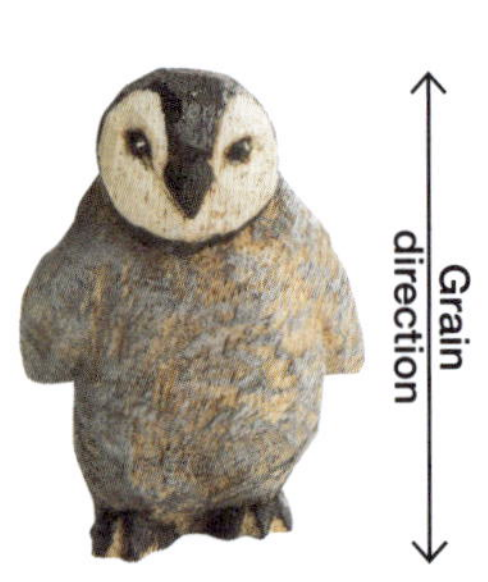

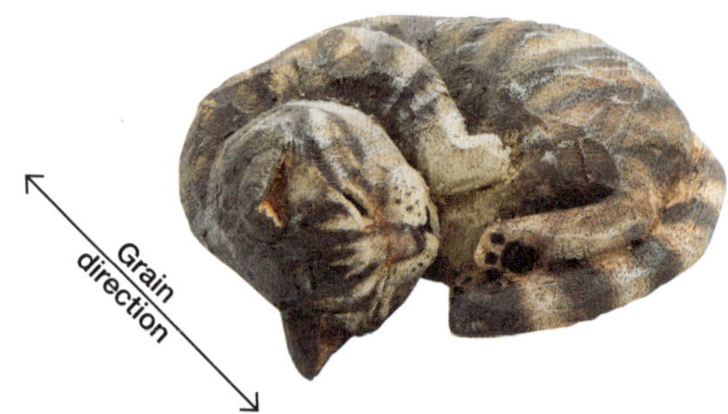

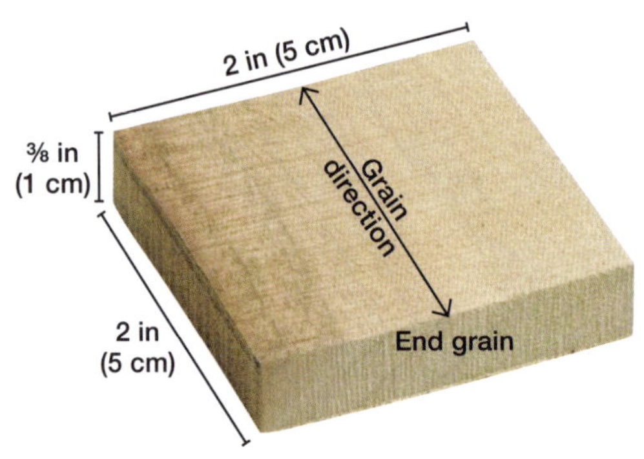

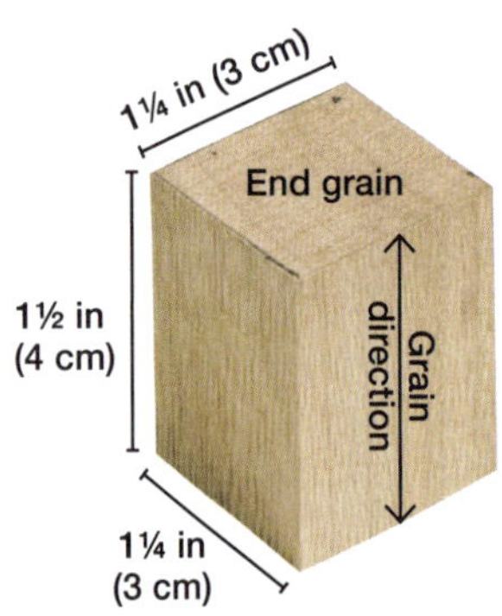

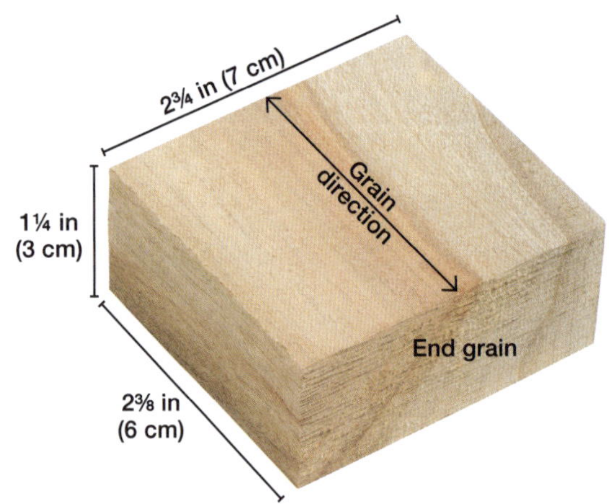

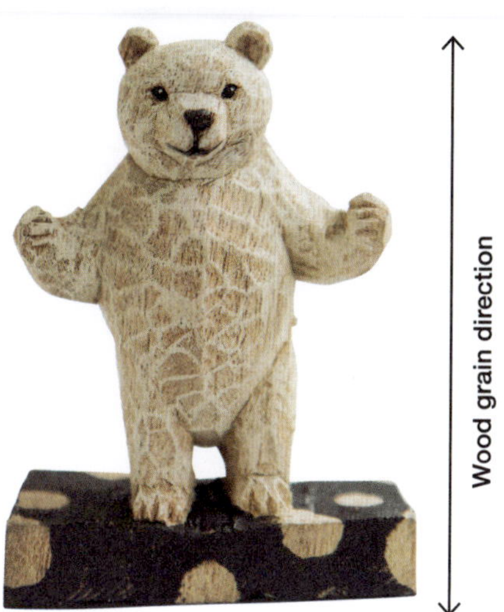

Wood grain direction

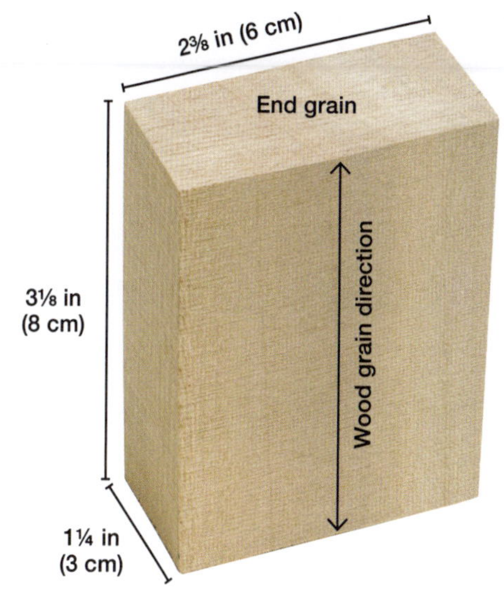

2⅜ in (6 cm)
End grain
3⅛ in
(8 cm)
Wood grain direction
1¼ in
(3 cm)

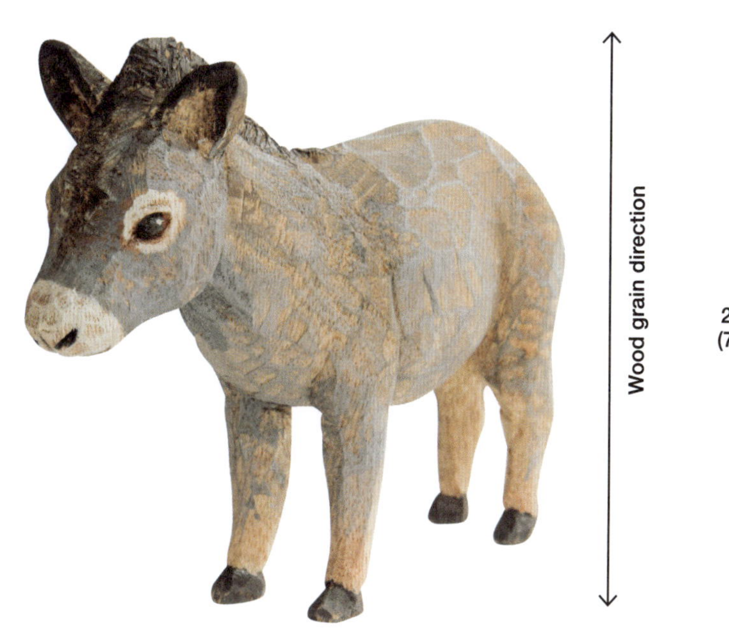

Wood grain direction

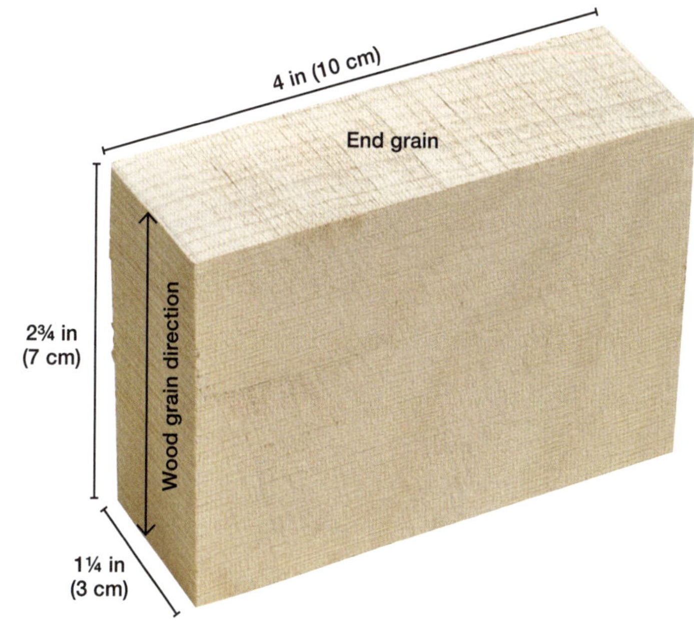

4 in (10 cm)
End grain
2¾ in
(7 cm)
Wood grain direction
1¼ in
(3 cm)

Ten Rules for Carving

1. The true nature of sculpture lies in its three-dimensional effect. Moreover, the life of sculpture lies in its poetic spirit.

2. Think about the structure. Where there is no structure, nothing exists.

3. Your attitude is like a river, and your movement is like the flow of water.

4. The depth of the carving lies hidden within the fusion of forms.

5. Get the whole story. Capturing a certain moment, a certain expression, or a certain aspect is not the essence of sculpture.

6. Discard all effects of chance. Do not be misled by touch.

7. It's disrespectful to superficially position details side by side. They should exist in harmony, not in sequence.

8. Do not aim merely to imitate. If you achieve structure and form, likeness will come naturally. Be ashamed of common likeness.

9. The secret to carving wood lies in constantly sharpening the blade. It is not to show off the sharpness, but to use the tool as if it were part of your hand.

10. Observe nature at all times. Sculpture is filled with nature.

Published in Kotaro Takamura's "Essay on Modeling" 1926 (*Beauty of Modeling*, p. 220, Chikuma Shobo, 1942)

Conclusion

The first time I made a wooden carving of an animal was a sculpture I carved to remember a cat that had run away from home. That first sculpture was extremely difficult; despite having lived together, I couldn't recall anything about the cat! I remember feeling a bit sad, wishing I had looked more closely and remembered better.

Over the years since then, whenever the thought occurs to me, I have always made sculptures of animals. There are many challenges involved: things not going as planned, not being able to create as well as I'd like, not having enough physical stamina.... However, I've come to appreciate the irreplaceable moments these sculptures commemorate, allowing me to touch that lost pet again and encounter the landscapes they inhabited. I hope that others can also experience these precious moments. I encourage everyone to try making small wooden carvings of animals. Someday, your surroundings will be filled with beloved animals and those you have encountered. Sometimes, looking at these sculptures brings tears to my eyes as I vividly recall each animal. Even a tiny sculpture can bring a surge of warmth to your heart when touched. The landscapes where your future sculptures will be placed are sure to be beautiful and joyful, enriching your life.

About the Author

Mio Hashimoto has always had a special affinity for animals. She studied art at the Zokei Art Academy in Tokyo and after graduation began receiving commissions for animal sculptures and held solo exhibitions across Japan. Recently, she has organized traveling woodcarving workshops and exhibitions featuring touchable animal sculptures in collaboration with her sculptor friend, Emiko Honda. Mio lives in Japan, where she continues to create sculptures with her black Shiba Inu dog, Tsuki-kun, by her side.

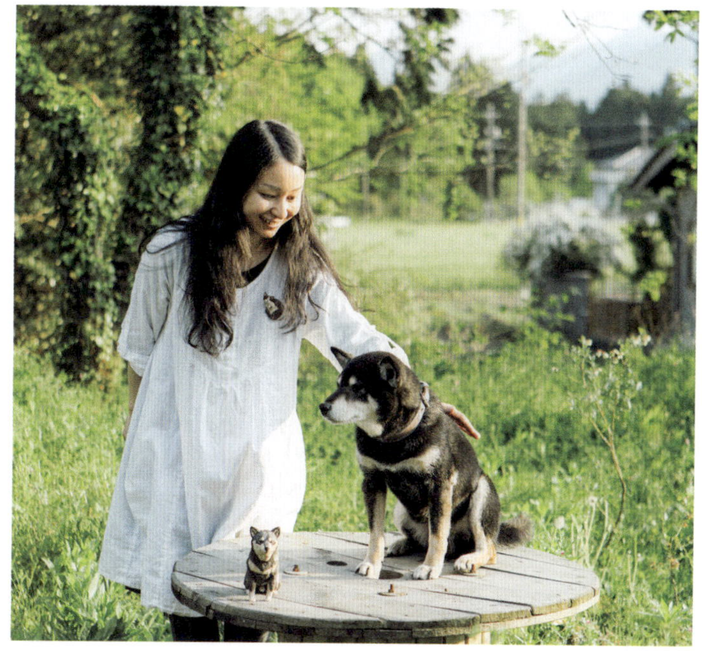

Published by Tuttle Publishing, an imprint of Periplus Editions (HK) Ltd.

www.tuttlepublishing.com

ISBN 978-4-8053-1894-2

Hajimete no Kibori Dobutsu Tenaraicho
Copyright © Mio Hashimoto 2015
English translation rights arranged with Raichosha
through Japan UNI Agency, Inc., Tokyo

English translation © 2025 Periplus Editions (HK) Ltd

Printed in China   2412CM

29 28 27 26 25   10 9 8 7 6 5 4 3 2 1

Distributed by:

North America, Latin America & Europe
Tuttle Publishing
364 Innovation Drive
North Clarendon
VT 05759-9436 U.S.A.
Tel: (802) 773-8930; Fax: (802) 773-6993
info@tuttlepublishing.com; www.tuttlepublishing.com

Japan
Tuttle Publishing
Yaekari Building 3rd Floor
5-4-12 Osaki Shinagawa-ku
Tokyo 141 0032
Tel: (81) 3 5437-0171; Fax: (81) 3 5437-0755
sales@tuttle.co.jp; www.tuttle.co.jp

Asia Pacific
Berkeley Books Pte. Ltd.
3 Kallang Sector, #04-01
Singapore 349278
Tel: (65) 6741-2178; Fax: (65) 6741-2179
inquiries@periplus.com.sg; www.tuttlepublishing.com